Stoneware and Porcelain

The Art of High-Fired Pottery

STONEWARE
& PORCELAIN
The Art of High-Fired Pottery

DANIEL RHODES

CHILTON BOOK COMPANY
Radnor, Pennsylvania

Photographs on cover: upper left, "Stoneware Form"
by Val Cushing; upper right, "Covered Jar," porcelain,
Ching Dynasty, China; lower left, "Porcelain Jar"
by Rudolph Staffel; lower right, "Salt-glazed Jar" by
Don Reitz.

Photo credits are as follows: Figures 5, 35, 69, Christman-
Marchello; 41, 63, 77, Margaret Dhaemers; 16,
Nathan Lyons; 1, 12-15, 18, 19, 21, 22, 26-29, 31, 32,
37-39, 43-47, 49, 50, 55, 58-60, 64, 68, 70, 75, Daniel
Rhodes; 17, Oppi Untracht; 33, 53, 79, John Wood

13 14 15 16 17 18   6 5 4 3 2 1

For Lorna and Aaron

Preface

During the past few years there has been an enormous increase in the number of people interested in pottery as a creative medium, and particularly an increase of interest in high-fired ceramics. In many ways stoneware and porcelain are ideal mediums for individual expression in ceramics, and I feel that we are only at the beginning of a renewal of vitality in this ancient art. It is difficult to realize that only a few decades ago knowledge of the techniques of stoneware and porcelain was restricted to a mere handful of individual potters and to those engaged in the commercial production of tableware. It is natural that this revival of interest has been accompanied by an intense curiosity about high temperature bodies, glazes, and firing, and potters have pursued the intricacies of their craft with an intensity which has amounted almost to obsession. Too often testing, experimentation, and the various processes of surface involvement have become ends in themselves, and pots, instead of being expressive or fitted for their purpose, have been merely the vehicles for a display of dexterity and technique.

We have now come to a point, I believe, where the relationship between technique and the essential values of the pot has become clear. It is obvious that the validity of any handmade ceramic today resides in its quality as a work of art, rather than in its utility as a vessel, or in its technical virtuosity. Our pots, if they are to live at all, must be really good. They must be individual, expressive, full of character and vitality—*beautiful*. Though made of lifeless clay, they must suggest awareness of life and the continuing force which makes us search for new formulations of the meaning of existence. If our pots are dull, academic, pretentious, or inept, we are only making objects for future rummage sales.

To make really fine pots, to achieve in pottery a truly authentic statement, is a challenge. To meet this challenge, the potter must train himself in his craft until technique can become assimilated into himself so that it no longer exists as a thing separate from the essential purpose of the work. His technical control and his creative insights must be part of the same thing.

I believe that the idea that craft, method, or technique existing separately from meaning, idea, and form is false. These two, the method and the meaning, must melt together so as to become indistinguishable. I believe that art and craft cannot be separated, and it is notable that in the Chinese language there is one word which expresses the perfect fusion of these two ideas. In our society the "craftsman" has often assumed that, because he is working in a "craft" medium, he is somehow absolved from the disciplines of art—disciplines which involve the development and the freeing of creative intuitions at the highest levels of perception. It is perhaps only fair to say that, on the other hand, the "fine artist" has sometimes considered himself above craft and has neglected means in a preoccupation with ends. To me, the "artist" and the "craftsman," although they may work in different mediums, are faced with essentially the same problems.

In this book I have tried to present a useful exposition of the materials and the methods which are available for making stoneware and porcelain, and to suggest the esthetic potential of these methods. I have also tried to express the feelings which I have about pottery, which make it meaningful to me. The standards implied are entirely personal, and are the outcome of my direct experiences with clay. I hope that potters will find in it not only information but perhaps inspiration as well.

I am indebted to James Marshall Plumer for his valuable suggestions, to John Wood and to Nathan Lyons for their help and advice on the illustrations, and to David Shaner for his assistance in testing some of the glazes and clay bodies presented in the text. I greatly appreciate the courtesy extended to me by the Freer Gallery of Art in Washington, D.C., and The Royal Ontario Museum in Toronto, Canada. In both of these institutions I was able to study and to photograph examples from their collections. The illustrations for the book could not have been assembled without the co-operation of the potters who supplied photographs of their work. Above all, I wish to express my gratitude to my wife for her encouragement and for her help in the many phases of thinking and work which have resulted in this book.

DANIEL RHODES

Alfred, New York

Contents

With Portfolio of Illustrations, pages 87–142

Stoneware and Porcelain

The Art of High-Fired Pottery

Chapter 1

Stoneware and Porcelain, A Great Tradition

1. The beginnings of high-fired pottery in ancient China

High-fired ceramics are of great antiquity, dating back to about 500 B.C. in China. Prior to this time, all pottery the world over was earthenware, that is, porous, nonvitrified ware. The origins of the early stonewares of China are lost in the obscurity of time, and we can only conjecture as to how they came to be made and as to the techniques employed.

At the time of the appearance of the first hard and vitrified pottery in China, the Chinese potters were technically far behind the potters of the ancient Near East, and it is surprising that hard stonewares were not made first in Persia. Glazed ware had been made in the Near East for hundreds of years, and the control of color and texture was far in advance of that achieved by the Chinese. It is hard for us now to realize what a difficult thing it must have been to achieve a range of glaze colors which included green from copper, yellows and browns from iron, blue from cobalt, and purple from manganese. All these colors had to be refined from natural minerals and mixed and blended with the glaze ingredients without the benefit of any exact knowledge of mineralogy or chemistry. It is no wonder that the old potters guarded their secrets jealously, and passed them down from one generation to the next. Firing, too, was a technique

which could only have been worked out over a long period of trial and error, and some of the achievements of the potters of the Near East in the pre-Christian era, such as the massive architectural reliefs in glazed tile of the Assyrians, are evidence of a high degree of control over firing temperature and atmosphere.

Several factors may have prevented the development of higher temperature wares in the Near East. One factor is that the design and construction of kilns remained at a relatively primitive level. The typical kiln throughout the Near East was a simple updraft chamber, fed through one or more fire mouths around the base and vented through a short chimney at the top. The flames from the wood or brush fires traveled upward through the ware, which was protected by saggers. Judging from present-day kilns still in use in the area, the walls of the kilns were made of a clay similar to that from which the pottery was fashioned, and were insulated with mud or dirt on the outside.

Although such kilns were adequate for the firing of low-temperature earthenwares and lead and alkaline glazes, they were not well designed for the full utilization of the heat from the fuel, and the higher temperatures could not be obtained in them. Moreover, the materials used in constructing the kilns were not very refractory, and even if temperatures in excess of 1100°C could have been reached, the clay walls of the kiln would have begun to soften.

Another factor which perhaps inhibited the use of higher temperature was the scarcity of refractory clays. But it seems likely that if kiln design had permitted higher temperatures, materials and techniques would have been found to take advantage of them. Certainly the potters of the Near East were not lacking in inventiveness, and their achievements in color, decorative processes, and the scale and quality of their work could only have resulted from a willingness to experiment.

Compared to the colorful, highly decorative, and sophisticated wares of Egypt and the ceramic centers in Asia Minor, the productions of the Chinese potters prior to the Han Dynasty, 206 B.C.–A.D. 220, were rough, mostly unglazed, and were characterized by a strength and virility of form. The potter's wheel, which had been in use in Egypt since about 3000 B.C., was apparently known in some simple form, perhaps contemporaneously, in neolithic China, yet the knowledge of it is generally believed to have come indirectly through the civilizations of Asia Minor and Central Asia.

Much of the pottery which has survived from ancient China has been preserved in tombs, and we do not know to what extent these wares were made for daily use. Tomb fittings were important to the ancient Chinese because of their religion, which centered around ancestor worship. The principal tomb objects, and perhaps the principal art form of the Shang and Chou dynasties were bronze ceremonial vessels. These mysterious and magnificent forms, which show an extraordinary degree of skill in metallurgy and casting, must have had profound symbolic meanings. The idea of the symbolic vessel appears early in Chinese art, and the great importance which the Chinese have attached to pottery throughout their history seems to stem from the early use of vessels of bronze, pottery, jade, and lacquer in religious ceremonies. There comes to mind the symbol of the Holy Grail in European mythology.

Much of the pottery found in tombs from pre-Han times may be a kind of poor man's bronze. Many of the shapes are obviously inspired by or are parallel to those of bronze vessels, and were meant for ceremonial rather than for any strictly practical function.

For reasons which remain obscure, the refinement of these early tomb-wares of ancient China took the form of higher firing, denser and more vitrified clay bodies, and whiter clays. Perhaps the change came about in the effort to simulate bronze more effectively. Or perhaps it came entirely through technical improvements in the kilns and refinement of the material. In any event, during the second or third centuries immediately preceding Han, the Chinese had succeeded in making a ware which was dense, impervious to liquid, and which had a stonelike ring when struck. This development, which was probably a gradual one taking place over a considerable period of time, was to mark a great turning point in ceramic history, and the beginning of the centuries long advance of Chinese ceramics, whose main glory was to be high-fired stonewares and porcelain.

2. The early high temperature kilns of China

Too little is known of the development and construction of pottery kilns in ancient China for us to be able to do anything but guess as to their exact size or design. It is safe to assume, however, that kiln types of our day are the outgrowth or survival of types that were centuries old. Figure 1 shows a typical Chinese chamber kiln. The kiln was usually built on a hillside, and in some cases an artificial hill was created by piling up a great mound of earth. The kiln consists of a group of beehive-shaped chambers built in a series up the hill. Each chamber is connected to the next by a small open-

4

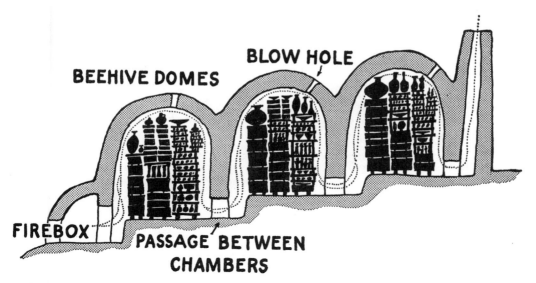

BEEHIVE DOMES

BLOW HOLE

FIREBOX

PASSAGE BETWEEN CHAMBERS

Fig. 1. ORIENTAL CHAMBER KILN

Only three chambers are shown, but six or more might be built one after the other. Most of the ware would be packed in saggers. All chambers after the first one have small stokeholes where additional fuel may be introduced to raise the temperature. Wood or brush is used for fuel.

ing near the base. The first chamber has a sizable firebox where the fuel, usually wood, grass, or brush, is burned.

The ware in the first chamber is protected from the direct impingement of the flames by a wall of brick or saggers, which also deflect the flame and hot gases upward to the crown of the kiln. Saggers are known to have been in use at least as early as the 13th century A.D. From the crown, the hot gases are drawn downward through the ware and out through the hole at the bottom, and so into the next chamber. Here the gases are again deflected upward. Thus the heat is made to pass from chamber to chamber, and a maximum exchange of heat takes place between the flame and the ware being fired. When the desired temperature is reached in the first chamber, firing is stopped in the main firebox, and the temperature in the second chamber is advanced by stoking fuel into small openings near the base of the kiln. Each succeeding chamber is fired off in this manner, and the cumulative heat raises the temperature in the last chamber so that

very little additional stoking may be necessary to finish it.

It will be seen that the design of the Chinese chamber kiln conserves a maximum amount of heat; in fact, chamber kilns operating on a similar principle were, until the recent development of the tunnel kiln, the most efficient method of firing bricks, tiles, and heavy clay products in Western countries. Through the use of a downdraft, and the conservation of the heat from one chamber to be used in the next, the Chinese were able to reach a much higher temperature than was available to potters elsewhere. In the downdraft kiln, the natural tendency of the hot gases to rise is prevented by diverting it first upward to the top of the kiln, and then forcing it to travel down through the ware to a flue near the bottom. This prevents an excessive amount of heat from escaping up the chimney.

The Oriental high-fire kiln was cleverly designed, of refractory materials essential for withstanding high temperatures. In some cases the kilns were made out of raw, unfired blocks of sandy fire clay, which became fired or partially fired in use. Similarly, a natural sandstone was used in this country during colonial times for the construction of kilns and blast furnaces. Or, the kilns were made out of prefired bricks. Usually the kilns were fairly thin-walled, and were insulated on the outside with a coating of clay or mud. Their dome shape required no bracing, and was well adapted to the expansion and contractions of heating and cooling. The slope of the chambers up the hill furnished a natural draft, and little or no chimney was required at the flue of the last chamber. Fragments of broken tea bowls of the Temmoku type, made in northern China prior to A.D. 1300, have been refired in modern kilns to determine the original firing temperature. No further shrinkage occurred when the refiring was carried to as high as 1250°C and the glaze remained practically unchanged. This would indicate firing temperatures of cone 9 or higher as common in the old kilns.

Kilns in the Orient were often large. The modern ones at Ching-tê-chên are as large as 12 feet high inside the chambers. Such kilns will hold thousands of pots. The need for pottery was always great in an agricultural society such as that of China and at an early date, perhaps by the time of the T'ang dynasty, the Chinese potteries approached the size of factories, employing whole communities of workers.

One kiln commonly fired the wares of several potteries or of numerous individual producers. The firing of a large chamber kiln is an exciting and dramatic event as described by those who have seen it in modern China. Preparations include the apportioning of space in the kiln, the setting of the various chambers, and the gathering in of fuel. A large kiln requires many cords of wood for one firing. When all is ready, the doors to the chambers are bricked in and mudded over, and the fire is lighted. For several days the fire is held to a low heat to insure the complete drying of the ware. Then the heat is gradually increased by constant stoking. Day and night the firemen ply the fires until the draft creates a steady roar, and red heat is seen in the spy-holes of the first chamber. Draw trials are hooked out of spy-holes in various positions on the wall of the chamber, and when full heat is reached, and the trials indicate that the ware is sufficiently fired, the stoking is moved up to the second chamber, where thin sticks of wood are poked into narrow holes provided at the base of the kiln. The kiln resembles a wheezing dragon, with smoke and flame breathing from every chink. After perhaps several days of continuous firing, the last chamber is judged finished and the firing ceases.

Such firings, which involved tremendous quantities of ware and the participation of many workers, demanded a high degree of organization and co-operation. Of course we have no way of knowing exactly how large the production units of ancient potteries were, but the vast quantities of pottery which have survived indicate the immense importance of pottery in the life of China, during the last millennium, particularly, and it is likely that the potteries from very early times were busy industries employing many people.

As the art of firing was perfected and the higher temperatures became possible, a new type of ceramics was a natural result. Refractory clays are abundant in China, and it must have been observed that pottery made from these refractory clays, when fired to a higher temperature, became hard and dense. With this obvious improvement in the ware noted, it would be only natural for the potters to increase the temperature of firing in an effort to obtain still harder and more durable results.

3. Early vitrified pottery in China

Pottery made in China prior to the beginning of the Han dynasty, 206 B.C.–

6

A.D. 220, is typically unglazed, and of a strong, straightforward, virile shape. Foreign influences up to that time had not been very important in the art of China, and while certain technical methods, such as the use of the potter's wheel, are generally understood to have been borrowed from the West, these early wares may be considered purely Chinese in their concept of form. The early Chinese pots always have a strong, clarified shape, and if decoration or surface interest is present, we always feel that it takes a subordinate and completely integrated part in the expression as a whole. The outstanding characteristic of Chinese pottery throughout its long development has been the persistence of this vital, clarified form, and although the forms change from one period to the next they are seldom weak or lost in surface interest.

Many of the early vitrified pots have a rough, rather grainy surface. In color they tend to be gray or buff and many examples show flashings from the fire.

Many of the pots are in the form of jars with swelling profile and a fairly narrow mouth. Although the pots are unglazed, their surfaces are usually enriched with incised pattern or texture. In some cases this pattern is repeated in such a way as to suggest that it was achieved by beating the damp pot with a textured paddle. Other surfaces have a fabric-like texture or textures which appear to have been made by pressing string against the damp clay.

Some of the pottery made before the Han dynasty has a partial glaze, usually appearing on one side or on the shoulder of the piece. Undoubtedly these traces of glaze are the result of ashes from the fire settling on the ware during the firing process. In any firing which makes use of wood, grass, or brush for fuel, a certain amount of ash is carried with the draft of the kiln through the chambers containing the ware. The fusible ash melts to form a thin glaze on the ware. Actually the only way to prevent such

glazes from forming in a high temperature firing where wood is used for fuel is to protect the pots from the draft of the kiln by placing them in saggers.

We find, then, that the basic techniques for making glazed stoneware had been developed before the Han dynasty. These techniques included a knowledge of building and of firing kilns to reach the relatively high temperatures required, a knowledge of refractory clays from which to make both the kiln and the pottery, and a knowledge that certain readily available materials will melt at high temperatures and form hard glazes. Once the higher temperatures, in excess of 1100°C, had been attained, it must have frequently occurred that fusible material was observed to melt in the kiln, either by accident or intention. Common red clay, for example, melts at this temperature to form a brown or black glass, and most feldspathic rocks or granite melt at about 1200°C. The fusible nature of wood ash when in contact with clay must have been obvious to those who fired the kilns, because it tends to glaze the inside of the kiln, the saggers, and the pots if they are exposed. Putting these observations together, potters even before the Han dynasty created the first true glazed stoneware.

4. The stoneware of the Han dynasty, 206 B.C.–A.D. 220

Perhaps the most common type of Han pottery is of earthenware, and is outside the scope of this study. This type consists mostly of funerary jars, usually made in imitation of bronze shapes and glazed with soft green lead glazes. In most specimens the glaze has decomposed to form an iridescent gray-green color. These pots, which are very noble in form and which often have decorative friezes in bands about the neck or belly, show the influence of the Near East in the use of the lead glaze. The knowledge of the use of lead for glazes was undoubtedly brought from the Near East, rather than developed independently in China. It is possible that the actual materials for the glaze was imported over the caravan routes of central Asia. The appearance of lead-glazed ware in China is another example of a long and interesting interchange between the potters of the Near and the Far East.

In addition to lead-glazed ware, the Han potters produced large quantities of glazed stoneware. These stonewares are unique in shape and surface, and represent a tremendous advance in the potter's art. In noble grandeur of form and monumentality of conception they have never been surpassed. Most of the Han stonewares are jars with fairly narrow mouths and either straight or swelling sides. The form is sure, controlled, carefully proportioned, and yet seems free and plastic. The dependence on bronze shapes is slight, although there are often small vestigial handles, and rings on the sides of the pieces which suggest metal. Many examples show a surface treatment which consists of bands and texture applied in the soft clay while the piece was still on the wheel. The scale and extent of these bands are always in keeping with the shape, and while they add to the character of the form, they never dominate it. In these early Han stonewares, we see a masterly use of the potter's wheel, and a mature, vital, and monumental expression of form.

In surface, these early stonewares are very interesting. The glazes, as such, are not of a very ingratiating character; the usual color is a gray-green or brown, rather cloudy, and with a tendency to run and to accentuate surface variations. The experienced potter will recognize the surface quality of these glazes as being derived from wood ash. It seems quite sure that these earliest of stoneware glazes were made from ash, probably from the ash collected from the fire mouths of the kilns. The brown-green color results from iron in the glaze fired in a reducing atmosphere. Very similar glazes may be made by mixing hardwood ash and common red clay in about equal proportions. On some pots the glaze has drawn up into globules or spots of slightly greater thickness, giving a mottled appearance. In Han wares, this simple glaze is invariably used in a natural state without coloring agents added, and in fact the potters knew of no coloring material to use, and were probably greatly intrigued by their accomplishment in being able to make a glaze at all, no matter what the color.

With the great early indigenous stonewares of the Han dynasty, Chinese pottery reached a maturity of style, and the beginnings of a technical development which was to carry it ultimately to the refinement of pure white translucent porcelain.

The wares of Han seem to reflect perfectly the stability, the order, and the respect and veneration for the past of Confucianism. Despite radical technical innovations, Han stonewares are never whimsical or personal, but rather they are somber, quiet, restrained, with a suggestion of the past about them. We might be inclined to assign them to an ancient period of Chinese civilization, even if no external evidence pointed to such a dating. The term "protoporcelain" is sometimes given to these early vitreous wares, and this is accurate in the sense that they were certainly the forerunners of the whiter and more vitreous pottery which followed. The difference between true stonewares, such as were made in Han times and porcelain is one of degree rather than kind; in fact, the Chinese use only one word, *tz'u*, to denote any resonant, vitrified piece of pottery, whether stoneware or white translucent porcelain.

It is possible that the body of the Han stonewares included some feldspar in its composition, although it is certainly possible to make similar bodies out of combinations of fire clay, stoneware clay, and red clay. Feldspar was possibly used in the glaze also. It is thought that the widespread use of minerals for pharmaceutical purposes in China may have given the Chinese potter a ready source of supply for ground and prepared mineral powders of various sorts. In any case, feldspar is such a common mineral that its inclusion in high temperature mixtures was bound to occur sooner or later, and in these wares from Han, that intimate relationship between body and glaze which is characteristic of the best stonewares of later times is certainly achieved. An interesting problem arises from the fact that most of the early wares that have come to light have survived through grave burial, and that we do not know to what extent they represent the everyday wares of this remote time. Was the ware made for daily use more refined, or more crude, than that which was buried with the deceased? We do know that utensils of other materials, notably lacquered wood, were in widespread use. It is possible that the Chinese did not greatly value pottery for use in the household or in the court at this time. But it is much more likely that the populous plains of the Yellow River basin supported, even at this early date, a great many potteries for the production of useful, everyday wares, and it is interesting to speculate on what their products were like. Chinese literary references are of little help.

By the 2nd or 3rd century of the Christian era the directions which Chinese ceramics were to follow for the next thousand years were established. For one thing, Chinese pottery was to follow an essentially conservative course, deeply respectful of tradition. Each generation of potters added to the tradition, but even during the political and social upheavals which separate the various stable dynastic regimes, no radical changes occurred in pottery, and some types of ware were apparently made continuously for hundreds of years. This tendency of various types of pottery to persist for long periods of time has made the exact dating of specific examples difficult. Chinese pottery, as a result of this veneration and conservation of the achievements of the past, reflects the philosophical and spiritual values of the Chinese in a particularly immediate and authentic way.

Technically, Chinese pottery moved steadfastly in the direction of higher kiln temperatures, and the refinement of the materials which resulted in the ultimate achievement of white translucent porcelain. While earthenwares, and the rougher sorts of stonewares continued to be made and collected, imperial patronage and the greatest enthusiasm was reserved for the more refined products of the kilns. This tendency toward refinement resulted in the eventual degeneration of the art, but only after centuries of remarkably profound achievement. One important characteristic of Chinese ceramics which was quite apparent during the Han dynasty, and even before, was the ability and the willingness of the Chinese potters to make use of the natural character of ceramic materials and processes. Effects were seldom forced. They grew directly out of the available clays, rocks, and minerals, and out of the insight and the relaxed working habits of the potters.

5. The T'ang stonewares and porcelains

Insofar as stoneware is concerned, there is little that we know between the Han and the T'ang dynasties, with the important exception of the Yüeh ware, which indeed appears to have bridged the long gap. Historically, the interval between A.D. 220, the end of the Han period, and A.D. 618, the beginning of the T'ang, was a time of frequent change of dynasty, and of, on the whole, political confusion. During most of this interval, north China was occupied by barbarian invaders. Although the period between Han and T'ang is sometimes referred to as China's "Dark Ages," it did see the advent of Buddhism. The T'ang dynasty was marked by an imperial expansion which penetrated into central Asia, and south to Indo-China, exceeding even the

9

Han precedent. A long period of stability, prosperity, eager absorption of foreign influence, and artistic fertility followed. The T'ang is held by many to be the golden age of China, its era of greatest fulfillment.

Buddhism was introduced into China about the beginning of the Christian era, and as time went on, its influence on the thought, life, and art of China became more and more important, and in the T'ang dynasty, a dominating factor. Buddhism gained a strong foothold during the social and political disintegration which followed the stable, Confucianist Han dynasty. Buddhism tended to be mystical and concerned with meditation and the inner life, as contrasted to the pragmatic, ethical nature of the doctrines of Confucius. More important for art, perhaps, was the fact that Buddhism placed an importance on images in its religious observances, and as a result, sculpture and painting proliferated in China as never before. When Buddhism reached China, its traditional images and forms were already tinged with Hellenic influences acquired in northern India; and Chinese art, in particular sculpture, but to a lesser extent pottery and other art forms, was henceforth marked by a curious but well-assimilated blend of Greek, Indian, and native Chinese features. The T'ang period was one of great religious tolerance, and Buddhist monasteries prospered alongside those of the Nestorian Christians. Confucianism, however, remained the official religion of the state.

Many foreign influences were at work in China at this time, partly as a result of the expansion of the Chinese Empire, and partly as a result of improved transportation across the trade routes of central Asia. Regular communication existed between China and Persia, with interesting results as far as the pottery of both areas was concerned. Many travelers from the West reached China at this time and recorded their impressions of its greatness.

As might be expected, the art and the pottery of the T'ang dynasty is vital, creative, inventive, restless, and full of vigor. Whereas in earlier Chinese times only a relatively few types of ware were made, during the T'ang period dozens of different kinds of pottery were produced, both earthenwares and vitreous wares. It is during the T'ang dynasty that the first true porcelain was made. This has been established beyond doubt by findings made on the site of the ancient city of Samarra in Mesopotamia, which was abandoned in 883. Many fragments of Chinese pottery have been found at this site, which is evidence of a lively trade between East and West, and also furnishes sure proof that all the types of pottery found there were made during the 9th century or before.

Vitreous T'ang wares of three distinct types exist. First is a class of stonewares, quite similar to those made in earlier times. This type of pottery undoubtedly represents the continuation of an earlier tradition. The glazes, applied over dark or gray clay, appear to be feldspathic in character, perhaps with the addition of ash as a flux. They are usually of a brown, or greenish-brown color, and the glaze tends to run thin over raised decorations in the clay.

Another remarkable type of T'ang high-fired ware is the Yüeh. Apparently its manufacture began before the beginning of the T'ang dynasty and continued well into the 10th or 11th century, a period of several hundred years. The Yüeh is a type of celadon, probably the first true celadon to be made. The glaze on this type of pottery is gray-green in color, sometimes tending to a somewhat brown-green. The body of the piece is usually carved in low relief to form a decoration which is emphasized by the tendency of the glaze to pool and settle in the low spots. The effect is one of great subtlety and beauty, and this technique of low relief carving or incising became a favorite of the Chinese potters, and appears on numerous kinds of ware. The Yüeh wares, while never translucent, are dense, high fired, and approach porcelain in their hardness, and in the hardness of the glaze. The gray-green color of celadon was highly prized in China for its resemblance to jade and countless literary references mention this similarity.

The outstanding technical achievement of the T'ang period was the production of vitreous white stoneware, and of white and translucent porcelain. In making these white wares, certain difficulties had to be overcome in the mining and preparing of the clay, in shaping the ware, and in the firing, and the mastering of these techniques put the Chinese centuries ahead of the Western world in ceramics. Making white stoneware or porcelain requires the use of relatively iron-free kaolin. This type of white clay is fairly common in China, but it almost always occurs, in nature, mixed with a certain amount of mineral fragments of quartz and feldspar. To recover the finer fractions of clay, some separation process is necessary. In China, it is the usual practice to mix the clay with a great quantity of water, and the resulting thin slip is then run into a series of settling ponds. In each pond some of the coarser material sinks to the bottom, and the finer clay is drawn off into the next pond. In the final pond the clay is allowed to completely settle, and is then dried to a plastic condition. This flotation process, which eliminates all but the very finest particles of clay, results in a plastic and workable material. It is also common in China to store the clay over long periods of time in order to develop greater plasticity by aging. Without proper washing and aging, it would not be possible to make, from kaolin, the wheel-thrown pottery forms such as were made during T'ang times.

The secret of hard stoneware and of porcelain is to mix with the kaolin a certain amount of feldspar, which, in the high heat of the fire, causes the clay to fuse, harden, and glassify to the point of becoming translucent. In order to maintain the whiteness and smoothness of their clay bodies, the potters of the T'ang dynasty must have learned to select their materials with great care, and to grind and prepare them so as not to contaminate them with any iron-bearing material which would discolor the final result. The white pottery of this early time was not as white as that made in later times, and the development of clean white, translucent, and thinly potted ware occupied several hundred years.

The glazes on the T'ang stonewares and porcelains represent a refinement of earlier stoneware glazes. They were probably composed largely of feldspar, quartz, limestone, and clay. Although these minerals are common and easy to find in most localities, it must have been very difficult then to achieve uniform results, and to control the selection, grinding, and apportioning of the glaze materials. The simple feldspathic glaze became the basic glaze for nearly all Chinese high-fired ware. By differing the proportions and source of the materials, and by varying the firing treatment, a great variety of textures and colors were achieved.

Many of the T'ang stonewares are creamy white in color. In some cases the white tonality is achieved by coating the body of the piece with a white engobe and covering this with a transparent glaze. In other examples the body of the piece is light, giving the effect of off-white when covered by a semitransparent glaze.

The distinction between the stoneware and the porcelain made during the T'ang dynasty is a matter of thinness, refinement of the materials, and perhaps the intensity of heat to which the ware was fired. While the clay body of the T'ang porcelains is relatively coarse, and tends to be somewhat gray or buff in color compared to later white wares, the general effect is one of purity of color and refinement of substance.

One of the remarkable things about

the early porcelains is that in spite of their having been made out of relatively nonplastic white clays, they are free, spontaneous, and claylike in shape. The Chinese genius for sure, fluid forms persisted no matter what medium was employed. Many of the pieces have spouts, handles, and lids, and these are invariably made and attached with seeming ease. Most of the T'ang whitewares are not decorated, and it is probable that the unusual quality of whiteness was considered of sufficient interest by itself. The simple surface treatment of these pieces is certainly testimony to the fact that beautiful form combined with beautiful substance is adequate means for expression on a high level.

6. The Sung dynasty stonewares and porcelain

The Sung dynasty, A.D. 960–1223, was a time of mellow fulfillment in Chinese art. Although the social, military, and artistic surge of the T'ang dynasty had subsided, the artists of this time brought to perfection many of the qualities in the art of the previous eras. The art of the Sung dynasty is perhaps more subtle, refined, and sensitive than that of the T'ang. To us it seems classical, with a quality of completeness and finality.

The Sung pottery is perhaps more varied, mature, and beautiful than that of any other time in China, or, for that matter, of any other time or place. The surviving Sung pieces are almost all of stoneware or porcelain. Lead-glazed wares, though still produced to some extent, lost favor. By this time the custom of burying pottery figurines with the dead declined, but household wares of every quality supplanted them. Besides those Sung ceramic masterpieces which have been found in tombs, many pieces have survived in collections since that time. Other pieces have been found hidden in wells, in gardens, in attics, in storehouses or have survived in temple use or been handed down in families. Nearly all of the Sung pottery was monochromatic, although there are some classes of ware which were decorated.

During the Sung dynasty, pottery making was greatly stimulated and influenced by imperial patronage. The emperors, and their followers and families at court, were avid collectors of art, and pottery, second, perhaps only to painting, seems to have enjoyed special favor. The emperors built whole factories, employed master potters, encouraged new designs and glazes, and used large quantities of ware. The wares which were favored by royal patronage became popular and everywhere in demand, although there were always more plebeian types which were eagerly collected by connoisseurs.

In general, the various types of ware are associated with specific localities, and the name for some of the types is of geographical origin. Local sources of supply for clay and for glazes must have had a great deal to do with determining the kind of ware which any given kiln produced. No great commercial wholesale supply houses such as ours existed, and each pottery worked out its own techniques in terms of what could be found to make the various bodies, glazes, and colors. Once a pottery established a ware that had a following at court or on the open market, the tendency was to go on making such a ware for a long period of time without changing it radically. We know that some types made during Sung times persisted for hundreds of years after that. The perfection of Sung pottery is due in part to the gradual but very complete solution to technical problems such as the mining and the refining of the clay and other raw materials, the techniques of shaping, and perhaps most of all, to the refinement of firing techniques. A number of old kiln sites from the Sung dynasty have been found, and the "wasters" which have been excavated give some idea of the tremendous quantity of successful pieces that must have been produced. But we also learn much of the potter's technical problems from pieces found at the old kiln sites. Pots stuck to their saggers, pieces which are over-fired, or underfired, and pieces on which the glaze did not develop properly in color or texture, all are evidence that pottery then, as now, was not a sure-fire process. It is probable that potteries in the Sung dynasty were numerous, and often large. Production of the larger and more prosperous kilns is believed to have been exported from China as early as the 8th century. Pottery was a group effort, and there is no record of this potter or of that one gaining individual fame or notice. The pots are essentially anonymous, and perhaps the idea of an individual potter who would perform all the operations of pottery making himself would have been unthinkable to the Chinese of that time. Their master potters were probably individuals who knew the secrets of making various bodies and glazes, the exact procedures for acquiring and processing the raw materials, and the management of the firing for the achievement of certain results. It is a fact that groups of potters from the Yüeh kilns who emigrated to Korea, Japan, and Indo-China succeeded in making there some wares similar to those being made in China, and this would indicate that a well-rounded knowledge of the pottery processes could move beyond a limited locality. The perfection of the Sung pottery leaves no doubt that every attention and care was lavished on its production, and certainly no such works of art could have been made in factories, where individual workers are usually concerned only with a minor portion of the work and do not contribute to its design. The Sung ware was made by men who loved the art and craft of pottery, and who practiced it with great vigor and sensitivity.

In general, Sung pottery is quiet and restrained, both in shape and in finish. It seldom has that flamboyant quality so common in the T'ang wares. An effect of dignity and monumentality is achieved by the subtle proportions of the piece, by the relationships of one part to another, and by the use of color, glaze quality, the relationships established between the glazed portions and the bare clay, and by the suitability of glaze to form. The forms are usually of a sort which can be made on the potter's wheel without too much difficulty, and there is an ease about them which one associates with an almost effortless production. Most of the Sung pieces are not in any way extreme or sensational in either form or glaze, and the more spectacular Chinese glazes, such as five colors, peach bloom, and ox blood came after the Sung period, in the Ming dynasty and later. The Sung potters seemingly felt no remarkable desire to be novel or original, and were generally content to refine the old forms and to restate them in a thousand subtle and different variations. Seldom have two pieces been found which are exactly alike, and this indicates a certain freedom in the potteries; unlike the modern mass production worker, the potters were able to give an individual character to each piece. Molds were sometimes employed, but rarely to the detriment of the pots, though quantity and cheapness were, in some instances, desirable. Some of the finest and most carefully made ware, such as the Ying-ch'ing, was made also in a cheap or poor man's version.

The celadon made in Sung times continued the tradition of the Yüeh ware, but with more refinement of both body and glaze. The body of most of the celadon pieces is a light gray or whitish color, very dense, and well vitrified. The potting, in the best examples, is thin and delicate. The glazes are of almost indescribable hue, ranging from a sea-green through olive-green, blue-green, yellow-green, to gray-green.

Many of the celadons have a pattern either incised with a tool or impressed by a mold. The incised patterns are of a marvelous delicacy, and are subtly emphasized by the pooling of the glaze. Many of the molds have been found which were used to make this kind of ware. They are made from fired clay and were evidently used as a sort of hand jigger mold to achieve a piece with a design in relief on the inside face. The celadon glazes were clear, highly feldspathic glazes, which were fired in a heavily reducing atmosphere. The iron was probably introduced into the glaze by the addition of a small amount of red clay or other iron-bearing mineral. The celadons produced in the north of China during the Sung period are referred to as northern celadon, and these are typically darker, and somewhat more olive in color than the southern celadon. An effect similar to the northern celadon can be readily produced by adding iron to a feldspathic glaze, and perhaps the northern potters employed some glaze material which contained sufficient iron to produce this color, and did not add iron as such to the glaze. Celadon glazes were highly prized. The earliest, known as *pi-sê*, or "secret color," was for a time reserved for the princes of Yüeh. Celadon wares were admired for their resemblance to jade, and at their best, celadon glazes may have the look and feel of precious stones.

The famous type of ware known as Chün includes several distinct kinds. The ware was made in the ancient district of Chün Chou, and elsewhere. The clay body of these stonewares is a fine grained gray or buff color which frequently burns to orange at the unglazed foot. The glazes are thick and opaque, and are typically of a cool lavender, green, or bluish color, marked or splotched with plum color. In one type, the glaze colors run together, giving a crushed strawberry look, and this glaze treatment is frequently used on pieces which are made from slabs or are molded in shapes reminiscent of bronze, including the three-legged *ting* or so-called bulb bowls. More attractive, perhaps, are the Chün pieces with either

a simple blue-green glaze or those which have distinct red markings.

In many specimens, the glaze is almost a robin's-egg blue, with red markings which may appear to have been either placed rather carefully or to have appeared in unpremeditated spots. The glaze on these is marvelously deep and opalescent, and has a beautiful surface which is neither shiny nor dull. It frequently slips down a bit in the firing to form a roll of glaze near the foot.

The Chün wares are technically very interesting. The bluish color of the glaze is quite hard to duplicate. The color, as indicated by chemical analysis of old specimens, derives from iron, fired in reduction, and its opacity and opalescence is probably caused by the presence of phosphorus, no doubt introduced in the form of an ash, perhaps bone ash. The red splotches are caused by small amounts of copper in the glaze, which may have resulted from a wash of some copper-bearing slip under the glaze, or from an application of patches of a copper glaze over the glaze of the piece. These red markings on Chün ware are the first appearance of copper red glazes in Chinese ceramics and are thus the ancestors of the flambe, the oxblood, and the peach bloom of later times. In some specimens of Chün ware the blue-green and red variations on the same piece may be due to flashing in the fire. The discovery of saggers made with holes to admit the flame in certain spots would seem to indicate this, and some specimens which have been analyzed do show traces of copper in the blue portion of the glaze as well as in the red portion. But most Chün blue derives its blue color from a very small amount of iron in the glaze.

The Chün wares did not receive imperial patronage on a scale comparable with some of the other types of Sung pottery. The Ju and the Kuan wares, however, were strongly patronized by the court, and these wares were seemingly an outgrowth or refinement of the Chün ware. The Ju and the Kuan wares were thickly glazed with a very dense and smooth stoneware glaze, usually greenish-blue or blue in color. Not many specimens of this ware survive. Many of the shapes seem to derive from those of the ancient sacrificial vessels, and were slab-built rather than thrown on the wheel. The glazes are exceptionally refined, both in color and in texture, and have that unctuous, smooth, luminous quality characteristic of high-fired reduction glazes at their best. As in the case of the Chün ware, the cool colors result from small quantities of iron, well dispersed in the glaze.

One of the greatest achievements of the Sung potters is the Lung-Ch'uan celadon. This type represents the pinnacle in the development of the celadon glaze. The body of the Lung-Ch'uan ware is a very dense porcelanous stoneware; by Chinese definition it is porcelain. The glazes are typically very thick, and are usually crazed, sometimes in a wide and handsome network of cracks. The color is a somewhat cloudy bluish-green, sometimes appearing over an incised or combed pattern which is dimly revealed under the glaze.

One of the most beautiful of the Sung wares is the Ting. This ware, which was greatly favored by the court, is either a cool white, or a creamy, ivory-like color. The ware is very delicately made, is usually quite thin, and is decorated with incised patterns in low relief. Frequently these white wares were fired on the rim instead of the foot, a method used to prevent warping, and the unglazed rim was later finished with metal. The dark metal band at the lip of a bowl which is otherwise pure white can be very handsome, and these metal edgings were put on many pieces even though there was no unglazed part to conceal. The Ting ware probably represents the utmost in refinement of body and glaze which was possible for the potters of that time. The body of the ware is of exceptional purity,

and while it is seldom stark white, it rarely shows any coarse impurities which would cause specks. It is smooth, very fine-grained, and quite translucent where thin. The glaze likewise is very smooth, and colorless. In most cases it fits the body without crazing, and the glaze appears more as a natural surface of the clay than as a distinct and separate layer of glass. The surface of the glaze is lustrous and jadelike. The incised decoration, when it appears, is not emphasized by the glaze, as in the case of the celadon wares, but is sharply defined by its form alone. The specimens which are ivory color were probably fired in an oxidizing atmosphere, and the small amounts of iron present in the body and in the glaze were sufficient to cause the warm tone. The Ting pieces which are cooler white are no doubt those which were fired in reduction, and may have been identical in body and glaze to the ivory-colored ware.

Besides the highest quality of Ting, which is known as Pai Ting, other grades of the ware were produced, and these were presumably cheaper and more plentiful. In some of these wares the white color was achieved by coating over the body with a white engobe rather than by using a white body.

The Tz'u Chou wares of the Sung dynasty include several different types, but they are all stonewares of a rougher, more earthy type than those already described. They are easily identified by the style of potting, even though widely differing techniques were employed in glazing and decoration. The Tz'u Chou wares are distinguished by a masterly use of brushwork or sgraffito lines and by the superb integration of form and surface variation. They are all finished in subdued colors of black, brown, gray, or white. The Tz'u Chou wares were probably closely related to the wares then in general everyday use, and as such they did not enjoy imperial patronage, or for that matter the particular esteem of contemporary critics and writers. In style, the Tz'u Chou stonewares are vigorous, sure, and have the look of having been made with rapidity and verve. Many of the pieces are quite large and show considerable virtuosity in wheel technique. Of all the Sung wares, the Tz'u Chou has perhaps had the most influence on contemporary studio pottery, particularly in England and the United States. Potters feel sympathetic to its spontaneity and its frank use of ceramic materials to achieve natural earthy textures and colors.

Tz'u Chou is one of the few localities where pottery is known to have been made continuously from the Sung dynasty until modern times. We can only speculate on the organization of the potteries in those days, but in all probability production was carried on by small units, each one of which had a special style which was passed on from one generation to the next. A few pieces of Tz'u Chou ware exist which are signed by the makers, as "made by the Chang family" or "made by the Ho family." These are unusual, and most of the ware, like all Chinese pottery of all periods, is unsigned and anonymous.

The Tz'u Chou wares were probably produced under conditions not too different from still-surviving methods in China, Korea, and Japan. Pottery centers in these countries frequently have large communal kilns capable of firing thousands, or even hundreds of thousands, of pots at one firing. The kilns are set with wares from many small producing units, certain spaces in the kilns being assigned to certain potters. The potters co-operate in securing fuel and in the work of firing. Within the small producing units a certain specialization exists. Throwers, for instance, seldom do any decorating or glazing. The decorators tend to work with patterns which have been used for a long time, and which they know well. The manual work of preparing clay and mixing glazes is done by apprentices or special classes of workers. The work proceeds in an orderly rhythm of production.

Such a system of making pottery has certain advantages over individual production. Designs have a chance to "ripen" over a long period of time, during which subtle refinements of shape or decoration can be made. The potters, by long repetition of certain processes, become highly skilled and can work without any sense of strain or uncertainty.

The Tz'u Chou wares owe much of their quality to the organization of production in this way. The throwing is skillful, and the forms are relaxed and "easy." The decoration is almost invariably done with a seeming effortlessness which can come only from familiarity and skill in carrying out a more or less pre-established pattern. While each pot has a character of its own, it is still a member of a family and is recognizable as such.

The group of producing potteries at Tz'u Chou must have felt a certain identity with each other, because the wares they made are all conditioned by similar standards and values. But at the same time each pottery must have taken considerable pride in its own type of pots, and worked at perfecting and perpetuating its own individual style.

One common type of Tz'u Chou pottery is decorated with a sgraffito line, cut through a light-colored engobe, which is covered over with a transparent glaze. These sgraffito designs are often carried out with great freedom and grace, usually in patterns based on floral motifs.

Another related technique is the carved slip glaze. In this method, the pot was glazed in the raw state with a brown or black slip glaze. Before firing, the glaze was cut away in part, or incised with a linear pattern, thus forming the decoration by revealing the color of the unglazed clay in contrast to the glaze. It is certain that these pots were once-fired because the incising tool has, in many examples, dug into the clay. The glaze is not always particularly attractive in itself, but the contrast between the brown or black of the glaze, with its dull luster, and the beautiful earthy color and texture of the clay makes a handsome and sometimes dramatic color scheme.

Although a few T'ang wares were decorated by painting, the art of painting in slips or pigments did not really come into its own in Chinese pottery until the Sung dynasty. This development coincides with the perfecting of calligraphy as an art considered equal in expressiveness to painting, and the decoration of Sung pottery has much in common in style and spirit with the brushwork of Chinese writing. In the best examples of Tz'u Chou brush decoration, the brush strokes are swift, sure, well defined, and perfectly adapted to the form of the pot. In some examples, thick slips were brushed onto the body of the pot with substantial brushes, and then glazed over with a transparent glaze or a semiopaque glaze which clearly reveals the thick to thin gradations of each separate stroke.

In other examples, the body of the pot was covered over with a light-colored slip, and the decoration done on that in a pigment containing considerable iron, perhaps composed largely of red clay. Under a clear feldspathic glaze, the painting appears brown, black, or iron-red, and the quality of each brush stroke is well revealed.

Another important group of Sung dynasty stonewares which are earthy and dark like the Tz'u Chou pottery, rather than light and porcelanous, is the dark-glazed Chien ware, and the dark-colored wares of Honan. In the Chien wares, the surface interest depends almost altogether on events in the glaze, which is limited in range to blacks, browns, tans, and other earthy colors. Although the glazes are dark, they are nevertheless full of depth, surface quality, and interesting variations. The Chien pots are nearly all tea bowls of various shapes and sizes. Apparently, judging from the number of these bowls

which have survived, they were made in great numbers and must have been a kind of a household item.

They are glazed with dark slip glazes, and in most examples the glaze runs somewhat, collecting in a thickened roll near the foot, which is left unglazed. The bowls, as is proved by many wasters found at the old kiln sites, were each fired in an individual sagger, and the saggers were piled one on top of the other in high bungs. The glazes were no doubt composed largely, or entirely, of some common red clay, and refirings of fragments have indicated that the firing temperature was around cone 10, in a fairly oxidizing atmosphere. Glazes very similar to the old Chien ware can be made from red clay, particularly from those dark-burning, fusible clays which have considerable impurities in them, such as lime and sulfur. The impurities cause the melting slip to go through a boiling phase, and the streaks or spots in the finished glaze can be accounted for as the remains of bubbles and healed-over craters. In specimens where the glaze was quite fluid, these spots tended to run down and cause streaks of brown or bluish-black in the darker brown or black glaze. Chien glazes of this type are known as "hare's fur," or as "Temmoku," the Japanese designation.

During Sung times, dark-glazed wares were apparently made at many sites in Honan, and the Honan wares include not only bowls of the hare's-fur type, but many other interesting pottery types as well. In some specimens the black glaze is smooth, and uniform in color, the so-called mirror black. Other pieces show spots of silver color or brown on a black field, and these have been called "oil spots," which, in fact, they resemble. The oil spot glaze is a variation of the slip glaze and depends on an exact firing treatment of some natural slip glaze. Eruptions or blisters, which occur in the surface of the glaze during firing, cause the spots in the smoothed-out finished glaze. An oxidizing fire is necessary for this effect. Another unique glaze effect found in another type of Northern Sung ware is the subtle decoration which appears on the inside of some of the bowls. Leaf patterns and other markings may appear in brown or gray on a black field. These effects were apparently secured by various thickness of glaze, and are, typically, somewhat blurred.

The Chien wares and the other dark-glazed Northern stoneware are not only notable in themselves, but are also interesting because they had such a strong influence on Japanese stoneware. The Japanese admired the rustic, natural quality of these dark stonewares and collected them for use in the tea ceremony. A great deal of Japanese stoneware has been made either in imitation of the Chinese Sung wares or has proceeded out of similar philosophical and aesthetic premises.

It will be seen that the pottery of the Sung dynasty is quite various, ranging from the restrained and dignified elegance of the Ju and Ting wares to the robust, earthy expressions of the Tz'u Chou and Honan wares. But there is a common denominator for Sung pottery. It is a completeness and perfection of form and finish, no matter what the idiom. This pinnacle of perfection could not be sustained indefinitely, and in subsequent times, although there are many examples of splendid potting, the trend was downward toward overrefinement, toward an emphasis on technique for its own sake, and toward the sensational in both form and color.

If the Han dynasty pottery exemplified the Confucian virtues, and the T'ang wares owed much to a Buddhist outlook, it might be said that the Sung wares were essentially Taoist and expressed a spontaneous creativity and identification with nature. Varied as the Sung wares are, they are all dependent for their effects on naturally occurring reactions in the making and the firing, and they all rely on materials which must have been ob-

tained locally. Many students and chroniclers of Chinese ceramics have assumed that Chinese glazes and colors could have been arrived at only by complex, super-refined techniques and controls, and with materials and methods not now known. Actually, the bodies, the glazes, and the colors of these classic wares were the natural outgrowth of process, and the genius of the Chinese potters, practical and down to earth as they were, was to make the most of what they found near at hand.

7. Later stonewares and porcelains of the Ming and the Ching dynasties

The porcelains of the Ming dynasty, 1368–1644, and later, were formerly considered to be the crowning achievements of Chinese ceramics, but contemporary taste tends to give this place to the Sung dynasty wares, and to consider the later work as decadent. Actually the earlier pottery was not well-known until about 50 years ago, when extensive railroad building in China led to the excavation of numerous tombs and the unearthing of quantities of pottery of types previously rare.

The Ming dynasty restored native rule to China after the Mongol rule of the Yuan dynasty; the time of Genghis Khan, and the visit of Marco Polo to China. Ming was a time of expansion, prosperity, and great artistic and cultural activity, and the period has been compared to the Renaissance in Europe. The writers, the artists, and the potters of the Ming dynasty took the same sort of interest in the T'ang dynasty and its achievements that the men of the Renaissance in Europe took in classical Greece and Rome. As a result of increased contact with the peoples of central Asia and of the establishment of secure overland trade routes, foreign influences became once more a very important factor in the art of China, particularly in pottery.

Radical developments occurred in the production of pottery, especially in the making of porcelain. China began to export porcelain in quantity, and in response to large demands, a great industry sprang up at Ching-tê-chên. The factories at Ching-tê-chên, actually the first true factories the world had seen, were to remain for several hundred years the main ceramic production center in China. Hundreds of workers were employed there in mining clay, preparing materials, forming, and firing the ware. The work was arranged on the basis of the division of labor, and in decorating, even the different parts of the decoration on one piece were often done by different people, just as it might be done in a factory of our own time. Mass production had the inevitable effect of bringing about some standardization in the product, and, whereas Chinese pottery had formerly had the flexibility of form and decoration characteristic of relatively small-sized producing units, it now took on a more impersonal character.

An important technical innovation of Ming times was the introduction of blue underglaze painting on white porcelain. Cobalt blue had been used in Persian and Mesopotamian pottery for a long time, and its use in China may have resulted from the importation of the cobalt ores necessary to produce the color. Or, the knowledge of how to locate, grind, and use the ore may have been gained from Near Eastern sources. In the early blue and white ware, the cobalt color was prepared from somewhat impure ores which gave a grayed quality to the blue. Later, the underglaze painting was carried out in colors which were clear and strong. At the same time as the blue pigment was being perfected, the porcelain itself was being refined and, in general, Ming porcelains are whiter, thinner, more translucent, and more smoothly glazed than any of the Sung wares.

The enthusiasm of the imperial court, the collectors, the critics, and the foreign trade for blue and white wares was immense, and this type of porcelain became known the world over as the finest product of the Chinese potter.

Unfortunately, the preoccupation with painted patterns coincided with a loss of interest in the form of the pottery, and never again was the serene and monumental quality of the Sung wares recaptured. However, the early Ming wares do have a virility and a verve about them which is highly pleasing if not profound. During the long centuries of the Ming and Ching dynasties, fine wares were produced, not only in porcelain, but in stonewares and earthenwares as well. Many of the stonewares were made in imitation of or as actual copies of the classical wares of the Sung. Many types, such as the Tz'u Chou and celadons, continued to be made.

The identification and classification of the Ming and Ching porcelains has occupied scholars for years. The habit of the Chinese of copying earlier wares and of putting on them various misleading marks has made this task very difficult. But dozens of distinct types of blue and white porcelain are established.

The potters of China during the Ming and the Ching dynasties achieved an astonishing technical proficiency. Overglaze enamel decoration, which had been practiced to some extent during the Sung dynasty, became refined and elaborate. In spite of the refinements in the body of the ware which resulted in extreme whiteness, and which must have been accompanied with some reduction in plasticity, a wide range of intricate shapes and some pieces of very large scale were made. Many monochrome colors were perfected, including yellows, copper red, blue, black, and brown. While the exact controls of material, process, and firing for all these effects represents a major technical accomplishment, it must be admitted that the aesthetic quality of the ware seemed to deteriorate rather than improve as a result.

During the Ching dynasty there was a revival of interest in monochrome ware glazed with earthy colors, somewhat in the manner of the Sung dynasty. These stonewares tend to be very refined and closely drawn in shape, and the glazes are smooth and lustrous. The textured brown and tan glazes of this time are known as "tea dust" glazes. These rather severe wares were the inspiration of some European individual potters during the latter part of the 19th century.

A great deal has been written about the porcelains of the Ming and later periods in China, and the present work is hardly the place for a detailed description of the dozens of different kinds of ware as they are classified by connoisseurs and art historians.

The average potter, or pottery enthusiast, of today finds the classification and the distinctions between these wares not only confusing but meaningless. And for a variety of reasons, the later Chinese porcelains arouse little enthusiasm. They are the work of large-scale producing units, and while hardly comparable to the mass-produced wares of modern times, the forms and the decorations are lacking in that individuality and personal quality which is almost universally felt in the earlier Chinese pottery. More than that, much of the late work seems to have been made as much in response to the demands of the export trade as it was to any strictly Chinese taste. Although much of the Ming porcelain retained a certain virility, later work tended to become more and more effete, overdecorated, and symptomatic of China's cultural decline.

8. Korean and Japanese stonewares and porcelain

Korean pottery is very interesting both technically and in design. The Koreans had a special flair for ceramics. Their pottery, no matter how dependent it was, technically, on Chinese models, always had a very strong flavor of its own, and it is usually quite easy, even for one not schooled in the finer distinctions of pottery styles, to tell Korean work from either Chinese or Japanese.

The earliest Korean wares known to us are those of the Silla dynasty, 57 B.C.– A.D. 936. Many of these early pots are unglazed and are decorated in an overall fashion with impressed designs. They are formal in shape and surface, yet very freely executed.

The Silla wares also include some vitrified stonewares with brownish feldspathic glazes. These pots are similar to the stonewares of the Han dynasty in China, and were no doubt made with the same technical methods and with similar materials. Wares of the Silla period have that same remote, rather mysterious, quality of the early Chinese pots, and we feel that they belong to a distant past. The forms are strong and archaic, and were probably made for ritualistic functions.

The Koryu period in Korea, A.D. 936–1392, corresponds to the Sung and Yuan dynasties in China, and the pottery made during this time is closely related to the northern Chinese wares. Many of the finest Koryu stonewares are glazed with a celadon color quite similar to the color and quality of the Yüeh ware, and a favorite decorative technique was an incised pattern emphasized by the slight pooling of the green glaze in the low spots.

Another favorite technique of the Korean potters of the Koryu period, and one which was apparently original with them, was the inlaid slip pattern. In this method, the surface of the raw ware was scratched or incised with a fine tool in the intended pattern, then the incisions were filled with white or black slip, and any excess above the surface was scraped off. The lines of slip so achieved were then covered with a celadon glaze. This technique is commonly known by the Japanese term, *mishima*.

The decorations on nearly all the inlaid mishima pieces are very precise and carefully done. The surface treatment of each piece must have taken a great deal of time and painstaking labor. In spite of this inherently rather tedious method of decoration, the inlaid pots invariably retained a freshness and liveliness characteristic of all Korean pottery. The combination on these pots of the beautiful blue-green or gray-green field of glaze with the delicate lines in lighter green and black, with sometimes a hint of copper red, is among the most subtle and beautiful color schemes in any pottery. Besides the mishima technique, the Koryu potters were masters of other techniques of decorating, most of which relate to the Tz'u Chou wares of China. Fine pieces survive which are decorated in white and black slips, painted on the ware, or applied to the ware and then cut through to form various designs. There are also many examples of pottery painted with an iron-bearing slip or pigment, which, when covered with a transparent or semi-opaque glaze, gives a deep, rich, reddish-brown color.

In 1392 the Yi dynasty began, and the later phase of Korean ceramics occurred during the following centuries, which were marked by depression and poverty, and by the invasions, first of the Chinese under the Ming emperors, and later, in the 16th century, by the Japanese. In contrast to the polished and often rather elegant wares of the Koryu period, the Yi period produced some ware of a much rougher and more spontaneous sort. In particular, the brushwork became more rapid and casual, many designs being carried out with incredible freedom and sureness.

Much of the Yi dynasty pottery has the look of being made by rather crude techniques; the bowls may be warped or show other kiln imperfections, the bases of the pots frequently have sand adhering to the glaze, and the glazes and slips are applied with an almost reckless abandon. The rather primitive quality of this class of Korean pottery may be the result of the deterioration in the social and economic life of the country which tended to eliminate refined tastes and refined patrons. On the other hand, there is no need to regard such wares as inferior; in fact, besides being rich in a style indigenous to Korea, they are among the most ruggedly beautiful pottery which has been made anywhere.

Korean pottery is interesting not only for its inherent beauty of form and surface and its unique plastic quality but also for its relationship to Chinese pottery on the one hand, and for its influence on Japanese ceramics on the other. Korean potters looked to China for technical improvements in their wares, and no doubt some Chinese potters emigrated to Korea, carrying with them knowledge of Chinese methods of raw materials preparation, kiln construction, and firing. But in spite of this rather close technical relationship, Korean pottery remained a distinctive style, and Korean pottery is easily recognized as such. Chinese models must have been well-known, but were not slavishly copied.

Korea served as a gateway to Japan for the transmission of many cultural values, and the pottery of Japan from early times has shown very strong Korean influence. Much Japanese pottery, at least up until fairly modern times, was more like Korean pottery than it was like Chinese.

The first wheel-made pottery in Japan dates from around A.D. 100–500 and is known as Sue. It is very similar to the Silla wares of Korea, which are contemporary. The ware is unglazed, and seems to have been made primarily for ceremonial purposes. The forms are frequently set on high feet, and, as in the Silla ware, the feet are sometimes cut through to form arabesque-like patterns. These early Japanese wares may be thought of as a sort of provincial or countrified version of the Korean pottery of the time.

During the period corresponding to the T'ang dynasty in China, Japanese potters began to make glazed ware. The expansionist character of the T'ang regime in

China must have resulted in increased trade with the Japanese. The Japanese lead-glazed wares of this time are colored with iron and copper just as the T'ang glazes, and the ware is typically splashed or streaked with color. In most cases, however, the effect seems a little stiff compared to the Chinese models. An important group of lead-glazed pottery, green and white, has been preserved since the 8th century in the Shosoin, or imperial treasure house, at Nara.

As in Korea, the Japanese potters gradually improved their techniques through the influence of Chinese wares and Chinese methods. It is known that true stonewares and celadon glazes were made in Japan as early as the 9th century. Sometime during the 12th century Seto became the center for the making of crude vitreous wares in Japan, and this area continued for hundreds of years to be one of Japan's most important ceramic locales. Prior to the 12th century, Japanese pottery was relatively primitive and did not have a strong, distinctive character of its own. But with the establishment of the Seto kilns, Japanese pottery, although still strongly influenced by foreign models, began to achieve a maturity of style. Production at Seto was well established during the 14th and 15th centuries.

Seto wares are related to those of the Koryu period in Korea and to the Sung period in China. Many different shapes were made, including bowls, pitchers, bottles, incense burners, and bowls of the Temmoku type. While many of these forms were based on Korean and Chinese wares, which were being imported at this time into Japan in large quantities, other shapes are peculiarly Japanese, and do not have much direct relation to Continental models. The production at Seto was notable for its wide variety both of form and of surface treatment.

The most characteristic Seto ware was decorated with incised patterns and glazed with a yellowish iron glaze. The yellow Seto glaze is no doubt very similar to a celadon glaze, but is fired in a more oxidizing atmosphere. It is not known whether this oxidized color was preferred by the Japanese, or whether it resulted from firing techniques peculiar to their kilns. Other early Seto glazes are mottled and textured and apparently derive from wood ash. The Seto wares clearly show a character which has been quite constant in Japanese ceramics down to the present time; this is a variety, diversity, and multiformity which is quite unlike the Chinese wares. In China, pottery styles changed slowly, and while there are subtle differences between each piece, all the old wares fall within distinct types. These types ripened and matured over long periods of time, and the Chinese potter seems to have been quite content to work within the framework of a given style and to direct his creative energies toward its refinement. In Japan, on the other hand, pottery from one locality, such as Seto, was made in dozens of different styles, and the variations in decoration, form, and glaze treatment indicates an inclination on the part of the potters to experiment, to seek various surface effects, and to accept the natural happenings of the fire which, by another standard, would perhaps be considered imperfections.

Toward the end of the 16th century, Japan, under the leadership of the war lord Hideyoshi, invaded and conquered Korea. Many Korean treasures were carried back to Japan, and soon Korean pottery became fashionable in the tea ceremony. It is interesting that for the tea ceremony, the quality in Korean ceramics which appealed to the Japanese was not the smoothness and perfection of the Koryu period wares but the rough and earthy style of peasant pottery. The tea ceremony as it was practiced in Japan had a very important influence on pottery. The ceremony required certain utensils such as tea bowls, tea caddies, waterpots, and the like. Since the tea ceremony involved a return to naturalness and the appreciation of simple natural beauty, the style of the pottery most favored by the tea masters tended to be very unassuming, and without artificial refinements. Korean pottery was admired for its "imperfections," which seemed to reflect a direct and unsophisticated vigor. These imperfections took the form of pitted or crawled glazes, very rough and casual trimming, warped rims, and kiln accidents, such as bits of clay or sand stuck to the glazes or to the feet of the pots. The appreciation of such flaws as an evidence of process was, of course, a measure of the sophistication of the Japanese. Many Korean pots were copied by Japanese potters, and the influence of Korean pottery on Japanese wares, always strong, became dominant.

The 17th century marks the beginning of modern times in Japan, and the Japanese style in pottery, as well as in other arts, reached maturity during the Edo period, 1615–1868. In the early part of this period, large-scale manufacture of high-fired wares was continued at Seto and at Karatzu. The Karatzu wares are typically rougher than those of Seto, with much use of techniques such as the beating and deformation of thrown forms, and the use of rough slips. The manufacture of porcelain began at several localities. The early Japanese porcelains were patterned after the Yi dynasty porcelains of Korea, but later, in the Edo period, the enameled porcelains of the Ming dynasty in China became the dominant source of inspiration. A large class of stonewares and porcelains originated at Satsuma. The Satsuma wares are frequently distinguished by double glaze effects which give a mottled or irregular surface color.

During the Edo period, porcelain manufacture was centered at Arita, and this locality, with its many kilns and hundreds of pottery workers, became the Japanese Ching-tê-chên. As in China, technical advances made possible the development of pure white translucent wares of great refinement. Great quantities of blue and white porcelain were made. These were, technically, similar to the Ming porcelains. But the decoration on Japanese porcelain was carried out in a style of painting quite different from the Chinese. It is more asymmetrical, and, in general, freer in design. However, many Japanese porcelains are decorated with figures, floral patterns, or landscapes which, though rather casually placed, are much more realistic than the typical Chinese decoration. As in China, the perfection of overglaze techniques and the development of a technical virtuosity which brought all kinds of shapes within easy reach, resulted in overelaboration, affectation, and a loss of the strong, direct qualities of the earlier porcelains, which had been more related to the Yi dynasty wares of Korea than it had to Chinese prototypes.

During the last half of the 17th century, individual potters began to gain renown in Japan. Prior to that time, pottery in Japan, as in China and Korea, was an anonymous art, and only rarely were pots signed by individual makers. The first potter in Japan to gain a wide reputation was Ninsei, 1663–1743. A prolific worker, he made many pieces both in the older Korean-inspired styles and in enameled porcelains. The work of Ninsei shows that already the tendency of Japanese artists to look back toward the past for their inspiration was in evidence. Perhaps the most famous and admired potter in Japanese history is Ogata Kenzan. Kenzan was a pupil and follower of Ninsei. Kenzan's talents were decorative, and he is best known for his decorated plates. These are done in slips and underglaze pigments, and have a broad, simple, expressive style which was much copied in the work of later potters. It is probable that the actual pottery forms of these and other early masters were made by artisans working under their supervision, and that only the decoration, and perhaps the glazing, was done by the master potter, who signed the piece.

This practice is still common in Japan today.

Many well-established early styles of pottery persisted for centuries in Japan through the productions of relatively isolated country potteries, some of which still exist. An example of this is the Bizen ware, which has been made since the Edo period. Bizen, a sturdy utilitarian ware made for use in cooking, is made from a vitrified brown clay. It is not glazed in the usual way, but parts of the ware may have a gloss caused by flashing in the fire or by ash glazing.

The study of Japanese pottery presents some unusual difficulties. The practice of copying earlier pieces was widespread, and the certain attribution of most wares is practically impossible. Further confusion arises from the practice of Japanese potters of skillfully copying foreign pieces. In many cases this makes it difficult to distinguish between Japanese and imported pottery from Korea or China. Japanese pottery marks or signatures mean little because of their practice of copying old marks. Besides these difficulties, the student of Japanese pottery must contend with a bewildering profusion of names, and these names may refer either to kiln sites, towns where pottery was or is made, styles or types of ware, individual potters or names of potteries, or the techniques employed in making the ware.

Japanese pottery has been made in a tremendous variety of styles and in all kinds of techniques and clay bodies. But despite this, and despite the fact that much of it is imitative of Korean and Chinese models, Japanese pottery does have a distinctive character of its own. It is closer to the ways of thinking and working of contemporary studio potters than any other kind of historical pottery, and for this reason much Japanese pottery, even that which was made hundreds of years ago, has for us a fresh and new look, and we find it easy to understand and to appreciate. The immense variety in Japanese pottery suggests that among the potters there was a considerable reliance on individual impulse rather than on strictly traditional forms. Pottery made at the same locality in Japan and during any one particular period is of diversified form and surface treatment. Underlying this diversity, however, is the connecting factor of an attitude toward materials and processes. Much of the best Japanese pottery has a relaxed and informal quality. The evidences of craftsmanship tend not to be hidden or obscured but to be used directly and enjoyed for their own sake. For example, in Japanese pottery the marks of the fingers resulting from the process of throwing are frequently allowed to remain, and the crisp texture of the clay where it has been cut by the trimming tool is not smoothed over. Deformations caused by lifting the pot while damp and soft, or the warping which occurs during firing, were not regarded so much as flaws as the natural outgrowth of process. Decorative processes were often dependent almost as much on accident as on intent, and rapid and somewhat casual glazing techniques resulted in frequent runs or drips of glaze. These running or cascading coatings of glaze have a fortuitous but often very beautiful quality. In firing, the Japanese potter also tended to accept variations of color due to flashing and the unpredictable effect of ash glazing as a part of the whole rhythmic process of pottery making. It is sometimes difficult for one who accepts the Western idea of perfection in pottery as being somehow related to smoothness and to the concealment of the processes of making, to accept the Japanese concept that any evidence of process is not out of place on the finished ware, especially if it speaks of the intent of the potter and does not conflict with the purposes for which the ware was made.

Paradoxically, much Japanese pottery, particularly from later periods, which is made according to a philosophy that values simplicity and the acceptance of natural materials and processes for their own beauty, seems marred by affectation and the untrue quality which is apt to result from the adoption of, or clinging to, techniques which are out of their true context. For example, many of the Japanese wares inspired by Korean prototypes were carried out with a roughness and disdain for finish which was not necessarily characteristic of Japanese craftsmanship, but was a borrowing from the more unself-conscious, devil-may-care methods of the Koreans. This fault in Japanese pottery we should be quick to forgive, since we too are not a little prone to it. We have learned a great deal from the Japanese potters. There is scarcely a technique in pottery which they did not explore in an inventive and open-minded way. Although Japanese pottery is seldom monumental, it is seldom dull. It has a liveliness of form and a spirited use of color, texture, and decoration which is often inspiring. The willingness of Japanese potters to experiment and to search out new values in pottery has resulted in some work which is trivial, merely sensational, or badly done, but the best is among the finest of the world's expressions in this medium.

We have learned much from the Japanese also in attitudes toward the craft of pottery, and in the enjoyment of pottery as an art form rather than as something used either for ostentation or for merely utilitarian or humdrum purposes. The Japanese potters obviously practiced their craft with gusto and enjoyment. We are given the feeling that not only is the finished work important, but that the *making* of it is important too. It is out of the actual process of potting and out of the attitudes, values, skills, and sensitivity of the potter to his material that the real meaning of the pottery finds embodiment. This is in contrast to much European pottery, which is more planned out in advance, more "designed," and which depends on craftsmanship merely to carry out an idea already established, rather than to create the idea along with the pot.

Japanese pottery must be understood in terms of the way it is used. The Japanese value pottery as they would any other art form, and the fact that pottery is useful in certain practical ways does not make them think the less of it. The Japanese collect pottery with great enthusiasm and the best-known Japanese potters today cannot begin to satisfy the demand for their work. Valued pieces are kept stored in boxes, rather than exposed in cupboards or cabinets. They are used in tea drinking, in cooking, or for flower arranging, and all these functions are thought to demand pottery of the finest expressive quality and individuality. Even though a pot may be rather humble in shape and finish, and may perform some simple and routine function, such as storing grease from the stove, it may nevertheless be a prized possession and may give the user the same kind of aesthetic enjoyment that we would normally expect only of a painting or a piece of sculpture. Art, in other words, is allowed to enter into and to fructify all phases of life.

9. European stonewares

European stonewares and porcelain are of relatively recent origin and do not have the continuity of development of the Oriental wares. To describe European pottery fully, the productions of each factory and its peculiar contribution must be taken into account, and for this reason, most treatises on the subject are a confusing welter of details which are of real interest only to the antiquarian. European wares have been produced in great variety, and many influences, both technical and aesthetic, have determined their design and character.

Both technically and aesthetically, European pottery has lagged far behind Oriental pottery, at least until very recent times. The greatest periods of Chinese pottery, the T'ang and the Sung dynasties, coincide with the Dark Ages in Europe, when nothing but the crudest kind of unglazed earthenware was being produced. By the time stonewares and porcelain were being made in Europe, ceramic art was already decadent in China, after more than a thousand years of high achievement. Until quite recently, technical achievement in European ceramics meant learning to do what had already been done in the Orient. And it must be admitted that it was usually done better in the Orient.

The earthenware traditions of Europe prior to the 17th century derived largely from the Hispano-Moresque pottery of Spain and North Africa, and indirectly from the Islamic pottery of Persia, Mesopotamia, and Egypt. Although some pieces of Oriental porcelain are said to have been brought back to Europe by the crusaders, this type of ware remained legendary until the revival of trade during the Renaissance brought it to the West in larger quantity.

The earliest type of vitrified ware made in Europe was probably salt-glazed stoneware. This type of pottery, which originated in Germany, was perfected at a surprisingly early date. Its manufacture was highly developed by the 15th century, and its earliest beginnings, about which very little is known, may go back a hundred years or more before that. The development of salt-glazed stoneware required two separate inventions: (1) the perfection of a kiln capable of relatively high temperatures; (2) the discovery of the method of glazing by the use of common salt. Salt glazing is perhaps the only technique of pottery making which is exclusively a Western invention and which, moreover, has never been used to any great extent in the Orient.

Early European kilns for firing earthenwares were simple updraft structures based on Roman prototypes. At some early date German potters made improvements on this type of kiln, making use of more refractory materials in the walls,

and also placing flue holes at the bottom of the kiln instead of the top, thus creating a downdraft. These early German kilns permitted the firing of ware to perhaps as high as 1150°C, sufficient to vitrify the ware and to make a true stoneware.

The discovery of salt glazing was such an original and unprecedented development that it may have originated in some accidental firing. When kilns are fired with wood, especially at temperatures above about cone 4, some vapor glazing resulting from the dusting of ash through the kiln is sure to occur. Potters, noticing this, may have sought ways to make this natural glaze thicker and more uniformly spread over the ware. Perhaps the accidental use of wood which had become impregnated with salt, such as driftwood, led to the discovery. In any case, the earliest known salt-glazed wares are vitreous and have a uniform and well-distributed coating of glaze. In salt glazing, common salt is thrown into the fireboxes of the kiln when the highest temperature is reached. The salt volatilizes, and the sodium from the salt combines with the activated silica of the ware to form a thin glaze.

The Rhine River valley is the original home of salt-glazed stoneware. The earliest wares were made at Cologne, and potteries there have continued the manufacture of stoneware for centuries. The earliest salt-glazed stoneware was similar in form to contemporary earthenware, although many of the shapes appear to have been influenced by the forms of metal containers or leather flasks. Perhaps the best known of the early Cologne forms is the "gray-beard" jug. This is a narrow-necked piece intended for storing liquids which has, just below the neck, a bearded face modeled or stamped in low relief. In many examples, the modeling is wonderfully enhanced by the thin, slightly pooled, salt glaze. Mugs, pitchers, and other useful forms were made in the early Rhenish stoneware potteries.

26

These early stonewares illustrate a distinction between Oriental and European pottery. In the Orient, pottery early acquired a value which made it highly prized by collectors, patronized by the court, and used for ceremonial occasions and for the most refined expressions of civilized living such as the tea ceremony. In Europe, on the other hand, pottery was not much used by the nobility, who preferred wares of pewter, wood, or silver to the unsanitary and coarse earthenwares which were the best the European potter had to offer, technically, until modern times and the introduction of porcelain. As a result, European pottery was largely an expression of the needs and tastes of the peasantry, rather than of the upper classes. Utilitarian shapes predominate, and the character of the ware tends to be earthy, robust, and casual.

These qualities are certainly characteristic of the early German stoneware. The jugs, steins, and tankards were made for a beer-loving people, and the potting, although it incorporates much fine detail, is broad, sure, and full of vitality. The pieces were skillfully made on the wheel. Templates were commonly used to determine the final shape, which gives the throwing a precise and almost metallic quality, very different from the more fluid and sensitive shapes of Chinese pottery. A distinctive feature of the ware is the decoration in low relief, which frequently covers most of the entire surface of upright forms such as mugs. These decorations were often adaptations of contemporary engravings. They were first pressed as flat clay sprigs in shallow molds carved from wood and then fastened to the damp, freshly made pots with slip. Some of these sprig designs are composed of floral patterns or oak branches, others are rich with animal and figure motifs carried out in considerable detail. Sprigs were an ideal decorative technique for salt glazing, which is at its best over impressed or relief pattern, and these old German pieces have a rich, complex, and

beautiful surface. Many of the pieces are fitted with pewter lids.

The stoneware made at Cologne and at nearby Frechen and Eigelstein was mostly brown, with a mottled and slightly orange-peel texture. At Sieburg, a white stoneware clay was used, and the salt-glazed ware from this neighborhood is very light in color, with accents of blue or brown achieved through touches of slip or oxide. At Westerwald, salt-glazed stoneware figurines were made.

Although the potteries of the Rhine Valley have continued to make quantities of stoneware until our own day, much of it for export, the quality of the forms and the decoration deteriorated in the 17th and 18th centuries. In part this was the result of the influence of the then popular rococo style in design, which led to overelaboration and an excessive preoccupation with surface effects.

The German potters apparently did not discover the use of feldspar as a basic material for high-fired glazes and did not experiment with types of stoneware glaze other than salt glazing. Nor did stoneware production become common in Europe generally before 1700. Rather, it remained a specialty of the Rhenish potters, and its production methods were apparently a closely guarded secret and were the envy of earthenware potters, especially in England, where the Cologne stoneware was greatly admired.

The first stoneware in England was made by John Dwight about 1680 at his pottery at Fulham, a village near London. It is not known whether Dwight discovered the salt-glaze process by independent research or whether he learned the technique from immigrant German potters. In any case, he applied for a patent in 1684, and was granted the exclusive right to manufacture salt-glazed stoneware in England. Dwight was an energetic businessman, and soon the expanded pottery at Fulham was producing salt-glazed stoneware mugs, tankards, and teapots in a sturdy, vigorous style which, although it resembled closely the German ware technically, was quite English in character. Sprigged and embossed decoration was used at Fulham from the start, though not so lavishly as on the Rhenish models. The early Fulham ware, a direct and honest expression of contemporary tastes and needs, remains one of the finest achievements of English pottery. However, Dwight was perhaps best known for the statues and figurines which were made in his pottery. These were probably not modeled by Dwight himself but by sculptors hired for the purpose. The figures, covered with a thin salt glaze, are realistic and laboriously detailed, and to us are of no more interest than any second-rate sculpture of the period made in other materials.

Soon after Dwight began making stoneware, the Elers brothers discovered the secrets of salt glazing and began making a similar ware. The Elers are sometimes erroneously credited with introducing salt-glazed stoneware to England. Dwight sued the Elers brothers in 1693 for infringement of his patent, and won the case. His patent, however, expired in 1699, and soon numerous potteries were producing stoneware. Staffordshire at this time was already an important pottery center, making entirely earthenwares which were decorated with slips and glazed with lead compounds. Stoneware production developed rapidly here and for about 50 years vitreous salt-glazed wares were made in great quantity and variety in the Staffordshire district. About 1720 white clay was imported from Devonshire, and the light cream-colored pottery made from this clay soon began to displace the earlier gray or brown wares. Common forms of this time are mugs, teapots, platters, and other utilitarian wares. Teapots especially were in great demand during the early part of the 18th century, when tea drinking was just becoming popular. At this time the dinnerware set, as a group of related shapes including plates, cups and saucers, tea-pot, platters, and the like had not been developed, and most of the production of the potteries seems to have been in single items, rather than sets.

Whatever its shortcomings may be, early Staffordshire stoneware is charming. German influence gradually gave way to a truly English expression. Incised and embossed decorations appeared on nearly all the ware, and some of the shapes, the teapots especially, have a delightful exuberance and gaiety. Moreover, the ware is hard and durable. Salt-glazed figurines were also made at Staffordshire, many of them in a true folk-art style which seems more genuine than the more sophisticated figurines made contemporaneously on the Continent.

Toward the middle of the 18th century the pottery industry in England changed radically. The old handcraft methods of Staffordshire were no longer equal to the demands of a growing population, and the impact of the industrial revolution changed the whole method and character of production. This was a time of rapid and profound change in all manufacturing, and many industries, including the pottery industry, underwent a complete transformation within a few decades. The most important features of this change were the introduction of steam power, and the introduction of the principle of the division of labor. Josiah Wedgwood perfected his Queen's Ware in 1762. This ware was a durable, glazed earthenware which could be produced more cheaply than salt-glazed pottery, and soon salt-glazed ware became only a minor part of English pottery production. About this time pottery molds came into general use, and the result was an inevitable standardization of form. Wedgwood introduced a much greater division of labor than had been common in the potteries before, and he also was the first to introduce power machinery and more exact controls over the firing process.

The late 18th century brought important changes in pottery design. Largely as a result of Wedgwood's work, tableware became more functional, simpler, and the penchant for covering every piece with embossed decoration gave way to a preference for plain smooth-glazed surfaces. The production of tableware increased enormously, in response to a seemingly unlimited demand. On the other hand, the design of "artwares" as distinct from useful pieces designed for daily service was strongly influenced by the prevailing vogue for the neoclassical. The sturdy and indigenous English pottery tradition, as typified by the earthenwares and stoneware made prior to 1750, was lost, and throughout the 19th century the English potteries poured out vast quantities of pretentious, overelaborate, and imitative work.

Wedgwood's important technical innovations included a variety of clay bodies, some of them vitrified and made in various colors. His Jasper ware and Basalt ware were actually unglazed vitreous stoneware. As a result of Wedgwood's work, and as a result of the accumulation of technical knowledge coming from the Continent, where porcelain production had reached a high degree of perfection, English potters had gained control over the whole range of pottery substance and decoration.

10. Porcelain in Europe

The first true porcelain was not made in Europe until early in the 18th century. That the discovery of how to make porcelain was delayed so long is a significant indication of the primitive state of European technology prior to 1700. Many attempts were made, since porcelain from the Orient was a well-known and highly prized substance, tremendously admired and wondered over. Early attempts at making porcelain took the form of adding glass to white earthenware to make it more fusible and thus translucent and vitreous. Such an attempt was made in Florence under the patronage of the Medici family as early as 1575,

and a few of the pieces which resulted from this experiment are still in existence. They are rather thick, and relatively crude, and could never be mistaken for the Chinese models which they imitated.

The most successful "imitation" porcelain was that made in France at St. Cloud during the latter half of the 17th century. This ware, the so-called soft-paste porcelain, was made in a variety of shapes and was decorated with over glaze enamels. It was much sought after in its day, and its manufacture continued for several decades even after the manufacture of true porcelain had begun in France. The ware was thin, well potted, and although somewhat glassy, was not unpleasant in surface. The body was composed of light burning clays combined with a fusible glass frit. The firing temperature was far below that of true porcelain. Several factories in France produced soft-paste ware of this type, including those at Chantilly, Vincennes, and Sèvres.

Since porcelain making is an art which involves no complex chemistry, only the burning at high temperatures of three rather common minerals—kaolin, feldspar, and flint—it is surprising that the process was so elusive. It must be remembered, however, that the occurrence of kaolin in Europe, as elsewhere, was relatively rare, and since the material then had no important use, the clay deposits had gone unnoticed. Actually the only kaolin being mined in Europe at the beginning of the 18th century was used as a powder for wigs. Feldspar, up to this time, was apparently not included among the materials used for pottery. In Piccolpasso's famous book, *Li Tre Libre Dell' Arte del Vasaio*, the first treatise on pottery making, written in 1548, no mention is made of feldspar as a glaze ingredient. The firing temperature needed for porcelain was another stumbling block. All the European earthenwares were fired at about 1000°C to 1100°C, and it is unlikely that the kilns then in use were capable of much higher temperatures. Potters may have thought of about 1100°C as the upper limit of the possible as far as heat was concerned, and they probably could not have even guessed that the Chinese wares were commonly fired to 1300°C or higher.

Little or no direct information about how to make porcelain came out of China. Chinese literature contained no "how-to-do-it" books, and the pottery recipes and techniques were for the most part held as family secrets. A few Chinese potters emigrated to Korea, Japan, and to southern Asia, but none strayed as far as Europe. If even one Chinese master potter in, say 1600, could have been shanghaied, taken to Europe, and put to work in a pottery, the whole history of Western ceramic art might have been altered.

The earliest detailed account of the manufacture of Chinese porcelain is that written by Père D'Entrecolles, a French Jesuit missionary who was stationed in Kiang-si. He wrote two letters about porcelain, one in 1712, and the second in 1722, both dealing with the potteries at Ching-tê-chên, which at that time were large and thriving industries. He described in great detail the mining of the raw materials, how they were purified and processed, the location of the mines, the manner of transport used, and the processes of throwing, trimming, glazing, decorating, and firing which he had observed at first hand. In the light of our present knowledge, his account is accurate and quite complete. He correctly identifies the two major ingredients of the clay body, kaolin and feldspar, the latter known by the Chinese as "petuntse." He wrote: "The material of porcelain is composed of two kinds of clay, one called *pe-tun-tse*, and the other kaolin. The latter is disseminated with corpuscles which have some shimmer, the former is simply white and very fine to the touch. While a large number of big boats come up the river

from Jao-chou to Ching-tê-chên to be loaded with porcelain, nearly as many small ones come down from Ki-men laden with *pe-tun-tse* and kaolin made up into bricks, for Ching-tê-chên does not produce any of the materials suitable for porcelain. *Pe-tun-tse*, which is so fine in grain, is simply pulverized rock taken from quarries, and then shaped into bricks. Every kind of stone is not suitable, or it would not be necessary to go for it, twenty or thirty miles away." It is interesting to note that, according to Père D'Entrecolles, "a rich merchant told me that the English or Dutch [the Chinese use the same name for both nations] bought, several years ago, some *pe-tun-tse*, which they took to their own country to make porcelain with, but, having taken no kaolin, their undertaking failed, as they afterwards owned. The Chinese merchant said to me, laughing, 'They wanted to have a body without bones to support its flesh.'"

But sometime before the letters of Père D'Entrecolles became known in Europe, the secret of porcelain making was independently discovered in Germany. Credit for the discovery is usually given to Johann Böttger, but actually the important facts leading to the making of the first porcelain were established by Ehrenfried von Tschirnhausen, a Saxon nobleman and scientist. About 1690 he conducted an investigation of the melting point of various mineral substances. For this work he used the heat of the sun concentrated by mirrors or burning glasses. Very high temperatures can be achieved by this method; in fact, until the first atomic fission was achieved, the highest temperature ever recorded by scientists was achieved in a sun furnace. From his experiments with the burning glass, Tschirnhausen soon found that some minerals had a much higher melting point than others, and that specimens of true porcelain melted only at relatively high temperatures. He then proceeded to make small porcelain-like speci-

30

mens by fusing various minerals together, and presumably his tests included both kaolin and limestone.

Tschirnhausen well understood the economic importance of his researches, and in his travels through France and Holland he visited many potteries and acquired as much knowledge as he could about ceramics and the then common methods of making and firing pottery. Returning to Saxony, he tried to interest the king, Augustus the Strong, in supporting his researches. He met Böttger in 1701. Böttger was in the employ of the king as an alchemist in search of methods of turning base metals to gold. Although Böttger's work was financed by the court, he was held practically as a prisoner by the king until 1705, when his work in alchemy was plainly a failure. At that time he had joined Tschirnhausen in a porcelain research project supported by the king. The two men worked together until the death of Tschirnhausen in 1708. The first achievement of their laboratory was the development of a vitrified red body from which tiles, artificial gems, and pottery was made. The character of this red ware, very dense and hard, suggests that the researchers had constructed a kiln capable of fairly high temperature. With the achievement of higher temperature, it remained only to find suitable clays and fluxes. White clay was found at Colditz, and at first lime was used as a flux. Vessels of true porcelain were made as early as 1708, but the glaze was not developed until later.

In 1710, as a result of the success of Böttger's experiments, a factory for the manufacture of porcelain was established by the king, and after several years of further experimentation, pieces were finally offered for sale in 1713. A better kaolin was discovered at Aue, and the problems of fabrication, glazing, firing, and decorating were all brought under a measure of control. Although the first pieces were somewhat crude, by later standards, the productions of the factory which was set up at Dresden soon reached a high technical quality. At first the ware had a yellowish color, but this defect was overcome when feldspar was used as a flux instead of alabaster. Böttger appears to have been a poor factory manager, and it was not until after his death in 1719, and the subsequent reorganization of the enterprise under a new director, that production on any scale was achieved.

It is significant that the first porcelain manufactured in Europe was made under royal patronage. For many years porcelain making continued to be a diversion of kings and princes, and factories were established and maintained, not so much for profit as to furnish wares primarily for court use and for the prestige which came from the patronage of such wares. The vast majority of the porcelains of the 18th century were made for the aristocracy, and porcelain continued to be so expensive as to be far beyond the reach of the ordinary man. The fact that the ware was made to please the tastes of the nobility and wealthy aristocrats accounts in large part for the character of its design. This tended, from the first, to be complex, elaborate, pretentious, and not very functional. Court life in the 18th century was marked by elaborate pageantry, and the ceramic pieces which graced the tables, sideboards, and mantels of the aristocrats were intended to display, if nothing else, a lavish richness of form, decoration, and color. Large showy pieces were in great demand as centerpieces or as decoration for the table, and a high percentage of the wares made during the 18th century, including the figurines, were made for this purpose.

It must be remembered that porcelain making began in Europe when the baroque style of art was in full swing, and the forms and the decorations of European porcelain continued to be baroque in inspiration down to the present day. It is interesting to speculate on what would have happened if porcelain had been introduced into Europe during the Renaissance, or during Gothic times. Perhaps an entirely different tradition would have taken root then, one not based to such an extent on ostentation, overelaboration, and surface interest.

It is impossible to avoid the conclusion that porcelain in Europe does not measure up, aesthetically, to the wares of the Orient. The taste for which it was created was a degenerate one, which valued the superficial and the elaborate, and which had no feeling for the form of pottery. Very soon after the discovery of porcelain, interest in it turned almost exclusively toward its decoration, and wares without profuse overglaze enameling were seldom made. As in the later Chinese ware, the form was thought of primarily as a base on which the painting could be carried out, and different styles and factories were distinguished more by the overglaze painting than by the form.

By all odds the best European porcelain was that made during the early part of the 18th century, when the art was still new. The early European porcelains, while they have a rococo exuberance of form, still show a management of detail which indicates some respect for the material. Decorations of this time, in the Dresden ware and in the early wares from other European factories, often used the popular Chinese styles of painting in blue, and the effects, while they do not always ring quite true, are often quite charming.

To properly appreciate the 18th century porcelains, one must, of course, place oneself in that time and imagine the effect produced by the rarity, the elegance, the refinement, and the high cost of the ware. Since it was made for the aristocracy, it was coveted by all lesser folk. To appreciate it one must also try to forget the flood of inferior ware which has been made in imitation of the best. After the French Revolution and the rise of the middle classes in Europe, the ceramic industry was not slow to expand its production to provide "china" for the millions of people who wished to identify themselves with the upper classes, and who regarded porcelain appointments as an important status symbol.

Although the secrets of the porcelain manufacture at Dresden were at first carefully guarded, various German princes succeeded in establishing rival factories at Vienna, Ansbach, Bayreuth, and other places during the first half of the 18th century. In France, the royal factory at Sèvres, which was already making soft-paste porcelains, succeeded in making true porcelain in 1770. The productions at Sèvres, as a result of exceptional technical control and refinement, became the standard of excellence everywhere. However, the design of the ware at Sèvres, and in fact at most of the other European porcelain works, suffered from the pseudoclassical style ushered in by the Napoleonic era, and the wares made throughout the 19th century are inferior, by almost any standard, to the productions of the earlier time.

In France, the production of soft-paste porcelain was gradually replaced by the hard-paste or true porcelain. The earlier soft-paste wares of Sèvres, which were discontinued about 1770, later became much sought-after collectors' items. In England, the manufacture of true porcelain never became very important, and the English variation of the soft-paste type of ware, bone china, has been the most characteristic kind of vitrified ware. Many factories were established, including those at Chelsea, Worcester, and Darby. In all of these, bone ash was employed as a flux, and the resulting fired ware was very thin, exceptionally translucent, and very white in color. The ware has a fragile, yet solid, substance which is very appealing, and it became tremendously popular. Besides the development of bone china, England also has the dubious distinction of having originated printed underglaze decoration. In this process, the design is printed with underglaze colors onto transfer paper, and then rubbed onto the surface of the bisqued ware, over which the glaze is applied and fired. Such prints enabled the production of inexpensive, yet highly decorated wares. At first transfer prints were used to apply blue underglaze decoration in the Chinese style. Later brown was also used, and a variety of subject matter and graphic styles were introduced. American collectors especially prize the printed wares made after the American Revolution for sale in the United States. Some of these picture the great events of the War for Independence, as well as portraits of George Washington and Benjamin Franklin.

11. The country stoneware potters of the 18th and the 19th centuries

The production of inexpensive utilitarian pottery was not much affected by the development of porcelain and whitewares. Potters continued making earthenware vessels of all sorts to meet the needs of everyday life, and porcelain or china continued, during the 18th and well into the 19th centuries, to be so expensive as to be out of the reach of the ordinary man. As we have seen, salt-glazed stoneware was largely replaced for table use by the cheap and durable earthenwares of the Wedgwood type. But salt glaze continued to be used for utilitarian wares such as jugs and crocks, both in England and in Germany. It was made in small- or medium-sized pottery shops, which often produced only for a local market. Such stoneware potteries persisted until almost our own time, and kept alive, in isolated spots, a tradition of sound handcraftsmanship which in general had succumbed to the factory system. Some of these "country" pots are fine examples worthy of comparison to the best folk art of any country. They are simple, direct, and unself-conscious. The forms made for everyday usage are not cluttered with extraneous frills or appendages, and the material, buff, gray, or

brown clay and a simple glaze, speaks for itself, usually without the addition of any surface decoration.

Stoneware was made in America as early as 1775. A salt-glazed jug bearing that date is known to have been made in New York by John Crolius. For many years stoneware production centered around New Jersey because of the excellent stoneware clays in that vicinity and its nearness to the market. Early in the 19th century, clay from New Jersey was commonly transported to New England to supply the pottery shops there. Good stoneware clays are common in the Ohio Valley and in the Middle West, and toward the middle of the last century a great many small potteries existed in many parts of the country, producing salt-glazed wares for local demands. One hundred years ago the predominately agricultural economy of the country created a great need for durable pottery. Vessels were needed for storing liquids such as cider, vinegar, beer, and whisky. The pottery churn was superior to churns made from wood or metal because of the ease with which it could be cleaned. Crocks and large jars were needed for storing pickles, butter, sauerkraut, and other foods preserved for the winter. Cooking vessels, including baking dishes and the familiar bean pot, were made. In addition to these common items, the stoneware potter was called upon to make inkwells, pitchers, cuspidors, doorstops, footwarmers and drainpipes, and sometimes in his spare time he also made fanciful things such as whistles, puzzle jugs, and figurines.

Many of the potteries which supplied these useful forms were small establishments employing only a few workers, and in many cases they operated seasonally, closing down in the summer when farming chores became demanding. Many of the potters had been trained in England or Germany, and the tradition of design from those countries persisted. Most of the potteries seemed to have been rather short-lived as businesses, and many of the throwers were itinerants who moved on to a new location every year or so.

The stoneware potteries produced wares with a minimum of equipment and with the simplest techniques. Usually only one clay was used, tempered, perhaps by the addition of some sand. The clay was mixed or pugged in a vertical mixer with revolving mixing blades which cut and recut the damp, lumpy clay. This device was powered by a mule or a horse walking patiently in a circle. The pots were thrown on a kick wheel. When large crocks and churns were being thrown, the wheel was spun by the unwinding of a rope on the shaft which was pulled out by a boy or an apprentice. The insides of the pots were glazed with Albany slip or with a mixture of Albany slip and lead. Albany slip as a glaze material apparently came into general use about 1840, and it was shipped to potteries in various parts of the country. Pottery forms were made in shapes which permitted them to be stacked one on top of the other in the glaze fire, thus eliminating the need for shelves or saggers to hold the ware in the kiln. The kilns were at first constructed out of firestone, a type of loose sandstone also used for making blast furnaces and smelting ovens. Later, firebricks were used for kiln construction. The kilns were usually of the downdraft type, sometimes built into the side of a hill where earth could be piled around the kiln for insulation. Firing was done with wood, or, in some cases, with coal. Wood firing is excellent for the salt-glaze process because the volatile ash which flies through the kiln contributes to the salt glaze. Common salt was thrown into the fire at the highest heat to achieve the glaze. After many saltings, which builds up a thick coat of glaze on the walls, the kiln produces more uniform results. Most of the 19th century salt-glazed stoneware was fired at about cone 8.

The typical stoneware pottery was utilitarian and was seldom decorated. Some pieces do have a blue decoration painted on the raw ware with a cobalt slip, and sometimes this coloring was used to accent an impressed or scratched decoration. Elaborately embossed or sprigged ware, such as that made by the Rhenish potters or by the English salt-glaze potters, was never made in the United States.

The best of the old salt-glazed stonewares have a rich, varied surface with an orange-peel texture, and some color variation caused by flashing in the fire. In color they may be warm gray, tan, or a rich golden brown. The combination of the claylike color of the salt-glazed portions with the dark, black-brown of the Albany slip on the inside can be very handsome. The forms of the ware were for the most part traditional ones, and were dictated largely by well-defined functions. But besides filling very definite functional requirements, many of the pots are distinguished by a certain generosity of shape, a fresh and spontaneous quality in the throwing, and a richness in surface texture which makes them beautiful as well as useful.

Chapter 2

Stoneware and Porcelain Today

1. Contemporary interest in high-fired pottery

Much as we may admire the great pottery of the past, it is clear that the conditions which brought it into being have disappeared or have been completely altered, and that whatever pottery may be in the future, it can never again be the same as it was in the past. By the end of the 19th century most of the old handcraft tradition in pottery, at least in Europe and America, had died out. The small producing pottery shop, manned by a few well-trained craftsmen who did all the work of throwing, glazing, and firing, has given way to the larger industrial unit which, by making use of molds, power machinery, and the division of labor was able to turn out pottery that was cheap, uniform, and adapted to distribution in a mass market. However, remnants of the older craft methods survived in various places. In England, France, Germany, and Scandinavia, some small pottery shops which used throwing as a production method survived until after the First World War, and in the United States a few small country potteries persisted in the southern highlands region until about 1930.

In pottery making, as in other kinds of manufacture, the initial impact of the industrial revolution had detrimental as well as beneficial results. On the good side, industrialization held the promise of well-made, attractive, practical pottery cheap enough to be used by everyone. This possibility was realized to a certain extent even during Wedgwood's day. In many ways, Wedgwood was an enlightened industrialist. He was one of the very first to realize the possibilities of steam power, and one of Watt's first engines was used for decades in his pottery. Wedgwood also realized the need for improved transportation for British industry, and was active in the movement to build canals for the transportation of coal and raw materials. He was very inventive in adapting or changing the old handcraft methods of the Staffordshire potteries, to enable increased production. Much of the early Wedgwood pottery was pressed in piece molds and luted together, but soon casting and jiggering were used, and the hand processes of throwing and modeling were practically eliminated. Many pottery processes, such as glazing, finishing, decorating, and kiln setting, are difficult to mechanize; in fact, they have been brought within reach of machine production only within the last few decades. But the use of molds and the transformation of the potteries into large establishments using machinery and considerable division of labor meant the end of the craft potter.

Industrialization had a profound effect not only on the way pattery was made but on the design of pottery. The old handmade pots, of Staffordshire for example, had an individual charm, a feeling of the rightness of the form for the processes of making, and a certain irregularity which gave to each piece a particular quality all its own. All of this

35

was lost in factory-made pottery. Instead, each piece was exactly like the next, and the processes of molding lent nothing to the design. In the late 18th century, and throughout the 19th century, designs for factory-made pottery were based largely on imitations of the kind of expensive wares which had been made on the Continent for the aristocracy. This type of ware, highly decorated and rococo in design, enjoyed a tremendous prestige among the masses, a prestige which has lasted to the present day. The refined substance of porcelain was imitated in earthenware and china, and bad hand-painted overglaze decoration was imitated in worse prints applied mechanically. In design, the mass of factory-made pottery (the same could be said for many other factory-made products of the 19th century) was vulgar, pretentious, imitative, and unsuited either to the methods by which it was made or the uses to which it was put. If the pottery of our time were to be judged by the majority of factory-made wares, it would rank as perhaps the worst from any age or place, and this in spite of the great technical advances which made pottery cheap and relatively easy to produce.

It is only very recently that a start has been made toward a design for mass-produced pottery which is dependent neither on the shapes or character of handmade things nor on an outworn tradition of elegance, gentility, and refinement. As has been so often stated, what is needed in the design of factory-made goods is an understanding of both the potentials of machine production in terms of form and of the realities of function in terms of present-day living. The facilities of a modern ceramic factory have made many pottery forms easily possible which could not have been done before, and which have no aesthetic precedent. The changed ways in which people use pottery has made many of the older forms cumbersome or unnecessary or has created new functions altogether. Some European fac-

tories, notably Berlin Porcelain, Arsberg, and Rosenthal, have made a promising start toward a kind of design which is sensitive to modern conditions. American manufacturers have also become more aware of the importance of design and are moving away from abject dependence on earlier wares. Although really well-designed pottery still makes up only a small percentage of things produced, at least a start has been made toward solving the problem of mass-producing beautiful pottery.

The future of mass-produced ceramics is in the hands of the industrial designer. The factory worker of today, unlike his counterpart in preindustrial times, has no responsibility whatever for the design of the things he helps to make, and usually he has no personal interest in the product, outside of the fact that its production gives him gainful employment. While a knowledge of handcraft methods may be valuable to the designer, he must be free to make use of new techniques without being hampered by the old. While he may be inspired by designs from the past, or even by works made by contemporary craftsmen, he should not be thought of as a craft potter who happens to be using his skills and abilities in the service of factory production rather than for the production of handcrafts. More and more the designer is becoming the co-ordinating intelligence which alone can bring together in a sensible way the often conflicting interests of production, public demand, and profits, and still shape a product sensitive to the real needs of today.

The old craft of pottery, practiced more or less anonymously for millenniums, expired as a result of industrialization. But after a hiatus lasting a few decades, it has begun to revive again. And, as is proper for reincarnations, it is taking a somewhat different form.

A great increase of interest in pottery as a craft, as distinct from its industrial importance, seems to have occurred beginning in about 1930. At that time there were few people in the United States who were interested in making pottery, at least compared to the numbers involved with it today. The contemporary interest in pottery seems from the start to have been only incidentally related to the idea of making things for profit, or to any connections between ceramics and teaching in the public schools. It has stemmed rather from a desire on the part of numbers of people to explore the craft for what it was worth, and to experience the satisfaction of making things entirely through personal, individual effort. Opportunities for people to create something which is entirely their own have been generally diminished by the conditions of modern life, and perhaps the revival of interest in pottery, as well as the other crafts, grows out of a widespread feeling of dissatisfaction with the socialization and standardization of human effort.

A generation ago, most efforts in craft pottery were carried out in earthenware. Kilns for firing stoneware or porcelain were not commonly available to the studio potter, and most craft potters did not have either an interest in or a knowledge of how to produce high-fired pottery. Most of the work was inspired by wares of a Mediterranean type, with bright, colorful, majolica glazes. But the last 20 years have seen not only a tremendous increase in the number of people who are making pottery, but also an increase in technical knowledge and control, and in the available equipment and raw materials for studio work. Potters have turned increasingly toward stoneware as an ideal vehicle for personal work.

Most handmade pottery today seems to have one thing in common: it is made not for profit but for the love of the doing. This puts the craft on an entirely different basis than formerly. There are no guilds or professional standards to be upheld, no strong tradition, either of design or of usage, no importance attached to efficiency or economy, and no apprenticeship system which enabled the potter in the old days to learn the craft in a thorough and orderly fashion. All of this is gone forever. Pottery has become a very individual matter, not based on group effort or stimulated by economic demand. As such it has, of course, lost status as a trade or a profession, but it has gained freedom. The potentials of this freedom, as yet largely unrealized, are great.

2. Japanese stoneware potters

Unlike potters in most other countries, contemporary Japanese potters have succeeded in building soundly on the old ceramic traditions of their country, and the best of them have been able to create an art which, though very Japanese and having obvious technical and stylistic relationships to older pottery, is yet creative and individual.

The coming of industrialization in Japan created problems differing from those of Europe, but no less far-reaching in effect. The rapid expansion of the export trade, mostly dealing in goods far inferior to the Japanese norm in design, with the attendant growth of large-scale factories, disrupted the old handcraft production methods, and threatened the extinction of the old Japanese styles of pottery and the other crafts as well. Industrialization came quickly to Japan, and its rapid and uneven spread in the early part of this century left many areas of Japanese life more or less untouched. Thus, in spite of the fact that Japan could boast a modern ceramic industry, making use of advanced machinery and tunnel kilns, there still existed country potteries such as those at Mashiko, which carried on the same ways of working that had been practiced for centuries. The product of such peasant potteries was taken as a starting point by a group of potters who early in this century set out to revive and to develop the folk-art tradition of Japan. Through their efforts, and through the work of the Folk Art

Museum in Tokyo, the movement has succeeded. Today there are hundreds of individual artist-potters working in Japan, and while their work is various, much of it shows a respect for ways of potting which are essentially indigenous to Japan. Folk pottery, the older Japanese ceramic wares such as Bizen and Seto, Korean pottery, Sung dynasty brown and black wares, and even the work of Bernard Leach must be counted among the influences which have been active in shaping contemporary work.

Perhaps the best known of the modern Japanese potters is Hamada-Shoji, who was born in 1894. He studied technical ceramics, but early in his career he decided to follow the way of an individual artist-craftsman and set up his shop in the pottery village of Mashiko. Hamada's pottery is marked by an unassuming modesty and a frank acceptance of stoneware qualities and effects as they result from a simple and direct treatment of the materials and processes. He does not sign his ware, but prefers to remain anonymous except as the distinction of his style identifies his work. His pots are nearly all simple functional forms such as plates, bowls, tea bowls, teapots, and flower vases. He works exclusively in high-fired stoneware and has limited his colors to gray, iron red, and the milky, semi-opaque qualities of high feldspar glazes. His glazed surfaces are achieved most simply, and the power of his work comes not from any unusual or spectacular surface effects, but rather from a relaxed, spontaneous, yet masterful command of form, together with an ability to impart to each piece some accent which seems to dramatize a moment of rare insight. For many years, Hamada has produced a steady flow of work which is consistent, full of vitality and warmth, and which has had a strong influence on other Japanese potters, as well as on the development of studio pottery in Europe and the United States. Hamada is especially well-known in England and in the United States, where he has visited and given demonstrations.

Another outstanding modern Japanese potter is Kawai-Kanjiro, born in 1890. His work has shown great variety in shape and finish, including much ware which is hand built rather than thrown.

Tomimoto, born in 1896, was one of the leaders of the Folk Art movement and was a close associate of Bernard Leach during the latter's first stay in Japan. He is best known for his beautifully brushed patterns on stoneware.

Kitaōji-Rosanjin has made much pottery which displays a deference to older styles. Some of his ware, for example, has been made in the manner of the old Bizen ware, but he has also done a great deal of experimental potting, some of it in low-fired wares which incorporate underglaze and overglaze techniques of various sorts. Kato-Hajime works in porcelain and stoneware and has become well-known for his enamel overglaze decoration. He is a versatile potter who works in many different techniques, and has gained a sure mastery over them all.

These and many other modern Japanese artist-potters, although they work in widely differing styles, share a philosophy of pottery making which might be summed up as follows: The potter must continue to serve the humble needs of everyday life. The potter should be loyal to pottery as such and not try to make it into sculpture or painting. But within the limitations of pottery form, profound rhythms may be discovered having an expressive potential which is different from, but not necessarily inferior to, that of the other arts. Meaningful proportions, forms, and surfaces will result from the submergence of self in the concentration on the making of the pot. The materials of the craft must not be forced too much, but should rather be allowed to take forms and colors which seem to occur naturally as a result of pottery processes. And what may have been considered a flaw by some false standard of mechanical perfection may actually be expressive of the true nature of the process as sensitively guided by a particular potter.

3. Some pioneers in contemporary high-fired pottery

The English potter Bernard Leach was born in the Orient and returned there as a young artist in 1911. Soon he became absorbed in pottery and was a fellow student of Tomimoto. He studied the ancient wares of Japan and China, started his own pottery shop, experimented with Oriental ways of forming, decorating, and firing, and in his work he tried to interpret the spirit of the old methods in modern terms. Leach became well-known in Japan, and there his pottery has commanded the respect of his fellow potters. After the First World War, Leach returned to England, where he started his pottery at St. Ives. Here, using a wood-burning kiln patterned after the Japanese chamber kiln, he began making high-fired stonewares.

Leach believes that the finest pottery seldom results from making one unique piece but is, rather, the result of that subtle refinement of form which is possible only when numerous similar pieces are made. He also believes that the humble piece intended for daily use may be just as profound an expression of the art of pottery as some pretentious and elaborate thing made for exhibit. The pottery at St. Ives has produced a steady flow of ware of high quality. It has never been a one-man pottery but has involved the productive and creative energies of several people.

Bernard Leach's influence has been effective not only through his pottery and through the work of his students, but also through his book, *A Potter's Book*. In this book, published in 1940, he forcefully states his philosophy of pottery making, and gives a vivid description of the Oriental approach to technique. The book became widely known in this country during the 1940's and had the effect of turning the attention of potters to Chinese and Japanese values in pottery, and to stoneware as an ideal material for the expression of something individual and yet universal in ceramics.

In his own work, Leach has used rather smooth stoneware clay bodies, usually gray or light tan, and glazes which are quiet in color but very rich in surface quality. Celadon, iron red, and an oatmeal gray are his typical glaze colors. His wares are cleanly made, yet always have an ease and naturalness about them. Most of his pieces are modest in size and are intended for use. His early training as a painter and draftsman has given him great facility in decoration, and his control of brushwork approaches an Oriental standard of fluency. Leach has had an absorbing interest in the pottery of the past, and his greatest contribution, perhaps, has been to make the techniques and the philosophy of Oriental ceramics more available to Western potters. His absorption in this task has perhaps prevented him from developing a truly personal style, or a pottery which seems in keeping with any dynamic or developing Western tradition.

Another English potter who has produced stoneware of exceptional quality is Staite Murray. He began working in high-fired stoneware during the 1920's, and he shared Leach's interest in Oriental techniques, especially in glaze effects. Unlike Leach, who maintained a regular production of more or less utilitarian pots, Murray produced mostly unique pieces, and worked more as an artist than as an artisan. His best pieces, many of which are impressive in scale, have a great individual beauty and dignity. They are exhibition pots; in fact, most of them have been sold through exhibition. Staite Murray, although he used clay and glazes in techniques similar to Chinese and Japanese pottery, succeeded in bringing into his work a personal vitality and individuality rare in modern pottery.

Charles F. Binns was an English potter who became an American and who had a great influence on ceramics in the United States. He was born in 1857. After his early training and work in the Royal Worcester works, he emigrated to the United States and settled in New Jersey, where he became director of a trade school for ceramics. In 1900 he was made the first director of the New York School for Clay-working at Alfred University, which later became known as the New York State College of Ceramics. During the 35 years that he directed this pioneer school of ceramics, it became the leading institution for ceramic education and research in the United States. In addition to his work as an educator and ceramic technologist, Binns was continuously productive as a potter. His work was greatly influenced by his admiration for the Chinese pottery of the Ching dynasty. During the time that Binns was forming his style of potting, later Chinese ceramics were much admired and the wares of the Sung period were little known. Binns believed in the ultimate refinement of the potter's art, both in form and in surface, and he spared himself no pains in achieving his ideal of perfection. His work showed no trace of the fussiness or elaboration so typical of the decorative art of his day. Many of his pots, which usually took the form of simple bowls or vases of modest size, were thrown with the aid of a template design, and were made in two pieces to facilitate the exact control of the shape. Binns's stoneware glazes, while very quiet in color and texture, were magnificent in their restrained and dense brilliance. Many of his glazes are reminiscent of the Chinese tea-dust effects. He fired his pots to cone 11 or 12 in a predominately oxidizing atmosphere. Binns's influence was effective not only through his pottery but also through his great enthusiasm for ceramics and through his teaching and writing. His book, *The Potter's Craft*, was for many years the standard work in its field, and many important

ceramists and educators were his students, including Charles E. Cox, Arthur Baggs, John F. McMahon, Marion L. Fosdick, and Charles Harder.

Sam Haile was a particularly gifted English stoneware potter who died in 1949. He studied at the Royal College of Art in London, and learned pottery from Staite Murray. Like Leach and Murray, Haile found his expression in techniques related to the classic early Oriental pottery—high firing, reducing atmospheres, and the simple direct use of high-temperature glazes and slips. But he succeeded in infusing into his work an altogether modern spirit. Taken as a whole, his pots were a statement far in advance of the time, and they were little appreciated while Haile lived. In form, Haile was not confined by precedents, and he stretched the scale and profile of his pots until, in some cases, they give the effect of great tension. His pots were usually monumental in concept if not in scale. Great anthropomorphic cylinders, swelling globular forms, massive and virile jars, spreading V-shaped bowls—of these he made a vocabulary of shape which was unique and unforgettable. He dared to decorate these forms with fearless brushwork and slip in patterns of barbaric intensity. Haile rebelled at the idea of "good taste" and "safe" proportions and relationships in pottery, and he was interested in breaking into new territory more in keeping with the searching and uncertainty of the modern spirit. In this quality of search (at the risk of finding nothing, perhaps), his pottery relates to modern art in general, and is far from the warmed-over rehash of values long dead which so many potters have been content to express.

Haile worked for a time in the United States, first in New York, where he built a kiln for high firing at the Henry Street settlement, and later at Alfred, where he worked for a year making stoneware pots. After a brief period teaching at the University of Michigan, he returned to England to serve in the war. His untimely death in an accident cut short his career at the height of his power.

4. Pottery today

Pottery making, far from dying out as a handcraft belonging to former ages, persists, and is very much alive today. Although the technical essentials of the craft have not changed, the function of pottery, and the reasons for making it have altered radically, so that comparisons between the pots made now and those made in former times are difficult to make and may be meaningless. Pottery has become an individual matter, not really dependent for its form or character on any factors which are beyond the potter's control, such as market demands, function, and tradition. The potter, like the painter and the sculptor, makes what he has an urge to make, and while he cannot escape the influences around him, any more than any other artist can, he is not, for the most part, making a commodity.

This tendency toward individualism, which has resulted from the declining economic importance of handcrafts as a means of filling everyday functional needs, has placed pottery making in somewhat the same position as painting and sculpture. These arts long ago lost any except the most fitful patronage, but have continued nevertheless, as vital expressive arts. As an individualistic art, pottery risks the defects which are apt to be inherent in any activity which is removed from the guiding and controlling influence of social integration. All of the individualistic arts which are divorced from the main stream of economic life, while they may and have arrived at statements of unique power, may also be afflicted with waywardness, amateurism, preciousness, obscurantism, lack of standards, and the uncertainties of forms which are not controlled to any extent by functional considerations. Thus in pottery today we have a field of activity which is extremely various, and which includes the work of some very highly trained potters whose work is guided by standards which would be high for any age or place, and who make pottery of exceptional quality. It also includes work made by beginners or amateurs who bring to the craft only the rudiments of skill or understanding, and who practice it perhaps for amusement or for therapeutic reasons. In this, pottery is no different from painting, which is practiced by some gifted individuals who contribute seriously and brilliantly to emerging culture, and also by innumerable dilettantes whose work has no significance, except, perhaps, for themselves. The modern artist, no matter in which country he works, and no matter what medium he chooses to work in, is essentially without artistic roots, and his task is more to create a tradition than to support or expand an existing one.

It is not reasonable to expect that pottery today should conform to any discernible standard applying to all potters, or that it should have any unifying sense of direction or purpose such as sometimes characterized it in certain past eras. It is only possible to judge pots on their own terms. At least the present conditions make possible a maximum freedom for individuality and imagination, and in many ways the craft of pottery has been revitalized during the last generation by the creative work of individuals who found in it ways of saying new things. As each person brings a different set of interests and abilities to the craft, each will find a different expression in it.

There has been a general blurring of distinctions between the arts and the crafts. Many established artists, like Picasso and Miro, have worked in mediums traditionally reserved for the craftsman, such as pottery, tapestries, and rugs, and have made, in these media, works in no way less significant than their statements in paint and bronze. On the other hand, a few outstanding artists who consider themselves primarily "craftsmen" because they use mediums which have been associated with the crafts, have produced works which are certainly as valuable as the vast majority of contemporary paintings and sculptures in authenticity, expressiveness, and meaning. It is clear that we can no longer relegate a work to a position of lesser importance just because it is made in a certain way, of a certain material, and is thus a "craft." This does not mean that all pots are works of art, any more than all sculptures or paintings are works of art. But a pot may be made from motives and for purposes similar to the motivation behind painting and sculpture, and it *may* also prove to be a work of art.

Most individual studio potters are inclined to concentrate on types of pots which are not particularly functional in the narrow sense. There is a general feeling among potters that the task of supplying plates, pitchers, cups and saucers, teapots and the like, is best performed by the factory, whether large or small, and that the proper field for the individual potter is in ware which gives more scope for the expressive vagaries of handwork. While this tendency to avoid forms which are utilitarian in an immediate way is widespread, there are at the same time numerous potters who prefer to make things for use in the kitchen or on the table, and who regard the function of the pot as a healthy base to which other values may be added in keeping with the abilities and insights of the potter.

There is today a great urge to experiment, to try new forms and new kinds of surfaces, and to break through traditionalisms which no longer seem valid. For example, many potters have questioned the idea that pots are best covered with smooth, unbroken glazed surfaces, or that tooled feet made in the manner of Oriental precedent are necessarily the best way to form the bottoms of pots, or that the relationships between the parts of the pot should be orderly and "classical," or that the potter's wheel should be used only in ways which were originally intended to result in rapid and efficient production. All experimentation involves the risk of failure, and if the traditional values of pottery are not to be relied on, it is to be expected that some of the results will remain groping and of uncertain value. Of course, work growing out of a genuine drive toward new shapes which is based on truly creative impulses must be distinguished from work which pretends to originality but which, in fact, only apes currently popular trends. Thus when pots with multiple spouts and openings first became popular a few years ago, they were, perhaps, the result of genuinely original ideas. Today every exhibition is cluttered with pots having a multiplicity of necks or spouts, and the idea has become merely a cliché. Original and valuable work, no matter how free or casual it is in the treatment of surfaces or in the way the shapes are established, will be found to result from mastery over the medium, and from the ability of the potter to make his materials respond sensitively to his intentions, even his unpremeditated ones. Unfortunately, the ineptitudes of the beginner may be mistaken for an inspired groping toward the unknown. But all experimental effort runs the risk of being indistinguishable from failures which had their genesis in lesser purposes.

Much pottery, then, is made to stand alone, deriving its value neither from usefulness in the everyday sense or from any nostalgic associations. As an object standing alone and signifying nothing beyond itself, there is a chance that it will be found eventually in the rummage sale, along with other outmoded objects which no longer serve any function. On the other hand, if it is a work of passion and conviction, the pot will have an enduring value which in no way depends on function (such as containing, pouring, storage) but which has to do more with the vision and imagination of the potter and his ability to give his work universal and symbolic meanings.

42

Chapter 3

Stoneware Clays and Clay Bodies

1. Natural stoneware clays

Natural stoneware clays are fairly abundant, though not nearly as common as red-burning earthenware clays. Any clay might be called a stoneware clay which can be fired to a temperature of 1200°C (or about cone 7) and which, as a result of this treatment, is of a serviceable hardness and density. Stoneware clay may burn to a buff, tan, gray or light brown, or to a dark brown or brown-black, depending on the amount of iron or other impurities present, and depending also on the exact temperature and atmospheric condition of firing. Most common, surface, iron-bearing clays are unsuitable for stoneware because they will not withstand temperatures above about cone 4 without excessive softening and loss of shape. On the other hand, very pure clays, such as kaolin and many fire clays, cannot be used by themselves for stoneware because they are too refractory and do not become hard and dense unless they are fired to cone 14 or more. Stoneware clays are commonly of the sedimentary type, and are found in seams or layers, often associated with fire clays, flint clays, or coal.

Stoneware clays vary considerably, not only in fired color but also in working properties. Some may be very plastic with an attendant high drying and firing shrinkage, while others may be relatively nonplastic and have a low shrinkage. The stoneware potter will search for a clay which first of all has the right reaction to the fire and produces a fired substance of the desired color and density. Beyond that he will look for good working properties such as plasticity, good drying, and not too much drying and firing shrinkage. Not very many natural clays will be found to be satisfactory on all counts, and for this reason it is common practice to make stoneware bodies from a blend of several clays and nonplastic ingredients. However, it is always wise to use no more materials in a clay body than are necessary, and if one fine natural stoneware clay can be found which will perform well without the additions of any other material so much the better.

There is no large market for stoneware clay such as exists for kaolins and ball clays, and only a very few stoneware clays are mined commercially. This makes stoneware clay hard to obtain in many localities. Another trouble is that many fine stoneware clays are found in relatively small deposits which do not justify large-scale mining, and so are available only to local potters. I have used fine stoneware clays from Colorado, Wyoming, and Iowa which were excellent for potting just as they came from the ground, without any additions. These were all from small pits, and the clay was not being mined or used commercially. If one is interested in locating and using native clay for stoneware, the surveys of natural resources which have been made in the various states can be of real help in locating likely deposits, and the geologists who are employed by many of the states can often give valuable advice. The Midwestern States are rich in clays of all sorts, including fine stoneware clays.

The slopes and silt beds lying on either side of the Appalachian Mountains have a great variety of clays, many of them suitable for high-temperature firing. The Pacific slope is relatively poor in clay, and the chance of finding really good natural stoneware clays in this region is small.

Stoneware clay is closely related to fire clay and might be thought of as a low-grade, plastic fire clay. Frequently deposits of fire clay which are being mined commercially will have an associated seam of material suitable for pottery. Anyone looking for stoneware clay should investigate the clays available at or near plants making refractory brick. Fire clay, while usually too refractory and nonplastic to be used by itself for pottery, can be a very valuable addition to stoneware bodies.

Jordan clay, mined in New Jersey, and Monmouth clay, produced in Illinois, are the two most commonly used commercial stoneware clays in the United States. They are quite similar in working and firing properties. They are fairly plastic, do not shrink unduly, and burn to a buff color when fired to cone 6 or above. While they may be used alone, most potters find them somewhat lacking in plasticity for throwing.

The characteristics of an ideal stoneware clay would vary, depending on the kind of ware to be made from it, but most stoneware potters would be pleased with a clay of somewhat the following description:

Physical Properties:
—Excellent plasticity for wheel work, yet with enough coarse material in it to give a slight tooth and to permit the making of larger shapes without slumping.
—Drying shrinkage of no more than 5%, and no tendency to warp or crack on drying.
—Freedom from alkalies which would cause scumming, or from excessive organic matter.

Fired Properties (cone 8–10):
—Firing shrinkage of not more than 6%.
—Absorption not less than 1% or more than 5%.
—Color in oxidized firing, medium buff perhaps with some texture or mottling.
—Color in reduction, light orange-brown, with pronounced texture.

Most potters will not have the luck to find a single clay with all of these virtues. But fortunately, blending of readily available clays and other materials will produce stoneware bodies which meet any practical or aesthetic requirement.

2. Blending stoneware bodies

Blending various clays and other materials to achieve workable stoneware bodies is actually a rather simple procedure. Stoneware bodies are easier to compound than either earthenware bodies or porcelain. In earthenware, unless natural clays are relied on entirely, there is the problem of selecting suitable fluxes, and of maintaining the plasticity of the body, perhaps in spite of the inevitably high percentage of nonplastics. In porcelain, the necessity of using iron-free clays, which are always relatively nonplastic, usually results in a compromise between the whiteness of the fired body and the workability of the plastic clay. Stoneware bodies are easy to compound and seem to happen just as a result of the nature of the materials employed, usually without any fine adjustments or compromises being necessary.

Whenever it is possible, stoneware bodies should be compounded using a high percentage of some natural stoneware clay. This not only makes the procuring and storing of raw materials simpler, and involves less work in mixing, but also usually results in a more satisfactory clay.

To arrive at a satisfactory body, the potter must first know what he needs and desires in the way of workability, toughness, temperature range, and fired density, color and texture. For example, if one could fire no higher than cone 8, and was limited to oxidation firing, a clay would be needed which might be quite different from one suitable for firing at cone 12 in reduction. When the practical requirements have been established, the blending or compounding of a body usually takes the form of *correcting* the deficiencies of some natural stoneware clay. Assuming that some stoneware clay is available, its shortcomings are apt to be one or more of the following:

1. The clay may be too sticky and plastic. This trouble is readily corrected by adding a less plastic clay such as kaolin, or by adding nonplastic materials such as flint, grog, or pyrophyllite. If a clay is too plastic and sticky it is likely to shrink excessively both in drying and in firing, and this tendency to shrink too much is helped by the addition of less plastic materials.

2. The clay may be short, mealy, and lacking in plasticity. In this case, more plastic material must be added, and the inclusion of ball clay usually serves to give the desired workability. Ball clays by themselves tighten and harden when fired to stoneware temperatures, but their shrinkage is so great that they cannot be used alone in pottery making. They are indispensable as an addition to bodies to improve plasticity. Most ball clays, while they burn to a light buff or tan color, do not materially affect the color of stoneware bodies. They do not have much effect on the maturing temperature of the body either. The selection of a particular ball clay is not a very critical factor in stoneware making, but some ball clays are somewhat more plastic than others and may need to be used in smaller amounts. In stoneware bodies a substitution can sometimes be made of one ball clay for another without much change being noted either in the working properties of the clay or in the fired results. Ten per cent of ball clay added to a stoneware clay will usually make a noticeable improvement in its plasticity. Additions in excess of 40% usually result in a body which is too sticky to work well and which shrinks too much.

3. The clay may, when fired, be too dense and vitrified, or may tend to warp, lose its shape, or slump. This means that the clay is too fusible at the temperature of firing. Either the clay must be fired at a lower temperature, or more refractory material, such as kaolin, flint, fire clay, or pyrophyllite must be added.

4. The clay may, when fired, remain soft, open, absorbent and chalky. In this case, the maturing point of the clay has not been reached, and either the firing must be carried to a higher temperature, or fluxes such as feldspar, nepheline syenite, red clay, or frit must be added to bring down the temperature of maturing.

5. When fired, the clay may be darker, or lighter, than the desired color. To lighten the color, light-burning clay such as kaolin or ball clay may be added. If the stoneware clay is very dark, however, a considerable addition of light-colored clay will be needed to effect the color. If the clay is a lighter color than desired, some red clay may be added, or coloring oxides such as iron oxide, manganese, ilmenite, or iron chromate, or combinations of these.

To make a stoneware body, the basic clay, or stoneware clay, should be first tested thoroughly so as to determine what additions may be needed. The clay should be tried out on the wheel, or by other methods of shaping, to gain an idea of its plasticity and workability. Sample bars should then be dried out and fired to determine the shrinkage, the fired density, and the fired color of the clay. When these tests are complete, a series of trial compositions can be planned indicating percentages of additions to the basic clay. It is best not to try too many different compositions at first, perhaps no more than half a dozen. These first tests can then be studied to see what further corrections need to be made. There is no scientific or exact way of arriving at clay body compositions, and the best one can do in the first trials is an educated guess. One might guess, for instance, that a stoneware clay would need about 15% of ball clay to make it sufficiently plastic for wheel work, and then find, after test-

45

ing, that 25% was necessary. In making a series of variations to test, it is well to vary only one ingredient at a time. For example, one group of tests might be aimed at determining the correct amount of ball clay needed, and another group of tests would be for the purpose of studying the effect of varying the flux. Once a basic stoneware clay has been selected, bodies made with it should be designed to capitalize on its good points rather than to alter it radically. If, for example, one had a fine gray clay with a slight specking in it, it would be foolish to change it to a dark brown or black.

If no natural stoneware clay is available, fairly satisfactory bodies can be made from mixtures of ball clay, kaolin, flint, and fluxes. The difficulty with this type of body is that kaolin is normally a very nonplastic clay, and a great deal of ball clay must be combined with it to make a satisfactory throwing clay. The working properties of such combinations never seem quite as good as that of a natural plastic stoneware clay to which only minor amounts of ball clay have been added. However, the color of bodies based primarily on kaolin and ball clay can be easily controlled through the addition of red clay or coloring oxides.

Another possibility, if no stoneware clay is available, is to base the mixture on a combination of fire clay and ball clay, or on combinations of fire clay, ball clay, and kaolin. Fire clay is ordinarily too nonplastic to be used by itself for pottery, but combined with ball clay or with other highly plastic clays its rough and open character may be exactly what is needed.

The commonly used ingredients for stoneware bodies are as follows, together with the usual maximum amounts used:

Stoneware clay	to	100%
Ball clay	to	50%
Kaolin	to	30%
Fire clay	to	75%
Sagger clay	to	75%
Red earthenware clay	to	25%

Grog	to	30%
Flint	to	25%
Feldspar	to	25%
or nepheline syenite		
Talc	to	10%
Pyrophyllite	to	20%

In formulating bodies there is a great deal of latitude possible in the amounts of the various ingredients used. A body which contains 25% sagger clay may be almost indistinguishable from one which contains 10% sagger clay. The amount of fluxes used, such as feldspar, or red clay, may be critical, however, and a few per cent more or less may make a very significant difference. Laboratory tests alone are not enough to prove the value of a clay body. It must be tested in use to determine its suitability for pottery making. Often a clay which seems promising in all laboratory tests will later prove to be unsatisfactory, for one reason or another. For example, a clay which is otherwise quite satisfactory may be found to be prone to warping when made into larger shapes. Or a clay which has an attractive dark color on small samples may be found to be subject to dunting when used for pots of certain shapes. Even though stoneware bodies are relatively easy to formulate and are quite free from technical flaws, such annoying difficulties do appear occasionally.

3. Materials for stoneware

The number of materials which may be used in formulating stoneware bodies is severely limited in number, and the physical properties of these materials and their reactions to the fire are easily kept in mind. A brief description of these materials follows (with the exception of stoneware clay, which has already been discussed).

BALL CLAY. Ball clays are all sedimentary in origin. They are extraordinarily fine in particle size and have the valuable property of great plasticity. To be classified as a commercial ball clay, a clay must not only be highly plastic but must also be fairly free from iron or other impurities, and must burn to a light color. Ball clay, while not highly refractory like kaolin, will nevertheless withstand temperatures up to about cone 15 without showing any sign of fusion. The clay will tighten at much lower temperatures than this however, and many ball clays when fired alone will be quite dense and hard at cone 8 or 9.

Ball clay is unusable by itself because of its great drying and firing shrinkage, which may be as high as 20%. It is used primarily as an addition to clay bodies to bring about an increase of plasticity, dry strength, and fired density.

While clays sold as ball clays do run quite true to type, there are some variations. Kentucky ball clay is relatively dark in the raw state because of carbonaceous matter in it. It is very plastic and quite light in color when fired. Tennessee ball clay is much lighter in the raw state but not quite as plastic. It burns to a very light color. The English ball clays, which have been used extensively in the white-wares industry, are very light burning and are perhaps more free of impurities such as iron and rutile than any of the American ball clays. English ball clays do have considerable lignite in them which may have to be screened out, but this contamination of carbon has no effect on the fired result. No matter what kind of ball clay is used, it is well to use the air-floated form. Air-floated clays are pulverized to a very fine powder and so are easily mixed or blunged with the other materials in the body. Lump ball clay slakes and disintegrates very slowly in the blunger.

Additions of ball clay to a body not only increase the plasticity and workability of the body but also greatly increase the dry strength, making the raw ware much easier to handle. It is important that a clay body has a good dry strength, especially if the ware is being once-fired. Ball clay also serves to make the fired body tighter, denser, and stronger without lowering its maturing temperature.

The selection of which ball clay to use for a stoneware body is not especially critical, and any commercial clay is apt to give good results. A different brand of clay may sometimes be substituted in a body without much difference being noted either in the working properties of the clay or in its fired appearance.

While ball clay does not much affect the color of stoneware bodies, it does have a tendency to inhibit the development of a burnt-orange color in reduced ware, and if this color is desired, the body should contain a maximum amount of fire clay and no more ball clay than is absolutely necessary for plasticity.

KAOLIN. Kaolin is not used in large amounts in stoneware bodies, but it will be discussed here in reference not only to use in stoneware but also its use in porcelain.

Kaolin is the aristocrat of clays—the only type which is not only used for pots but is also taken internally as a medicine and used in cosmetics. It is indispensable in ceramics because it is relatively free from iron and other associated mineral impurities and therefore fires to a very light color, and because of its refractoriness which permits its use in very high temperature firing.

Kaolin has the formula $Al_2O_3 \cdot 2SiO_2 \cdot 2H_2O$. Expressed as a percentage composition, pure kaolin would have 46.3% silica, 39.8% alumina, and 13.9% combined water. Chemical analysis shows many actual samples of kaolin to be very close to this composition, but small amounts of other oxides are always present in them, such as iron, titania, calcia, magnesia, soda, and potash. High-grade commercial kaolins contain no more than $\frac{1}{4}$ to $\frac{3}{4}$% of iron, not enough to materially darken the clay on firing. Shown on p. 48 are some analyses of various kaolins. It will be seen that though these clays originate in different places their chemical composition is very similar and that the mineral impurities are very slight.

47

	Georgia Kaolin	North Carolina Kaolin	English China Clay	Alabama Kaolin
SiO_2	45.3	46.30	47.00	44.74
Al_2O_3	39.14	38.28	37.72	39.47
TiO_2	1.54	.04	.15	1.29
Fe_2O_3	.27	.38	.96	.55
CaO	.13	.10	.19	.00
MgO	.04	.09	.18	.00
K_2O	.15	.34	1.57	.00
Na_2O	.10	.24	.23	.00
Ignition loss ..	13.71	13.73	12.37	13.89
	100.38	100.00	100.37	99.94

Kaolin is relatively scarce compared to other types of clay, and its existence was hardly known in Europe and America before porcelain making began in the early part of the 18th century. In Europe, kaolin occurs in Saxony and Bavaria, and there are smaller and less important deposits in France, near Limoges. The famous kaolin deposits of England, "English china clay," occur in Cornwall on the English Channel. These clay beds are of great extent, and were formed from the original granites of the area. The Cornwall kaolins were evidently formed deep in the ground by the action of hot solutions rising from below. The clay may be found at depths as great as 300 feet, and the material which is deeper in the ground tends to be more free from impurities. As the kaolin is found in the earth, it is too full of granular particles of mica and quartz to be used. These fragments of grit are removed by water washing and settling. English kaolin is not only relatively free from iron but it also contains very little titanium oxide or rutile.

The whiteware industry in the United States formerly depended to a large extent on imported English clays, but in recent times American kaolin has been extensively used. The most important deposits occur in South Carolina and Georgia. The clays in this region were evidently formed as primary kaolin from the granite masses of the Piedmont plateau, then were later transported toward the coastal plain and deposited in fresh water. There are large beds of clay of great uniformity and purity. These sedimentary kaolins contain very little mica relative to primary kaolins such as the English clays, but mica in small amounts and in very small particle size may be an aid to the working properties of a clay. The Georgia and South Carolina kaolins have a higher percentage of titanium oxide than English kaolin. This may cause them to burn somewhat darker, even though the iron content is no higher, or may be even less than that of the English material.

There are smaller and less important deposits of kaolin in the mountainous regions of North Carolina. The clay here occurs in pockets of primary clay formed by weathering on the site of pegmatite granite. As mined, the North Carolina kaolin contains considerable quantities of mineral fragments, including feldspar.

Florida kaolin is found in association with a fine, pure, silica sand. The clay occurs as a coating on the grains of sand and is recovered by washing. Florida kaolin is very fine-grained, and is evidently a secondary type of clay. It is much more plastic than either the English or the Georgia kaolin. It contains less rutile than Georgia clay, and therefore burns to a lighter color, even though the iron content is about the same. The Florida kaolins are important because of their beneficial effect on the plastic working properties of whiteware bodies. An addition of Florida kaolin to a whiteware body may increase the casting time, improve the plasticity, and add dry strength.

While some kaolins are more plastic than others, it should be emphasized that all kaolins are less plastic than the average earthenware or stoneware clay. The kaolin used in China is said to be plastic enough to work well on the wheel, but to what extent this is the result of more careful processing, and longer aging, rather than the quality of the clay itself, is a question.

Kaolin by itself is highly refractory and does not begin to soften until fired to around cone 30 (1650°C).

FIRE CLAY. The stoneware potter relies on fire clay to improve the workability of his clay and to achieve certain color and textural effects.

Fire clays as mined and sold are quite various, but they are all refractory clays with a softening point of cone 15 or higher. Most fire clays are rather coarse and nonplastic. Fire clay is ordinarily sedimentary in origin, and is frequently found associated with seams of coal. Extensive deposits of fire clay are found in the Eastern States, in the Midwest, and in the Rocky Mountain region. The more valuable commercial types are those which contain a high percentage of alumina, and are relatively free from iron, calcium, rutile, magnesia, or other fluxing minerals. The potter will be most interested in those fire clays which are plastic and have good working properties, and which lend a desirable color or texture to the fired body. Fire clay, because of its roughness and coarse grain size lends tooth to plastic bodies, and permits the making and drying of large shapes with little danger of warping and cracking. It tends to "open up" a body, makes mixing, wedging, and throwing easier, and hastens drying. Its coarseness gives a certain roughness and texture to clay bodies which otherwise might be too smooth and slick. This is especially noticeable

where trimming in the leather hard state reveals the grain of the clay.

Although fire clay contains a good deal less iron than most earthenware clays, it does usually contain an appreciable amount, and this iron may be concentrated in mineral fragments which fire to black or brown specks or splotches. Fire clays differ widely in the amount of iron they contain, and in the amount of texture they develop on firing, but nearly all fire clays will impart some texture when added to a stoneware body. Many fire clays when fired in a reducing atmosphere burn to a reddish brown or burnt-orange color, enriched with black or dark brown spots.

In selecting a fire clay to use as an addition to a stoneware body it is well to obtain samples of the different kinds which are available, and to try them out first without any additions. The relative plasticity and fired color can be determined in this way. The usual amount of fire clay which is added to plastic stoneware is from 10 to 30%, but if the fire clay is itself quite plastic, up to 50% may be used. Unfortunately, not as much control is used in the mining and processing of fire clay as in the preparation of ball clay and kaolin for the market, and the same brand of commercial fire clay may vary considerably in color and plasticity from one shipment to another.

Some fire clays which appear to be very coarse when first mixed with water slake down gradually over a period of time and become, in the well-aged body, fairly smooth and plastic.

SAGGER CLAY. Sagger clay is actually a type of plastic fire clay used for making saggers. Some kinds on the market are very plastic, burn to a light tan color, and by themselves are between a fire clay and a stoneware clay in working properties. Sagger clay can be a valuable addition to high-fired bodies.

RED EARTHENWARE CLAY. In stoneware bodies, red clay is used to darken the color of the fired clay and to serve as a flux to bring down the maturing temperature. Because of its low fusion point, only a small amount of red clay can be used in stoneware. It is a valuable source of color, however, and usually being plastic, it has no adverse effect on the plasticity of the body. Common red clay which matures by itself at around cone 04 will darken a stoneware body noticeably if used in quantities above 5%, and usually more than 10% will give darker colors than are desired, and may also cause warping and excessive vitrification or bloating. Red clay which matures at about cone 4 may be introduced into stoneware bodies in larger amounts, perhaps as much as 25%.

When dark brown, orange-brown, tan, or black effects are desired, red clay is, in general, a better colorant to use than iron oxide. It is inexpensive, easily obtained, mixes in well with the rest of the clay, and often gives an interesting color or texture to the fired body.

Grog. Grog is used in stoneware bodies to give a more open structure to the clay, thus facilitating drying and lessening the shrinkage. Grog is fired clay which has been ground to granules. It may be made from any sort of clay, but in making additions of grog to stoneware, only grog which has been made from a refractory clay can be used. Most of the grog sold on the market is made from fire clay. It may be purchased in various particle sizes, indicated by the mesh screen which the material will pass. Besides making a body easier to dry and fire, grog also adds importantly to the workability of a clay. When a clay body is composed mostly of very fine-grained materials, it may be sufficiently plastic but too smooth and lacking in "tooth" to stand in large, wheel-made shapes. Any clay intended for wheelwork needs some rough material in it. Grog seems to add "bones" to the clay, making it hold its shape better, especially in the later stages of throwing when it is quite soft and wet.

Grog may be added to a stoneware body in amounts ranging from only a few per cent up to 30% or even more, depending on the process which is being used to shape the ware. For throwing, the usual amount is from about 10 to 20%. The sizing of the grog is perhaps as important as the amount used. For throwing, the grog used should not be larger than about 30 mesh. For sculpture and large modeled pieces, the grog may be much coarser. Grog which passes the 30-mesh screen is likely to contain considerable fines, or very small particles and dust. There should not be too much of this extremely fine material in a throwing body, and better results are obtained if the grog is screened to eliminate all dust smaller than 80 mesh. Particles smaller than 100 mesh have an adverse effect on plasticity. The range of particle size between 30 and 80 mesh, together with the mass of very fine-grained clay, gives a dense packing and maximum strength to the body.

Grog gives a rough texture to the clay which in certain types of ware can be very appropriate. When ware has been thrown or cast, the particles of grog tend to lie just below the surface, and if a rough surface is desired, the clay must be scraped to bring up the particles of grog. Trimming the bottoms of pots reveals the roughness of the grog, and the contrast of the rough, trimmed surfaces with the relatively smoother surface resulting from throwing can be very effective.

If grinding equipment is available, grog may be made up from fired briquettes of clay, and the color and maturing temperature of the grog can be controlled.

Flint. Flint, or ground silica flour, is nearly always included in stoneware bodies. Flint adds the valuable property of hardness to the fired clay, and since it is a nonplastic substance, it also serves to "open" the body for better drying, and it lessens the drying and the firing shrinkage. Flint is a very refractory substance, and its presence in a body serves to raise the maturing temperature. It also has the effect of making the body less plastic, and in bodies designed for throwing, the quantity of flint should be limited to 15% or less. In casting bodies, which do not need to be so plastic, more flint is used, usually 20% or more.

The addition of flint to a body greatly simplifies the problem of getting glazes to fit without crazing. Clays which have less than 10% of flint may give trouble by causing most glazes to craze. On the other hand, if too much flint is used in the body, it may be found that glazes will shiver and peel.

FELDSPAR. Feldspar is used in stoneware glazes as a melter or a flux. Many stoneware clays, or clay bodies made up from largely natural stoneware clay, will require little or no feldspar to adjust the maturing temperature. But bodies which are composed principally of kaolin and ball clay may require considerable feldspar if the right degree of hardness and vitrification is to be achieved at the desired firing temperature. Feldspar melts at stoneware temperature, cone 8 to 12, and its presence in a body has the effect of tightening it, fusing it together, and reducing its absorbency. Too much feldspar will make the body slump or deform in the fire. Most stoneware bodies fired to cone 9 or higher will not need more than about 15% of feldspar. Feldspar, like flint, has an adverse effect on the plasticity of a clay, and in formulating throwing bodies, care must be taken not to let the nonplastic part of the body, including the flint, the feldspar, and the grog, exceed about 25%.

Feldspar is the ideal high temperature body flux, and seems almost to have been made by nature for this purpose. It is slow-melting and has a long firing range between the point where it just begins to soften and where it finally melts to a fluid glass. In this respect it is better than any of the fritted materials which are used as a flux in lower-fired clay

bodies. If only a little feldspar is used, the effect will be to only slightly harden and toughen the fired body, but if a lot is used, the body may approach the hardness and density of glass. Almost any kind of feldspar will be found to be suitable for use in stoneware bodies. Some feldspars, however, have lower fusion points than others, and this must be allowed for. In porcelain bodies the selection of a feldspar is more critical because the exact degree of fusion as well as the fired color are important.

Nepheline syenite is often used instead of feldspar as a flux in stoneware. Of course, nepheline syenite is a kind of feldspar, but it has a relatively low fusion point. Using it in a body instead of feldspar may bring down the maturing temperature 2 or more cones. Or, about 10% of nepheline syenite may be substituted for about 15% of feldspar without any effect being noticed in the density of the fired body. The use of some feldspar in a body tends to improve the fit of glazes.

TALC. Talc, a magnesium silicate, is sometimes used in bodies as an auxiliary flux, especially in low-fired bodies. It may be used in stoneware in small amounts to increase the density of the fired body.

PYROPHYLLITE. Pyrophyllite has the formula $Al_2O_3 \cdot 4SiO_2 \cdot H_2O$. It will be noted that its chemical composition is similar to that of clay except for the absence of combined water. It is especially useful in casting bodies. Its behavior in the fire is similar to that of kaolin, but in the raw state it functions as a nonplastic. Calcined kaolin may also be used in casting bodies to control plasticity and shrinkage.

4. Plasticity and shrinkage of stoneware bodies

A clay which is really satisfactory for use on the wheel must be highly plastic, and yet it should have enough coarse material in it to help keep it from slumping out of shape when made into larger or taller forms. Plasticity and workability in a throwing clay is a rather complex property, and results from several factors, including the plasticity of the clays in the body, the amount and sizing of the grog, the degree of aging and wedging, and the presence of plasticizers, such as bentonite.

For work on the wheel, the clay must be right, or all one's efforts will be frustrated. Throwing is a difficult process at best, and with improper clay, one is severely limited as to the shapes which can be made. Much of the seeming ease which characterizes the work of the professional thrower is the result of working with clay that is correct for the wheel, and it seems certain that the best examples of thrown pottery from the past were made with very plastic, well-aged, and well-prepared clay. Many amateurs blame their deficiencies in throwing entirely on their own lack of skill, but in many cases they are struggling with clay which no one, no matter how experienced, could manage well.

The first requirement for a body which is plastic enough for use on the wheel is that it contain an adequate percentage of clays which are in themselves plastic. This usually means a body which is made up of at least 75% of clay and no more than 25% of nonplastic ingredients, such as flint, feldspar, or grog. The clay portion of the body must contain a sizable percentage of very plastic clay, either ball clay, a plastic sagger clay, or a plastic stoneware clay. For this reason it is difficult to make a really satisfactory body using kaolin and ball clay in place of a plastic stoneware clay. In such bodies the percentage of plastic clay is apt to be too small for really good working properties.

The importance of the right quantity of well-sized grog has already been mentioned. But when a body has been made which is composed of the right quantities and kinds of clays and grog for maximum plasticity, there are still some other factors which have a very significant influence on plasticity. Proper wedging is one. When clay is stiffened by drying in plaster bats it frequently has a very open and spongy texture, full of minute air cells. Mixing and wedging is necessary to compact the clay, eliminate the air spaces, and develop a tight, dense, homogenous mass. Clay should be wedged before being put away to age and wedged again before use. If a mechanical mixer or pug mill is available to do this job, so much the better. In fact, a de-airing pug mill does a better job of wedging than could possibly be done by hand.

While the actual structure of a clay is not altered by wedging, the mixing and kneading of the clay prior to working on the wheel is most important to develop the full density and cohesiveness of the clay. Cutting and recombining the mass of clay will serve to mix the clay thoroughly and to force out the pockets of air. Spiral wedging, in which the clay is forced into a moving spiral shape, is even more effective. Any system of wedging, however, unless it is skillfully done, may result in pockets of air being developed in the clay instead of eliminating them.

Clay bodies tend to be quite short and not satisfactory to work until they have aged for at least a few days. The beneficial effects of this early aging is no doubt due to the more thorough wetting of the clay particles. But oddly enough, aging does not seem to begin until the clay is in the plastic condition, and clay when it is in slip form does not seem to gain much in workability from age. Aging seems to be promoted by proper wedging before the clay is stored. Aging has a very noticeable effect on plasticity during the first few days. The benefits of aging beyond 2 or 3 weeks, though slight, may nevertheless be worth-while. Long aging tends to develop a clay to its full plasticity. During an aging period of several months or longer, a bacterial growth occurs in clay which has a beneficial effect on plasticity. This growth of organic matter in clay is hastened by the addition to each new batch of clay of a portion of old, aged clay. Well-aged clay has a rich damp odor which is lacking in new clay. Anyone who has compared the workability of an old well-aged batch of clay with a new batch of exactly the same composition will not doubt the effectiveness of aging.

Shrinkage is a problem with all fired clay products, and in the case of plastic bodies designed for throwing on the wheel it is a particularly difficult problem. Shrinkage is the necessary price paid for plasticity, for when a clay is plastic, it is fine in particle size, and it requires a great deal of water to furnish lubrication between the individual grains of clay. When this water dries out, shrinkage occurs, and the finer-grained the clay is, the more shrinkage can be expected. In any clay plastic enough for wheel work a total shrinkage of 10% is not excessive. About half of this shrinkage occurs during drying, the other half during firing. Many bodies which are otherwise acceptable shrink a good deal more than 10%, perhaps as much as 15%. The potter must decide whether he wants the benefit of an extremely plastic clay at the cost of a very high shrinkage. The problem can be partly solved by the proper addition of grog, which, when properly sized and not added in too great quantity, does not have an adverse effect on the plasticity; rather the reverse—it improves the usefulness of the clay. At the same time it cuts down on the total shrinkage and makes drying and firing safer and more rapid.

Clays with a high shrinkage also have a tendency toward warping. Furthermore, when a high shrinkage clay is used it may be difficult to get handles and other appendages to stick on the pots without cracking during drying. But even aside from these practical problems, a high shrinkage is apt to distort the scale of the work. Even though one is very experienced with a particular high shrinkage clay, it is hard to be reconciled to the difference in size between the raw, wet pot, and the fired result. Inevitably, one makes things too small, too timid in scale, and the pottery comes from the kiln looking dwarfed. For all these reasons, it is well to keep shrinkage to a minimum, and this usually means some compromise with the ideal plasticity.

Bentonite can be added to a clay body to increase plasticity. Bentonite is unusable by itself because it swells when wet into a sticky, jelly-like mass. But when used in small amounts as an addition to a clay body it contributes very significantly to plasticity. The usual amount added to a body is no more than 2 or 3%. More than that will make the clay too sticky to work well. Bentonite makes the clay slower to stiffen or dry, increases the shrinkage somewhat, and may seriously aggravate any tendency toward warping or cracking. However, when used in small amounts it usually does not cause any real difficulty. When clay is mixed first as a slip, the bentonite may be added right in with the other ingredients. When the clay is made up directly into a plastic mass from the dry ingredients, the bentonite should be first slaked in water and added in this form. Even when used in very small quantities, bentonite may have a good effect on the working properties of a clay, and it should be tried whenever the clay is judged to be deficient in plasticity after the best balance of plastic clays has been found. Bentonite, however, is not a substitute for good plastic clay and can only supplement the plasticity contributed by clay.

5. Color and texture in stoneware clay

Fired stoneware can vary a great deal in color and texture. Although the color range is not brilliant, it is expressive of the earthy nature of the materials and of a process involving extreme heat. More than any other type of pottery, the color and texture of stoneware seems to relate to the rocks and minerals which form the source material of all ceramics. Stoneware may be smooth, dense, and light in color, like a piece of polished flint rock; or it may be very rough, mottled, and heavily textured like granite. It may express delicacy or strength. In color it may be cool gray, or off-white, or it may be a very dark brown or black. Or it may have a varied surface ranging through many shades of brown, gray, or orange-brown. Variations and flashing may suggest the licking flames of the fire. All these colors and textures are very natural to stoneware materials and processes, and are not especially difficult to achieve.

The color of a stoneware body is determined primarily by the selection of clays. Most of the clays marketed as stoneware clay are fairly light burning. Jordan clay, and Monmouth clay, for example, burn to a light buff color when fired to cone 8 or 9 in oxidation, and are gray or light gray-brown when fired in reduction. Ball clays and kaolin burn very light, and sagger clay and the various kinds of fire clay will usually fire to a light buff, brown, or toast color. The basic materials for stoneware, then, produce rather light-colored fired bodies, tending toward the warm colors in oxidation and in reduction either toward cool gray or an orange-brown. Some good stoneware clay, however, if it contains considerable iron and other dark-burning impurities, will burn to a dark color.

The color which develops in stoneware bodies is quite different in oxidizing and in reducing fire, and control of color will be more clearly understood if these two kinds of body colors are discussed separately. A more detailed description of reduction firing and reduction glazes is given in a later section.

OXIDATION BODY COLORS. In oxidation, stoneware bodies tend to be light in color. Iron oxide, which in lower-fired bodies produces a red or terra-cotta color, gives a medium brown in stoneware, or if present in only small quantities, it gives a buff or tan color. When fired in oxidation, stoneware bodies are the same color all the way through, that is, the color of the clay inside is the same as it is on the surface. Also, in a strongly oxidizing fire, there is seldom any flashing or variation in color from one part of a pot to another.

If light-colored clays are used in the body, without any additions of red clay or of any coloring oxide, the color of the clay in oxidation will be a warm buff color. The addition of 5 to 15% of red clay to the body will give a medium or rather subdued brown. Additions of more than 15% of red clay will result in a dark brown or black.

REDUCTION BODY COLORS. In reduction firing, stoneware bodies tend toward gray when only small quantities of iron are present. When more iron is present, the body color is dark brown, reddish brown, or black. In general, less iron, whether introduced into the body as iron oxide or as a red clay, is needed in reduction to produce the darker shades. In reduction, the color of the surface of the clay is often quite different than the color of the clay inside. Inside, the clay of a well-reduced specimen is apt to be dark gray or black. If some reoxidation has taken place on the surface (and this is nearly always the case), the surface of the piece may be brown, warm tan, or an orangy toast color. Paradoxically, the warmest hues are achieved in reduction, rather than oxidation, because of this tendency of iron oxide on the very surface of the piece to reoxidize on cooling, and one of the most attractive of all clay body colors is the effect known to connoisseurs of Chinese pottery as the "iron foot." This color is a light orange-brown and is achieved by firing a clay which has a small percentage of iron in quite strongly reducing conditions.

The color of stoneware bodies fired in reduction tends to vary considerably from one firing to another, and even from one part of the kiln to another. Color may also vary on the same piece from light buff to dark brown, depending on how the flame strikes the ware. These variations are natural to the process, and may be accepted and made use of. Iron oxide, especially, is extremely sensitive to the atmosphere of the kiln and will produce quite different results with seemingly small differences in firing procedures.

All of these stoneware body colors—the grays, the buff colors, and the browns come about very naturally and easily as a result of the kind of materials used and the kind and intensity of the fire. Certainly one of the virtues of stoneware is that the potter does not have to struggle to achieve the subtle and beautiful colors which develop in the clay.

One common characteristic of stoneware clay bodies is the presence of flecks or specks. These occur because of the tendency of high firing to melt whatever impurities exist in the clay, and many clays contain small concentrations of iron, or iron combined with other minerals, which fuse and give a broken or spotty texture. Fire clays in particular are apt to contain bits of iron which burn to dark spots. If spots are not desired, clays must be chosen for their purity and freedom from iron. Kaolin, ball clay, and some stoneware clays will produce a smooth surface without any noticeable specking. If specks are desired, fire clay or stoneware clay can be used which contain concentrations of impurities. Specks or spots are also very easy to achieve by making small additions to the body. One good material to use for this is ground-up common red brick. The clay from which red brick are made will melt at stoneware heat, and particles of red brick will cause an effective dark spot in the body. The size and frequency of the spotting can be easily controlled by the grind and quantity of the brick fragments added. One or two per cent will give a marked texture. Another material which gives

much the same effect is ground shale. Iron can be added to a clay in various forms to produce spots. Mill scale, rust, filings, or chopped-up steel wool, give spots of various sorts. Another way to achieve spotting in the clay is to add minerals containing iron or other dark-burning oxides. Black sand, iron pyrites, trap rock, ferrosilicon, iron chromate, slag, iron ore, slate, lava, copper ores, and many other materials may be used.

In stoneware, whatever impurities exist in the body are likely to have a strong influence on the glaze, and any material which is added to give textural interest, such as spots or flecks, is sure to produce spots in the glaze also.

For very pronounced spots or splotches which come through the glaze prominently, granular manganese may be used. Various grit sizes are available, but material passing the 40-mesh screen is coarse enough to give heavy textures. Granular ilmenite may be used in the same way, but it is not as active in the fire as the manganese and produces quieter effects.

Three-dimensional texture or roughness is achieved in clay by the addition of coarse material, usually grog or fire clay. Grog may be selected or prepared for color. White grog is usually obtained by grinding up china or porcelain rejects. Dark grog can be made by firing and grinding briquettes of clay to which some coloring oxide has been added. Four or five per cent of iron added to the body in use will usually suffice to give a very dark-colored material for use as grog. The mixture of both a light and a very dark grog can give a pleasing effect similar to the texture of granite.

Actually there are a great many possibilities in stoneware for interesting and unusual textural effects. The potter should always be alert to the resources of his own region, where perhaps he will find materials for his work which are easily obtained, valuable for his work, and more or less unique. By-products of mining, smelting, and metallurgical processing should be looked into, as well as the natural rocks, shales, clays, and sands of the neighborhood.

As an indication of the probable colors and textures which will result from the addition of coloring agents to a stoneware body, the following tests are given: A stoneware body was compounded of Jordan clay, 6 parts; ball clay, 2 parts; flint, 1 part; feldspar, 1 part. To this body, additions were made as indicated on the chart below, and the tests were fired to cone 10 in both oxidation and reduction with the color resulting as indicated:

intended for throwing, or modeling. All clay body compositions must be formulated with a view to the manner in which the clay is to be fabricated into objects. Throwing, as we have seen, requires a high degree of plasticity and carefully controlled grog sizing. Coiling, slab building, pressing, or modeling also require clays of considerable plasticity. For modeling or building large shapes or forms which are thick in cross section, considerable grog or other nonplastic material must be used in the clay to permit safe drying and firing.

Added Colorant	Color in Oxidation	Color in Reduction
½% iron oxide	light tan-gray	light toast color
1% iron oxide	warm tan	dark toast color
1% iron chromate	light umber	warm gray
½% iron chromate	light tan	light grayed tan
2% granular ilmenite	light tan, barely noticeable speck	grayed tan with slight specking
1% granular ilmenite, 2% granular manganese	warm gray with prominent black specks	warm tan with prominent black specks
5% ground red brick minus 35 mesh	light tan with very slight speck	slightly specked toast color
5% Barnard clay	warm tan	light umber
5% Barnard clay, 2% manganese dioxide	dark tan, slight specking	chocolate
2% black iron oxide	medium tan, fine metallic specking	light gray-brown, fine metallic specking

It will be noted that all the additions resulted in clay colors that were darker than the original body, which illustrates the fact that while it is easy to darken a clay by adding dark-burning materials, it is not possible to lighten a clay except by a radical change involving the addition of more kaolin and ball clay at the expense of the other darker-burning clays. The tests above by no means exhaust the possibilities of either color or texture, but are intended to show in a general way the effect of various added materials.

6. Stoneware casting bodies

A clay body which casts well requires quite a different composition than one

In casting, an excess of plasticity in a clay is a positive disadvantage because it increases the amount of water which must be used, and therefore slows down the casting time, increases the amount of water which permeates the molds, and increases the tendency of the ware to stick in the molds and to shrink and warp excessively. For these reasons, casting bodies are usually formulated with not much more than 60% of clay included, and bodies which are no more than half clay will work very satisfactorily.

Formulating casting slips for stoneware is no great problem. Many natural stoneware clays deflocculate satisfactorily, and have good casting properties. If a stoneware clay is being used, it is a good idea to run some deflocculation tests on the clay by itself to see if it responds to the deflocculent. A simple test can be made by preparing a sample of dried clay flour and a measure of water which weighs just half as much as the clay. To the water is added one half of 1% by weight of full strength sodium silicate. For example, if the clay sample weighs 500 grams, 2½ grams of sodium silicate would be added to the water. The clay flour is then slowly added to the water, with constant stirring. If all the clay can be added without the resulting slip becoming too stiff to pour, the clay has deflocculated and will probably be suitable for casting. More sodium silicate may be added to test the effect of a higher percentage of deflocculent, but more than 1% usually has the effect of making the slip more viscous rather than making it more fluid.

The same procedure may be used on a compounded clay body to determine its casting properties. It is wise to formulate the body first on the basis of fired characteristics, such as color, texture, density, and shrinkage, and when these have been adjusted satisfactorily, to determine how to make the body cast. Combinations of sodium silicate and soda ash are sometimes more effective than either by itself. While the usual percentage of deflocculent to the dry weight of the clay is between one third and one half of 1%, either more or less deflocculent may be required, and some tests must be made to determine the exact amount of both the deflocculent and water which will give best results.

To work satisfactorily, casting slips should contain not more water than one half the weight of the dry clay, and preferably the water content should be somewhat lower than this. Too much water in a slip will cause undue shrinkage, sticking in the molds, excessive mold wetting, and warping.

In making casting slips, it is convenient to use air-floated clays if they are available. If all the material used in the body is in a finely divided state, it may be added directly to water and blunged into a slip without preliminary mixing, screening, and drying. If the clay being used is in lump form, just as it comes from the mine, it may be necessary first to blunge it with a considerable excess of water, and screen it in order to get rid of bits of rock or other impurities. The clay is then dried out and added to the casting slip, together with the other body ingredients.

When it is desired to match a casting body in appearance with one which is used for throwing, nonplastic materials must be substituted in the casting body in place of plastic ones, and the fluxing ingredients may also have to be adjusted somewhat to obtain the same density and color in the fired body. This may require considerable testing, but it is usually possible to make two bodies, one for casting and one for throwing, which are indistinguishable in the finished product. As an example, two bodies are given below which are designed for casting and for throwing and which fire to a similar color:

Throwing Body:
Jordan clay 60
Ball clay 20
Flint 10
Feldspar 10
Iron oxide 1

Casting Body:
Jordan clay 40
Georgia kaolin 20
Ball clay 15
Flint 15
Feldspar 10
Iron oxide 1½
Water . . . . 50 parts by weight
Sodium silicate
            ¾ of 1% by weight
Soda ash . ¼ of 1% by weight

Stoneware casting bodies which contain considerable grog present a problem because the grog does have some tendency to settle in the slip, and also because during drain casting the rougher portion of the body does not appear at the outer surface of the cast ware but tends to be concentrated on the inside or nonmolded surface of the piece. If the grog is to show, the molded surfaces must be scraped after the piece comes from the mold to reveal the texture. By the use of grog in the body it is possible to cast very large and heavy pieces with thick cross sections.

Combination in the same pot of thrown parts with parts which are cast, offers intriguing possibilities. To do this, however, it is necessary to use the same composition of clay for both the cast and the thrown portions, and this usually means a compromise in plasticity. But most casting compositions, if they are prepared as plastic clay and are properly aged and wedged, can be used for modeling or for making simple shapes on the wheel. Handles, knobs, feet, or sprigs may be pressed or modeled and added to cast forms.

For jiggering, a clay body needs to be fairly plastic, but should not be as plastic as a throwing clay. The same body is commonly used for both jiggering and casting.

7. Temperature range and thermal reactions of stoneware bodies

Stoneware is by definition pottery which has been fired to the point where vitrification or fusion of the materials begins, thus making the structure of the clay dense and nonabsorbent. This point may be reached at a higher or lower temperature, depending on the materials used, and stoneware may be made at cone 6 or cone 14, depending on the composition of the body and glazes. Vitrified ware can be made at firing temperatures below cone 6 by the use of strong body fluxes, such as prepared frits or combinations of talc and nepheline syenite. But strictly speaking, such pottery cannot be properly called stoneware because of the softness of the glazes.

True stoneware which contains only natural stoneware clay or is fluxed by the action of feldspar, has a long firing range.

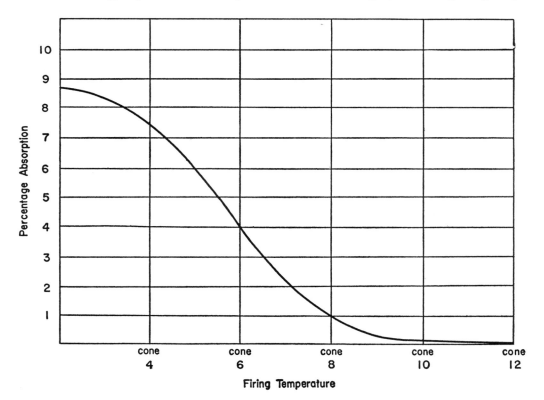

That is, from the temperature at which the body begins to tighten and vitrify to the temperature at which it is overfired and begins to bloat or to deform will be an interval of 4 or 5 cones. This long firing range gives a degree of latitude in firing stoneware which is not possible with earthenware. The chart on p. 58 shows the decreasing absorbency of a stoneware body as it is fired to progressively higher temperatures. It will be observed that after the body has reached a certain degree of maturity there is not too much change in it during advancing temperatures of several cones, and that the range from a point of reasonable density or maturity to the point of overfiring is long, in this case 4 or 5 cones.

The ideal density for stoneware varies with the intended use. For most wares intended to contain food, liquids, or for cooking, an absorbency of 2 or 3% is not objectionable. Chemical stoneware intended for containing acids or ware to be used where extremely sanitary standards must be met should have an absorbency of 1% or less. A low absorbency is always a practical advantage because it insures that even though the glaze of a piece may be crazed, liquids will not seep through the body. It is good too, to make ware which has a clear, bell-like ring when struck, although the quality of the tone will depend somewhat on the quantity of grog used in the body and on the fit of the glaze, as well as on the density of the body. On the other hand, the nearer the ware is fired to zero absorbency, the greater the shrinkage, and the more pronounced is the tendency of forms to warp and to slump.

The process of vitrification involves the formation of glass within the body, and the progressive melting of the various ingredients which are present. The mature stoneware body is a structure which, while it contains much material which is not fused, is tied together and made relatively compact and nonporous by the presence of glass between the particles.

Crystals of mullite may also be present in the structure, and these crystals give added strength.

The substance of stoneware, besides having the advantage of being nonabsorbent and leakproof, is exceptionally hard and durable. Stoneware is practically abrasion proof and is also much more resistant to breaking by impact shock than earthenware. The virtual indestructibility of stoneware is evidenced by the perfect condition of many specimens which are one thousand years old or more, and which, during the greater part of that time have been buried in the ground and subject to moisture. Stoneware is widely used in industry for containing and handling acids, and vats, pipes, valves, and the like are made of stoneware for this purpose.

The resistance of stoneware to heat shock and its suitability for use in oven cooking is of interest to the potter who wishes to make serviceable casseroles and other shapes for cooking. Most well-fired stoneware pottery may be safely used in the oven, provided it is not cooled too rapidly in use. The rapid cooling, for example, which would result from putting a very hot dish into cold water creates a severe strain which would be liable to cause breakage. Use in the oven over a long period of time may also cause glazes to craze which under ordinary usage do not craze.

When stoneware pottery breaks as a result of oven use, the difficulty usually can be traced to residual strains in the body. Such a strain may be caused by cooling the ware too rapidly in the glaze fire. All pots must become adjusted during cooling to a smaller volume. This slight shrinkage or contraction which always occurs during cooling must take place slowly or the ware will have a tendency to break later in use. Careful cooling is more important in making vitrified wares than it is in firing the more porous earthenware, whose structure, although not nearly as strong, is more elastic.

59

Another thing which may cause stoneware to crack when used in the oven is an excess of silica in the body. This excess silica may be in the form of added flint in the body, or it may be, in part, the silica present in very siliceous clays. Silica has a high expansion when heated, and this expansion is reversible, that is, the silica, when cooled, contracts to its original size. The contraction which occurs during the cooling of the ware may put the body under a strain which, while it may not cause the pot to break immediately, will make it incapable of surviving the relatively mild strain involved in oven use. So if a particular stoneware body is not giving durable service in oven cooking, the first adjustment to make to try to correct it would be to lower the silica content in the clay body. If this is not effective, substitutions of clays may be necessary, substituting clays which are high in alumina for those which are high in silica.

When silica is partially melted or fused together with some of the other materials in the body, it no longer has the characteristic of high expansion and high contraction. In fact, fused silica has an extremely low expansion. For this reason, firing the ware higher may make it much more resistant to heat shock, because it converts the silica from a high-expansion material to a low-expansion material. Holding the ware at top temperature for longer periods may also improve the heat-shock properties of the ware by increasing the development of mullite in the structure of the clay.

To make a ware which is exceptionally resistant to heat shock, and which can be used in cooking over a flame as well as in the oven, high firing temperatures are necessary—cone 12 or higher. Just enough feldspar is used to function as a flux to convert the silica in the body largely into fused or vitreous silica. The result is a very hard body composed of crystalline aluminum silicates and fused silica.

8. Basic stoneware body compositions

The following stoneware compositions are given as a basis for working out body compositions to suit particular needs. They are good, workable bodies which have been found to be free from defects or shortcomings in shaping, drying, or firing. They are not heavily textured or dark in color, but could easily be altered for color and texture. These compositions can be used as a guide or starting point in formulating bodies from available materials.

a. *Plastic Stoneware*

Stoneware clay (Jordan, Monmouth, or any other kind of stoneware clay) ..	60
Ball clay (any kind)	20
Flint	10
Feldspar (any kind)	10
	100

Grog can be added to these ingredients in amounts depending on how rough a body is desired. Five per cent will give a slight roughness, 20% will make quite a rough body and will also effect the plasticity. If the available stoneware clay is very plastic, less ball clay might be needed. If, on the other hand, the stoneware clay is very nonplastic, more ball clay would be needed. Similarly, the amount of feldspar might have to be adjusted, depending on the maturing point of the clays used. Fired color of this body is light gray-tan in oxidation, and light brown in reduction. Its absorption at cone 9 is 1%. Its shrinkage at cone 9 is 11.5%.

b. *Stoneware Based on Kaolin and Ball Clay*

Florida kaolin	25
Ball clay (any kind)	30
Red clay (any kind)	10
Fire clay (any kind)	15
Flint	10
Feldspar	10
	100

This composition is designed to be of use in case no stoneware clay is available. Kaolin, ball clay, and fire clay are generally available from suppliers, and the red clay could be any local, low-fire clay such as that used in most localities for making bricks. The working properties of this body may not be as good as the body given above, because in this case the composition contains no stoneware clay as a major ingredient. Grog may be added, or other materials for color and texture. In this composition, the kind of ball clay used might have a very noticeable effect, and several kinds should be tried. The fired color of this body in oxidation at cone 9 is gray and in reduction gray-brown. Absorption at cone 9 is 1%. Its shrinkage at cone 9 is 12.5%.

c. *Stoneware Based on Fire Clay*

Fire clay	40
Ball clay	30
Red clay	10
Flint	10
Feldspar	10
	100

This type of body, because of the large proportion of fire clay, is relatively coarse, and may not be ideal for wheel work. It is good for modeling or building. The kind of fire clay used is critical in this composition, and if a plastic one is available, a body of this sort may be very good to work with. The texture and color quality of the fired body will also depend on the kind of fire clay used. When North American fire clay is used in this body, it will fire to a tan-gray color in oxidation, and in reduction, at cone 9 or 10 will be a toast color. At cone 9, the shrinkage is 10% and the fired absorption is 15%.

d. *Casting Stoneware*

Kaolin	30
Ball clay	15
Stoneware clay	15
Red clay	5
Flint	15
Feldspar	20
	100

To make a slip, use 40 parts of water to each part of dry body. Before adding the clay to the water, dissolve in the water one fourth of 1% of sodium silicate, and one fourth of 1% of soda ash, to the dry weight of the clay. This body contains less plastic material than the other compositions given, and is not especially suited to throwing or modeling. It fires to a very dense and smooth structure, and at cone 9 in oxidation is a tan-gray color. In reduction it fires to a light warm tan color. Shrinkage is 12.5% and the fired absorption is 1%.

Chapter 4

Porcelain Clay Bodies

Unlike stoneware, porcelain can be made only from a body compounded of several ingredients and cannot be made from any single natural material. Unlike stoneware, only a few materials can go into the composition. However, the dividing line between stoneware and porcelain may be very subtle. Many stonewares are very hard, dense, and vitreous. They may be very light in color as well, gray or gray-white. Porcelain is distinguished from such stonewares only by its whiteness, and by the fact that where it is thin it is translucent. Historically, porcelain evolved as a refinement of stoneware, and it is exactly that.

Although the basic proportioning of ingredients in porcelain is quite simple, the exact adjustment of materials and the proper firing requires considerable control. Whereas in stoneware a small change of proportion in the body mixture may make little appreciable difference, in porcelain a change of a few per cent one way or the other may have a very marked effect on the ware.

Essentially, porcelain is achieved by combining kaolin with feldspar and firing the mixture to the point where the body is on the verge of melting or glassification.

1. Clays for porcelain

Making porcelain today is made relatively easy by the availability of fine, purified and prepared kaolins. Kaolin is produced in quantity not only for use in ceramics but for the paper industry, where it is used for coating white paper. Kaolin is discussed in the previous chapter in connection with stoneware bodies. Here its properties as an ingredient of porcelain concern us.

All kaolins are highly refractory. English China clay has a melting point of about 1800°C, and it softens to the point of deformation at about cone 35. If pottery were made from kaolin alone, it would have to be fired to at least cone 14 to be even as dense and as serviceable as a soft earthenware. The reason for the refractoriness of kaolin is its relative purity and freedom from any oxides other than alumina and silica, both of which have very high melting points. From the analyses already given of various kaolins, it will be seen that the percentages of sodium, potassium, lime, and iron are very small. From a geological point of view, kaolins might almost be considered freaks of nature, because the vast majority of all clays contain considerable percentages of these elements, and as a result, have much lower melting points.

For porcelain making, two properties of kaolin are of greatest importance: (1) the purity of the material, which determines the whiteness with which it will burn; (2) its plasticity, or lack of it.

Although all true kaolins are white-burning clays, there are subtle differences between the various clays which give slightly differing fired colors. As we have seen, Georgia kaolin fires to a slightly darker color than English kaolin because

62

of the presence of a small amount of rutile, and in spite of the fact that English kaolin has slightly more iron than the Georgia kaolin. The slight differences between kaolins as to fired color can be observed only when they are incorporated into a porcelain body and are fired with a clear glaze. Actually, the clays marketed as kaolins are all sufficiently light in color to meet most requirements as to whiteness.

As to plasticity, no kaolin is really plastic in the way that an earthenware or stoneware clay may be. In porcelain making it is a matter of finding ways to make pottery with a material which is not really good for throwing or for other plastic processes, and which in fact may be so low in plasticity that it is even difficult to cast. In selecting a kaolin to use in porcelain, the most plastic clay is the best choice, provided it compares favorably in fired color for the intended use. For this reason, Florida kaolin is valuable because it is relatively more plastic than other available kaolins, and at the same time fires to a very light color.

It is usually assumed that the kaolins in use in China were more plastic than those available to us. This assumption seems to be based mostly on the fact that the Chinese were able to make forms in porcelain which are natural to plastic clay—fluid, large in scale, and done on the potter's wheel rather than cast in molds. One thing which may have contributed to the plasticity of Chinese kaolin is their practice of carefully separating out the finer fractions of the clay by flotation. Another factor is their habit of aging the clay for long periods, sometimes for many years, to develop its maximum plasticity. Then, too, the Chinese were superb craftsmen and were able to overcome technical difficulties which seem almost insurmountable to us today, even with all our reservoir of exact knowledge and engineering skill. For example, we know for a fact that the Chinese porcelains were once-fired, and

that bowls of eggshell thinness were trimmed, dipped in glaze, and often transported for miles to the kilns and placed in the saggers for firing, yet a high percentage of ware came out of the kiln in flawless perfection.

English kaolins, while they are very free from impurities and burn to a very light color, are thought to lack strength during the vitrification period of firing, and it may be for this reason that little true porcelain was produced in England, but rather "china," which in many ways is easier to produce. On the Continent, one of the outstanding kaolins is the Zettlitz kaolin from Karlsbad, in Czechoslovakia. This fine clay formed the principal raw material of many of the famous European factories producing true porcelain. Perhaps the closest American equivalent to the Zettlitz kaolin is the primary kaolin found in North Carolina. Certainly, blends of Carolina and Florida kaolins can be used with success in porcelain.

It is common practice in factory production to use several different kinds of kaolin in one body mixture. This is done to minimize the ill effects of any change in the composition or firing behavior of any one of the clays. However, with clay mining and marketing now under exact laboratory controls, there is much less chance than formerly of the clay varying from shipment to shipment, and the inclusion of several different kinds of clay in the body may be an unnecessary precaution. It is common practice to use two kaolins, one of them a plastic kaolin and the other an English kaolin or Georgia kaolin.

To correct for the lack of plasticity in kaolin, some ball clay may be used in porcelain bodies. Ball clay, however, must be thought of as a necessary evil in compounding very white porcelain. The highly plastic nature of ball clay does, of course, correct the plasticity of the mixture, but only at the expense of darkening the body. All ball clays have enough iron in them to make them fire to a considerably darker color than kaolin. If a very white body is desired, the amount of ball clay should be held down to the absolute minimum which still enables the body to be cast. Ten per cent or more of ball clay will result in a slightly darkened fired color. European porcelain makers did not use ball clay, and were able to develop sufficient plasticity in the clay by very careful selection and preparation of the raw materials. Chinese porcelains also seem to have been made without any secondary clays of the ball clay type, and there is no reason to doubt the body composition as given in the Père D'Entrecolles letters, which indicates a body made up of only kaolin and prepared feldspathic rock.

In selecting a ball clay, the plasticity and the amount of iron and other impurities must both be considered. On both these counts, English ball clay is superior to the American clays because the English material is not only highly plastic but low in iron also. There are, however, many excellent American ball clays. Usually a ball clay which is dark in color in the raw state is apt to be highly plastic. The dark color is caused by the presence of carbonaceous matter, which burns off in the fire, having no ill effects on the color of the body.

Ball clay not only has the effect of adding to the plasticity and the workability of the porcelain mixture but also promotes an earlier densification and fusion in the body. Ball clays, although they are fairly refractory, usually fire to a very tight and dense structure at about cone 10 or 11, and they help in creating dry strength and early fired strength. This may simplify porcelain making, because objects made largely of kaolin are so fragile when they are dry that it is almost impossible to handle them. Also, when pots made largely of kaolin are bisque-fired at lower temperatures, they are extremely chalky and friable. The ad-

dition of ball clay to the body makes the handling of the ware much easier both before firing and after the bisque fire.

Air-floated ball clays require no preparation and may be added to the body mix as they come. Lump ball clays should be first blunged with plenty of water to a thin fluid slip, then passed through a 150-mesh screen to remove all particles of grit, lignite, or other foreign matter. The slip is then dried out and the clay is ready for use.

In the whiteware industry magnetic filters are used to remove particles of iron from the clay. The slip is run over a powerful magnet, which attracts and holds the metallic impurities. A magnetic filter is useful to remove impurities of iron which usually get into the clay during mining or transportation. Iron oxide, which is a part of the chemical make-up of the clay, is unaffected by the magnetic filter.

2. Flint and feldspar for porcelain

The selection of flint and feldspar for porcelain bodies is more critical than in the case of stonewares. Not only must these materials be considered from the standpoint of chemical purity and freedom from iron, but also for their exact firing behavior. Commercial flint is ground from various types of quartz, not necessarily from the mineral flint. Some quartz is transparent when fired, and some is more opaque. For this reason, the selection of quartz may have some effect on the translucency of the finished porcelain. Most of the flint prepared for the ceramic industry in the United States is ground from massive quartz of good fired translucency, and it also meets the potter's requirements as to purity and particle size.

For porcelain, potash feldspar is usually used. Many fine commercial feldspars are available in the United States. The material must be low in both iron and titania to yield the whitest finished ware. It is suggested that in selecting a feldspar to use in porcelain, the available feldspars be made up into "fusion buttons," or little mounds of dry powder which are fired at the glaze temperature to determine the degree of fusion and the color. The feldspar should fuse to a smooth, white, glassy mass. If a reducing fire is to be used for making the ware, the feldspar should not show any signs of gray discoloration from carbon as a result of the fire. Several kinds of feldspar are sometimes used in the body to reduce the chance of variation caused by changes in the composition of any one material.

As in the case of stoneware bodies, nepheline syenite may be used in place of all or part of the feldspar, with the effect of materially lowering the maturing temperature of the body. When a considerable amount of nepheline syenite is used and the maturing temperature of a body has been reduced to cone 8 or lower, some of the characteristics of true porcelain are lost, notably the hardness of the glaze and the ability of the body to stand or hold its shape during vitrification. However, smaller amounts of nepheline syenite can successfully lower the firing temperature of a clay body by 1 or 2 cones, so that, for example, a body which requires cone 14 for complete vitrification can, by the addition of about 5% of nepheline syenite, be made to mature at cone 12.

3. Proportioning of ingredients for porcelain bodies

Since porcelain consists of three main constituents, clay, feldspar, and flint, and since the correct amounts of these materials have been determined by long experience, the arrival at a suitable mixture for porcelain presents no great problem. The clays should total about one half of the body, including both the kaolin and the ball clay, if any. The remaining half of the body is divided about equally between the feldspar and the flint. The exact composition will be determined by the materials used and by the intended temperature of firing.

Chinese porcelains made at Ching-tê-chên were said to be composed of about equal parts of kaolin and *petuntse*. The petuntse was a feldspathic rock, which probably contained quartz.

A typical German porcelain body composition is:

Clay	54
Feldspar	20
Flint	25
Whiting	1

This is quite a refractory composition and requires about cone 14 for full maturity. French porcelain is apt to contain more feldspar, as in the following composition:

Clay	44
Feldspar	30
Flint	25
Whiting	1

As was noted above, few of the European porcelain compositions (or the Chinese) indicate any secondary or ball clay. However, to make a workable clay body for either casting or plastic forming without using any ball clay is difficult, and unless extreme whiteness is a goal, the inclusion of about 10% of ball clay in the body is a practical improvement. This addition gives the following composition, which might be taken as a starting point in compounding porcelain bodies:

Kaolin	40
Ball clay	10
Feldspar	25
Flint	25

This body will be mature at around cone 11. The kaolin in this composition could be broken down further into Georgia (or Carolina) kaolin, 25 parts, and Florida kaolin, 15 parts.

The further addition of 1% of whiting or dolomite to serve as an active auxiliary flux would give a body as follows:

Georgia kaolin	25
Florida kaolin	15
Ball clay	10

Feldspar 24
Flint 25
Whiting 1

To lower the maturing temperature of this body to about cone 10, the feldspar can be increased at the expense of the flint by 3 or 4 parts. To still further lower the maturing point to about cone 8 or 9, a substitution of nepheline syenite for some of the feldspar can be made.

Vitreous whiteware products are manufactured which are very similar in substance to porcelain, such as china, hotel china, sanitary ware, and tile. A distinction should be made between porcelain and china. In porcelain, the body and the glaze are both matured in the high fire. This makes possible a very hard glaze which is almost indistinguishable from the body. In china, the ware is vitrified in a high bisque fire, and glazed in a second and lower firing. This simplifies manufacture, because the ware can be supported on cranks (refractory plate setters) or by sand during the high fire, thus greatly reducing the chance of warping. Also, the ware can be supported on refractory "pins" in saggers or racks during the glaze fire, and this enables the setting of many more pieces in a given space than would be the case if each piece had to be set on a shelf by itself. Aside from this important distinction between porcelain and china having to do with the temperature and manner of glazing, the two kinds of ware differ also in composition, in that china usually contains more ball clay than does true porcelain and is therefore not as white. A typical hotel or restaurant ware china body is:

Kaolin 30
Ball clay 15
Feldspar 18
Flint 35
Whiting 2

China may be equally as transparent as porcelain, but hotel china is made thick in cross section and is therefore not translucent even though the body may be very glassy and capable of transmitting light. True porcelain tableware has not been made extensively in the United States, possibly because the pottery traditions and pottery techniques were inherited largely from England, where porcelain making was never highly developed.

The above compositions are designed to make translucent pottery of exceptional whiteness. This kind of fired substance is the classic ideal in porcelain, and to achieve it some difficulties must be allowed for, both in forming and in firing the ware. In forming, the lack of plasticity severely limits the ways in which the clay can be worked and the types of forms which can be made. In firing, porcelain bodies become soft at the highest temperature of firing, and this softening leads to a tendency toward deformation. This deformation can be controlled only by careful design and correct kiln setting and firing. More will be said about the limitations of both forming and firing in a subsequent section.

It is possible that the potter may not be interested in extreme whiteness or in translucency, but may wish to make rather a dense, completely vitreous ware which is slightly off-white in color and perhaps thicker in cross section than the average translucent porcelain. Bodies for ware of this type may contain considerable ball clay and may therefore be made to pot well without the difficulties which usually attend the making of white porcelain. There is, however, no sharp dividing line between stoneware and porcelain. The same ware might be correctly called either vitreous white stoneware or grayed heavy porcelain; it is merely a matter of classification.

To arrive at a suitable composition for a porcelain body, it is suggested that the temperature of firing be decided upon first. For true porcelain this should be at least cone 9, and preferably higher—cone 11 or 12 is an ideal working temperature. If the kiln has a top limitation of less than cone 9, approximations of porcelain may be made, but the extreme hardness of glaze and strength and clarity of body which are characteristic of porcelain at its best will be unattainable. After the temperature of firing has been decided on, the potter should next decide whether he is aiming for extreme whiteness and translucency or whether these qualities are secondary to form, glaze quality, and decoration. If whiteness is not a prime objective, the composition can contain considerable ball clay. The first trials (assuming that the temperature is to be cone 11 to 12) should be based on the proportion:

Clay (divided between kaolins
   and ball clay) 50
Feldspar 25
Flint 25

On the basis of the fired result of this mixture, subsequent trials can be varied to achieve more or less whiteness, translucency, or plasticity.

Actually, the difficulty in formulating porcelain bodies is not in arriving at initial compositions, for these are easily obtained on the basis of common practice. It is rather the evaluation of the body which is difficult. Any mixture made according to the proportions as given in this chapter will appear, in a small sample, to be suitable. The real test comes when some quantity of ware is made from the body. Then, in all likelihood, difficulties in forming, casting, drying, firing, and glazing will indicate the necessity for some alterations in the body, and the task is to make the adjustments which will successfully correct these difficulties. Another factor which makes the formulation of porcelain difficult is that there are many subtle factors which can cause failure in the kiln, and it is hard to determine whether failures are caused by the composition of the ware or by something which occurred during the preparation of the body, the forming, the drying, or the firing. For example, if porcelain is warping badly in the fire, one might be tempted to conclude that it was being overfired to a point where the pots were slumping out of shape. But actually, the difficulty might be traced to the way the ware was dried, the manner in which it was set in the kiln, or to numerous other factors. Successful porcelain has usually been made in shops or factories where the formulation and production techniques could be worked out over a long period of time, during which the various causes of failure could be isolated and corrected. Anyone expecting to produce porcelain in any quantity must be prepared to work out production methods during a period in which the failures coming from the kiln may far outnumber the successes. Skill in porcelain making has usually resided in the craftsmanship and knowledge of groups of people, including those responsible for the preparation of the raw materials, the casters, jiggermen, throwers, and trimmers who form the ware, and also the finishers, the glazers, and the kiln firemen. In Europe these skills were passed on from one generation of craftsmen to the next.

Of course, if one is interested in limited or one-of-a-kind production, many of the difficulties which plague large-scale factory production are not encountered. This is especially true if the shapes made are limited to hollow forms and no flatware, such as plates, platters, or low bowls are made. Of all pottery shapes, flat round plates are perhaps the most difficult to make in porcelain.

4. Plastic porcelain bodies

Many potters, although they may be interested in the qualities of porcelain, have avoided it because the lack of plasticity in porcelain clay bodies makes throwing difficult. It is certainly true that porcelain bodies are generally much inferior in plasticity to earthenware or stoneware clays, and an ideal clay body for wheel work cannot be made which will fire to a clear white color. However, if some compromise is made with whiteness, porcelain bodies can be made which,

67

though not ideal in working properties, can nevertheless be thrown with fair ease.

In arriving at such a body, the ball clay content is increased considerably above that which would be permissible where extreme whiteness is desired. The following composition, for example, is plastic enough to use for throwing simple shapes:

Georgia kaolin	10
Florida kaolin	15
Ball clay	25
Feldspar	25
Flint	25

At cone 11, this body fires to a very light gray, and under a glaze it will appear to be quite white. If such a body is compared directly with the whitest porcelain, it will appear to be somewhat dingy. If a still more plastic body is required, the clay content can be increased at the expense of the flint. For example, the above body could be altered as follows:

Georgia kaolin	10
Florida kaolin	25
Ball clay	25
Feldspar	25
Flint	10

Here the Florida kaolin has been increased from 15 to 25, which effects some improvement in the plasticity, with an increase, however, in the shrinkage. A point is soon reached beyond which plastic clay cannot be added to a porcelain body without seriously reducing the amounts of feldspar and flint. For a translucent body, about 25% of feldspar is an irreducible minimum, and if less than 10% of flint is used, it will be very difficult to fit glazes onto the body. About 65% of clay, then, is the practical maximum which can be used in the composition. And if the clay body is to fire to a light color, the majority of this clay must be kaolin, with a minor part of it being made up of ball clay. Thus with 65% of clay we seem to reach the limit of plasticity which can be achieved in a body and still have the fired result truly porcelanous.

One possibility remains, and that is the addition of bentonite to the body to increase its plasticity. Up to 5% of bentonite may be used without running into serious difficulties such as stickiness, checking, excessive shrinkage, or of warping and checking in the fire. Bentonite is not an iron-free material, however, and the addition of 5% of it will further discolor the porcelain toward a gray or buff color. When 5% of bentonite and up to 25% of ball clay are used in the body, the result is apt to resemble a light gray stoneware rather than a porcelain. However, if the ware is thinly potted, and if slightly opaque glazes are used, a very refined, hard, clean ware may be made which has most of the virtues of true porcelain.

Plasticity is strongly influenced by the manner in which the clay is prepared and by aging; for this reason, if a plastic porcelain body is desired for use on the wheel, it is important to give careful attention to the manner in which the clay is made up for use. If suitable equipment is available, it is advisable to ball-mill the body, rather than to blunge it. This disperses the plastic ingredients thoroughly, especially the bentonite, if this is used. To grind well in the mill, slip should not be too thin. After thorough mixing and some grinding in the mill, the slip is filter-pressed or dried in plaster bats to a plastic consistency. This process seems to have an adverse effect on plasticity, perhaps because the grains of clay are forced into a similar orientation, and the clay is improved, after pressing, by wedging or pugging. In Europe, wedging machines are used which roll the clay out and gather it up repeatedly, thus mixing it and dispersing the air in the clay. The de-airing pug mill mixes, wedges and de-airs the clay very effectively. Or hand wedging, if it is skillfully done, will put the clay into excellent condition. After wedging, the clay should be stored for aging. It should be rather moist when it is stored, just a little too soft for throwing. Some already aged clay added to a new batch will hasten the development of organic matter in the clay. Or the addition of a small amount of vinegar may help. The clay should be stored in tight containers, in a warm place, and it should be allowed to age for at least a week before use. Although the increasing benefits of aging will be less noticeable after one week, clay which has been aging for several months will be greatly superior to newer clay. Before using the clay, it should be thoroughly wedged again.

White bodies made in the manner described will be smooth, and plastic enough to the feel, and when tried on the wheel they will center easily and respond to shaping very well on smaller pieces, and on shapes which do not have extremes of overhang or curves. However, if pieces larger than about 8 inches high are attempted, it will be noticed that the clay does not stand well and will slump out of shape. Rather than struggle with what is a natural limitation of this kind of body, it is wise to confine the shapes made to those which come fairly easily. If very flat things are desired, such as plates or low bowls, considerable trimming may be necessary. Larger shapes can be made by joining two or more pieces together. The huge porcelain jars made in China were done this way.

If very thin, translucent, ware is desired, the shapes can be made fairly thin on the wheel, and then trimmed down to a thinner cross section when leatherhard. A very sharp trimming tool should be used to avoid chatter and tearing. The final thinning can be done by slightly sandpapering the piece, when dry, with flint paper.

Porcelain bodies are "tender," and must be handled with care at all stages of potting. Drying should take place in a draft-free place, and should not be too rapid. Whenever possible, open shapes, such as plates and bowls, should be inverted on smooth, dry plaster bats to dry. Porcelain bodies have a very low dry strength, and some losses are to be expected in finishing and kiln setting.

5. Porcelain casting slips

Casting is perhaps the best method of forming porcelain because it does not depend on extremes of plasticity in the clay. But even in casting there are some difficulties which need to be overcome.

It is advisable to arrive at a porcelain composition first on the basis of the fired characteristics of the body such as density, translucence, and color. When the fired properties of the body are thought to be satisfactory, some trials can be made to determine the proper amount of water and deflocculents needed to make a good casting slip. The usual porcelain body will not require more than 40% of water to form a slip, and perhaps as little as 35%. Sodium silicate and sodium carbonate in equal amounts should be tried as a deflocculent, and the total amount of deflocculent should be between one quarter and one half of 1% of the dry weight of the body. In the case of any particular body, experiment is necessary to determine the exact amount of water and the kind and amount of the deflocculent which will make the best slip. Some kaolins cast better when deflocculated with an organic deflocculent such as sodium tannate or sodium gallate.

The best way to prepare porcelain casting slip is to make the clay up first into a thin slip with water only, and blunge it thoroughly to intermingle all the ingredients of the body. The ball clay, if any is used, should be mixed and screened by itself first, then dried and added to the rest of the body. The slip from the blunger should be screened through a 100-mesh screen, then stiffened in a filter press or in bats to the plastic state, and dried. The dried clay is then shredded and added gradually to the water for the casting slip, in which the deflocculent has been dissolved. The slip is blunged for several hours, care being taken not to stir in air. The casting slip will improve with age, and although castings may be made with it immediately after preparation, its working properties will be improved after about a week.

Two difficulties are encountered in casting procelain: too rapid casting, and tearing when the spare is cut off. Porcelain slips, especially if little or no ball clay is used, will cast with rapidity. It may be found that sufficient thickness has built up in the mold after only 2 or 3 minutes, and this does not give enough time to gauge the thickness of the piece or to handle more than one mold at a time. One remedy for this is to wet the molds before casting, which has the effect of slowing down the absorption of water out of the slip. The molds will be found to work better and to cast at a more normal speed (about 10 to 20 minutes) after several pieces have been made and the mold has become partially saturated with water. The spare must be cut off with great care to prevent tearing at the lip of the piece. It is well to use a very sharp knife for trimming and to do the trimming as soon as possible after the molds have been emptied. Sometimes the spare is left on the piece and allowed to dry with it and is then cut or sandpapered off later. This, however, necessitates dry finishing of the edge, which is slow and increases the danger of cracking the ware during finishing.

Porcelain slip, being quite nonplastic, does not shrink excessively in drying, but in casting it does shrink rapidly at first, and this may cause the ware to crack in the molds before it can be removed. It is necessary to open the molds and to remove the ware as soon as it is stiff enough to handle.

Cast forms must be finished with great care, especially at the seams, if they are to show a perfection of detail when fired and glazed. When a clear porcelain glaze is used, minor imperfections are magnified rather than hidden. Wet sponging is effective for smoothing edges, but it must be done judiciously to avoid a worn-down, eroded look. Dry finishing is done in European factories with a switch made of the hairs from the end of a cow's tail, prepared by boiling into a tangled ball. Abrasion with a coarse cloth may do as well to give the surface of the piece a smooth polish.

Handles, knobs, etc., are easily attached with slip; in fact, even completely dry pieces can be luted together by applying slip to the parts to be joined and quickly bringing them together before the slip dries.

In making porcelain, the prevention of occasional dark specks or spots is a problem. The smallest impurity in the form of iron, or an iron-bearing mineral will cause discoloration. Iron may find its way into the clay either as an impurity in the raw materials or as tiny fragments picked up during the processing of the materials or during potting. There is not much that can be done about the occasional spot which appears as a result of impurities in the clay, feldspar, flint, or glaze materials. Grinding the body helps, because any dark impurity tends, during grinding, to be dispersed and so becomes less noticeable in the finished ware. In Europe, lumps of the flint and feldspar from the mine are sometimes picked and sorted by hand to eliminate dark spots. Commercial kaolins, feldspar, and quartz, as they are sold for ceramic use, are free enough from impurities to produce very clear, clean whitewares, and spots are usually the result of "tramp" iron which gets into the clay either when the body is being made up or when the pottery is being cast, finished, and handled. To keep the ware clean it is necessary to avoid using rusty tools or equipment, such as mixers or blungers which are in bad condition, and to keep the working areas clean. The remarkable whiteness of the Chinese porcelains may have resulted partly from the use of wood for nearly all the equipment of the pottery, which lessened the chance of contamination by iron. It is very difficult to produce white porcelain in a shop where dark clays are being used, and if both stoneware or earthenware production and porcelain production are to be carried on, it is better to have separate rooms for them to prevent contamination of the white clay. Porcelain slips and plastic clay must be stored in crocks or jars rather than in metal containers which might corrode and flake off.

6. Firing porcelain

Porcelain owes its unique properties of hardness, density, and translucence to high firing. There is no substitute for heat in making porcelain, and the approximations of porcelain achieved at lower temperatures do not have the beauty of substance which makes porcelain desirable. Cone 9 is probably the lowest kiln temperature which should be considered suitable for porcelain, and the general range of cone 10 to cone 12 is perhaps ideal because it permits a full use of the natural reactions of feldspar in body and in glaze, yet does not involve the expenditure of fuel and the wear and tear on the kiln and kiln furniture which occurs at still higher temperature. Temperatures of cone 14 to cone 18 have been used for European porcelains, and are used in the United States to fire technical whitewares, such as laboratory porcelain, insulators, and spark plugs.

Porcelain is a unique kind of pottery because it is fired to the point of melting; in fact, it somewhat resembles glass. The firing reactions which bring about this vitrification are very interesting. During the early stages of firing, porcelain reacts very much as any other type of clay. The water of hydration in the clay is driven off at an early stage of the fire. The clay grains tighten with advancing heat, and shrinkage begins. At about cone 04, the porcelain body will be found to

be still very soft and chalky, though bound together sufficiently for handling and glazing. Porcelain is usually bisqued between about cone 05, and cone 1. Although it is usual to bisque-fire porcelain before glazing, it is interesting to note that the Chinese commonly once-fired their stonewares and porcelains. In European factories, the ware was bisqued in the upper part of large bottle-shaped kilns during the glost fire. The lower chamber held the glazed ware. When ware comes from the bisque, it is still soft and may be further finished about the edges and on mold seams by sandpapering or scraping. The bisque is very fragile and must be handled with great care to prevent cracking. Also, the bisque kiln must be cooled very slowly to prevent dunting. Porcelain is especially subject to dunting because of its high silica content, and the soft bisque does not have the cohesive strength to survive the contractions of cooling unless plenty of time is given to the cooling cycle, especially during the period from 900°C to 700°C when the kiln is turning from cherry red to dark. It is during this period of cooling that quartz undergoes a sudden contraction.

The glost fire must also advance slowly in the range of 500°C to 800°C to prevent cracking from the sudden or unequal expansion of quartz. After the kiln reaches a bright cherry red, however, the advance of temperature can be quite rapid without endangering the ware. When about cone 9 is reached, the rate of advance should be slowed down. Ceramic reactions in the fire require time as well as temperature, and this is especially true in the vitrification of porcelain. With the advancing heat, the feldspar begins to melt. Feldspar does not have a very sharp melting point, and at first it softens into a very viscous glass. The feldspar in the porcelain body is present in more or less separate grains or particles, and these grains of feldspar lie adjacent to grains of quartz and to the much finer grains of kaolin. As the temperature advances and the feldspar melts, some of the quartz and some of the kaolin are drawn into solution. Quartz and kaolin, though they are both refractory, are fusible in the presence of the potassium, sodium, and lime of the feldspar. The virtue of kaolin, at this stage of the maturing of porcelain, is that even though it is drawn into partial solution in a mixture with an ever-increasing content of glass, it furnishes the strength and viscosity which prevents the ware from slumping out of shape. The ware can be considered matured when the desired degree of translucence is achieved. It will have been rendered very dense and nonporous at some stage before translucency is reached. The development of mullite crystals in porcelain is thought to interfere somewhat with translucency, which is a characteristic of the glassy state.

The maturing period in firing porcelain presents some problems which are not a factor in stoneware. For one thing, the high silica content of porcelain, which contributes to the hardness and clarity of the finished product, makes the ware more subject to dunting, or cracking on cooling. The fire must be carried to the point where a considerable portion of the silica goes into glassy solution. The vitreous form of silica has a low coefficient of expansion and does not go through the expansions and contractions on heating that the crystalline forms of quartz do. Therefore, when a portion of the quartz of the body is vitrified, the ware may be safely cooled without danger of dunting. The danger of underfiring, then, is that the ware may crack during cooling.

On the other hand is the danger of overfiring, which in porcelain making is a very real hazard. In stoneware, where the body is not carried as far toward complete vitrification, a firing range of several cones is possible, and the ware may usually be fired 2 or 3 cones above its usual maturation point without serious slumping or bloating. In porcelain, on the other hand, the ware is carried to the brink of melting, and if the top temperature is exceeded by even one cone or less, the ware may go out of shape. The first sign of overfiring in porcelain may be bloating. Any porcelain body, no matter what the process of fabrication, will have numerous small pores scattered through it. These pores are filled with air. When the ware reaches a certain stage of softness during the glost fire, the pressure of air within the pores will be sufficient to make the body swell or bloat, the process being similar to the rising of bread dough from the distention of gas bubbles within it. A further pressure is created in the pores of the body by the combustion of the small amounts of carbon which are present in the clay. The products of combustion within the sealed pores of the body must exert a sudden and strong pressure. In reduction firing, where the kiln is deprived of oxygen during certain periods of the fire, the carbon within the pores of the body cannot burn so completely, and for this reason, the tendency to bloat may be lessened. It is an observed fact that in reduction firing porcelain bodies have a longer firing range and do not tend to bloat at as early a stage as in the case of an oxidizing fire. The ware does not seem to slump as readily either, and this may also be a result of the lack of combustion within the body of the ware itself. Techniques of reduction firing and the effect of reduction of the color of porcelain are discussed in a later section. Also discussed later are the methods of setting porcelain wares in the kiln, and the management of the fire.

Chapter 5

Porcelain and Stoneware Glazes

1. The theory of high-fired glazes

One of the joys of working with stoneware and porcelain is the extreme beauty of high-fired glazes. In texture, in color, in tactile qualities, and in relation to the clay, high-fired glazes have a strong appeal. This is not to imply an inferiority of low-fired effects in ceramics, because the low-fired glazes also have their appeal—a beauty which can take the form of scintillating, melting color, or the sparkle and glint of polished glass. The high-fired glazes are more quiet, perhaps more dignified, and they seem suited to ceramic expressions in which form is the essential value.

And from a practical point of view, high-fired glazes have certain virtues not found in lower-fired glazes. Most important is an extreme hardness. Glazes differ greatly in hardness, depending on their composition and on the temperature at which they were fired. A very low-fired lead glaze composed largely of lead oxide is easily scratched, and a plate, for example, which has such a glaze will, after a period of use, develop numerous scratches just from the abrasion of silverware. High-fired glazes are scratchproof except from the abrasion of substances harder than the glaze. These would include only such substances as quartz, diamonds, and other materials which would never be used in connection with pottery. Along with hardness, high-fired glazes have the desirable property of resistance to the attack of acids. While this is of great importance in chemical porcelains and stoneware, it is of less importance in wares for everyday use. However, over a long period of time, centuries or millenniums rather than decades, the high-fired glazes have proved durable because of their resistance to corrosion. The most glorious periods of Persian pottery are now known to us mostly from specimens which are not in a good state of preservation because of the deterioration of the lead and soda glazes over the ages. The stonewares and porcelains of the Orient, on the other hand, are frequently found in a splendid state of preservation, even though they may have been buried for a thousand years or have been in continuous use for several hundred years.

More important than practicality to most potters is the beauty of high-fired glazes. This beauty arises from three distinct factors: the close relationship which exists between glaze and the clay body, the actual condition or quality of the surface of the glaze, and the quality of the color.

In earthenware the glaze tends to exist as a distinct and separate coating on the clay body. While it may be firmly stuck to the clay, it does not relate to it except as a covering. In high-fired pottery, on the other hand, the glazes tend to be part of the clay or an extension of the clay. In stoneware, the surface of the clay and the glaze are fused together, and the color of the clay has a very strong influence on the color and quality of the glaze. In porcelain the glaze and the body are so similar that there is no sharp distinction between them. The rims of porcelain cups are usually not glazed, yet this is barely noticeable, so glassy and smooth is the body. This close relationship between body and glaze, both in substance and in appearance, which characterizes high-fired ware gives a feeling of unity, rightness, and suitability about the surface that is difficult to achieve in earthenware. One of the difficult problems in design which the potter faces is the problem of keeping the glazed surface from seeming to be a superficial addition, an afterthought, or worse yet, a "decorative" embellishment intended to give interest to a form which otherwise might not be able to stand alone. The carver of wood or stone, or the worker in leather or metal, has no such problem because his material is the same all the way through and has no distinct and separate coating on the surface. In porcelain and stoneware this problem can be beautifully solved in various ways. A thick unctuous glaze does not seem out of place on very dense white stoneware, for example; rather, such a glaze seems like a very closely related substance which has been spread on the surface to enhance and slightly complement the substance of the clay. Or thin mat glazes on stoneware may appear to be films which bring out the character of the clay in somewhat the same manner as oiling brings out the beauty of wood, without in any way covering it up or concealing its color and grain. Or the glaze may give the effect of a polished or burnished surface rather than a coating. All of these possible surface qualities happen very naturally in the high fire; it is not a matter of involved technique, exceptional control, or unusual materials, but rather of allowing the materials to speak for themselves and to react in the most natural way possible. Work in high-fired glazes should always be directed toward finding out what the materials will do with the least involved or least forced techniques,

and toward the revelation of the natural beauty of the materials.

The surface quality of high-fired glazes is a very subtle thing. The fact that a glaze is matured at cone 9 or more is no assurance that it will not be harsh, unpleasant in texture, or ugly in color. In fact, high firing, since it tends to mute glaze colors and to develop brownish colors, frequently results in somber, lifeless, or overburned-looking pots. But the higher fire does make possible a range of surfaces which are close to those found in minerals and rocks. The similarity of many porcelain and stoneware glazed surfaces to jade has often been noted, and it is certain that the enthusiasm of the Chinese for stoneware and porcelain stemmed in part from their association of glazes with jade.

Low-fired glazes depend on the low melting fluxes, which include lead oxide, potassium and soda, and boric oxide. These are all oxides of low melting point which bring about the fusion of the more refractory materials in the glaze—silica, alumina, and the alkaline earths. Above about cone 8, the higher temperature makes possible the fusion of glazes composed of fewer materials, and fluxing is accomplished by feldspar and the alkaline earths—lime, magnesia, and barium.

Actually, very effective glazes for high firing can be made from a few easily obtained minerals. Granite, which is composed of feldspar, mica, and quartz, is in itself near to a glaze in composition, and a worth-while experiment is to select granite rocks (those with the most feldspar in them will be most suitable), grind the rock to a fine powder, and try it out as a glaze at cone 10. It is difficult to grind granite, of course, unless power grinding equipment is available. Feldspar is a very common mineral obtainable at least in small fragments in most localities, and it may be used for "found" glazes. Various combinations of feldspar, limestone, quartz, and clay will often give very interesting glazes, usually rather dark in color because of the iron and other metallic oxides which are usually present in common rocks. The labor involved in selecting and grinding rocks for glazes makes it rather impractical where any quantity of glaze is needed, or where uniformity is desired in the finished pots. But every potter should have the experience of making up some of his own glazes out of materials which are close at hand. It helps to make glaze composition less of a mystery which is dependent on chemistry and on raw materials suppliers, and more of an art which is based on the fire reactions of a few simple materials that are abundant and familiar.

2. Feldspar as the basis for high-fired glazes

The basis for most high-fired glaze is the mineral feldspar. Feldspar is like a natural frit. Most feldspar contains 10 to 15% of potassium, sodium, and lime combined. The remaining 85 or 90% is divided between alumina and silica, with silica accounting for 60% or more of the total. On a molecular basis, feldspar has the composition:

Na_2O, K_2O, or CaO . . Total of 1
Al_2O_3 1
SiO_2 6

Commercial feldspars vary widely, some having more or less silica than indicated in the above formula, and containing more or less of potassium, sodium, or lime, singly or in combination. Feldspars also have a variety of melting points, depending on their composition. However, all feldspars are fusible, and melt to a stiff glass at cone 10 or less. Since feldspar alone melts at stoneware heat, it is the ideal basis for stoneware and porcelain glazes. Most high-fired glazes contain about 50% of feldspar, and may be thought of as consisting primarily of feldspar, with other materials added for the purpose of lowering the melting point, increasing the hardness of the glaze, or for the purpose of controlling the color and surface texture of the glaze.

A good way to arrive at a high-fired glaze composition is to first test the available feldspars by melting them in the glaze fire without additions. A little mound of feldspar may be put on a fragment of brick and fired. Most feldspars will not melt sufficiently at cone 10 to flow in a thin coating of glaze, and the addition of other materials is necessary to make a fluid glaze.

3. Other materials for high-fired glazes

There are relatively few materials suitable for use in high-fired glazes, and the high-fired glaze is best made from a very simple combination of minerals. Since not too many different substances are involved, it is not difficult to learn the function of each in the glaze and to learn the usual proportions which will melt at stoneware or porcelain temperature. Feldspar, perhaps the most important high-fired glaze material, is discussed above. Nine other materials are commonly used:

FLINT. Most high-fired glazes contain about 20% of flint. Flint furnishes silica, which is the basic substance of all glass and glazes. It lends hardness, stability, and durability to the glaze. The presence of flint in the glaze also improves its fit to the clay and reduces the chance of crazing.

CLAY. Clay is added to the glaze to give it better adhesion to the pot in the raw state, and to help keep the ingredients of the glaze suspended in the glaze slip. It also furnishes alumina to the glaze, which increases the viscosity of the melted glaze and helps it to adhere to the walls of the pots without excessive running.

China clay is usually used in glazes, especially where a clear and colorless glaze is desired. If the glaze is to be dark in color, a clay containing some iron may be used. Ball clay is sometimes used because it improves adherence and dry strength, or a combination of ball clay and china clay. In glazes which contain a great deal of clay, a portion of the clay may be added as calcined clay. This prevents the excessive shrinkage which might otherwise result from a high percentage of raw clay.

WHITING. Whiting contributes calcium to the glaze. It may be used in amounts up to 15% in high-fired glazes. Although whiting is by itself a rather refractory substance, it forms a fluid glass when combined with feldspar, and its function is that of a flux.

BARIUM CARBONATE. Barium functions as a flux in high-fired glazes, but it must be used in limited amounts, usually not over 10%. When it is present in larger amounts than this it tends to make the glaze dry and to interfere with its melting. Barium together with boric oxide makes a fluid melt, and if some boric oxide is present in the glaze, more barium may be used. Barium may give the glaze a mat quality, and it also has important influence on the color of the glaze, as will be described in a later section.

MAGNESIUM CARBONATE. Magnesium carbonate furnishes magnesia to the glaze. Magnesia is a flux, and functions in a manner very similar to barium. About 10% of magnesium carbonate is the maximum which can be introduced into the glaze without producing excessive dryness.

DOLOMITE. Dolomite is composed of the oxides of calcium and magnesia in equal amount, and its effect in a glaze is similar to that obtained by the addition of these two materials separately.

TALC. Talc, which is a magnesium silicate, is used as a source of magnesia, and has an effect in the glaze similar to that of magnesium carbonate. It also furnishes some silica to the glaze.

COLEMANITE. Colemanite, which contains both calcium and boric oxide, is used as a flux. It is a very active flux, and in high-fired glazes can be used only in fairly small amounts, usually not more than 15%. Colemanite creates character-istic textural effects in glazes which are described in a later section.

ZINC OXIDE. Zinc is used as a flux in glazes, and is also sometimes used when crystalline effects are desired. Only small amounts are used, usually less than 5%.

4. Proportioning materials in high-fired glazes, and the formulation of new glazes

The relatively small number of ingredients in high-fired glazes makes the proportioning of them quite simple. Of course, the exact surface quality and character of a glaze may change radically with the change of only a few per cent in the quantity of one material. But it is not difficult to arrive at combinations of materials which will melt into acceptable glazes.

As a general rule, glazes designed to mature at temperatures of from cone 9 to cone 11 have about 50% of feldspar and about 20% of flint. The remaining 30% of the glaze is divided between clay, whiting, barium carbonate, magnesium carbonate, dolomite, talc, zinc, and colemanite. All of these materials are used in small amounts, and seldom are all of them used in any one glaze.

As a guide to the composition of glazes for the range of cone 9 to 11 the following chart is given, which indicates the usual *upper limit* of the amounts of the various materials which can be used:

Feldspar	50%	70% of glaze
Flint	20%	
Clay	0 to 15%	
Whiting .	0 to 15%	
Barium Carbonate	0 to 10%	
Magnesium Carbonate	0 to 10%	30% of glaze
Dolomite .	0 to 15%	
Talc	0 to 15%	
Colemanite	0 to 15%	
Zinc Oxide	0 to 5%	

76

The character of the glaze will be determined by the particular materials used, and by the amount of each. For example, a glaze which contains 15% of clay and a considerable amount of magnesia as well will be an opaque and rather dry glaze, while one which contains 10 or 15% of colemanite and some zinc is apt to be very fluid.

To formulate new glazes, 50% of feldspar and 20% of flint may be taken as a starting point. Then, the remaining 30% of the glaze may be made up of the other materials. Whiting is almost always used in high-fired glazes, and it should be included. Magnesia, barium, zinc, and colemanite may or may not be used, depending on the kind of glaze desired. If a good deal of magnesia or barium is used, the glaze is apt to be dry, while small amounts of these materials may, together with the flint and feldspar, result in fluid, clear glazes.

The limits indicated for the materials above are subject to many exceptions. The glaze may contain more than 50% of feldspar, or, in the case of glazes maturing at cone 12 or more, considerably less than 50%. Actually, some very interesting glazes can result from combinations of materials which depart rather radically from the "normal" proportions. For example, a glaze which is extremely dry and contains so much clay or barium that it will not melt normally, may, when used over an engobe which is loaded with coloring oxides, give an earthy surface halfway between a glaze and a slip. Or an extremely fluid glaze, which runs too much for ordinary use on the vertical walls of pots, may give spectacular results when used on the surface of plates or other flat surfaces where the tendency for the glaze to run and collect may be an advantage. Much depends on how the glaze is to be used. Many glazes which seem rather unpromising to the inexperienced eye will, if put to proper use, give highly interesting surfaces. This principle is illustrated in old Chinese pottery, much

of which is finished in glazes which by themselves are in no way spectacular, but which take on great beauty from the manner in which the glaze is used and the way it relates to the form of the piece.

Although the number of materials commonly used in high-fired glazes is limited, the variety of surface which can be achieved is considerable. Glazes may be clear or opaque, thick or thin, mat or bright, coarse and rough in texture, or smooth as a piece of polished quartz. An "experimental glaze" is very easy to make, especially if a likely combination of materials is used as a starting point. A 100-gram sample can be weighed in a few minutes, mixed with water, and applied to a bit of clay. Many handsome glazes have been arrived at in samples made in this way, and fired along with the regular glaze firing, and the excitement and interest in a glaze firing is always increased by the inclusion of a few "shot-in-the-dark" glaze tests.

5. Transparency and texture

The "normal" glaze is transparent and has a surface of high gloss. This is the result of the complete fusion of the ingredients of the glaze, and the formation of a smooth layer of clear glass on the surface of the piece. This is the condition of the glaze used on most porcelain. To achieve transparency and smoothness in the glaze, sufficient flux must be present in the composition to bring about melting at the temperature being used. Many glazes, although quite smooth, are cloudy and opaque. This results from combinations of materials which, at the maturing temperature, do not fuse completely. High-fired glazes which contain relatively high amounts of clay, magnesia, barium, or lime may be opaque, and to make a normally transparent glaze opaque, any of these materials may be added in progressively larger amounts until the desired effect is obtained. On the other hand, if a glaze is opaque and a more transparent effect is desired, the fluxing ingredient of the glaze should be increased at the expense of the more refractory materials. Or tin oxide or zirconium oxide may be added to the glaze to make it opaque. About 5% of tin oxide or about 8% of zirconium oxide is usually sufficient.

One of the advantages of working at the higher temperatures is the ease with which semiopaque effects can be achieved. In earthenware glazes, semiopaque effects are difficult to control because the slightest overfiring usually makes the glaze clear up. Or on the other hand, underfiring will make the glaze completely opaque. High-fired glazes have a much longer range than low temperature glazes and a glaze which gives a desirable semiopaque effect at cone 10 may also be semiopaque at cone 9 or cone 11. Semiopaque glazes are at their best when the opacity results from the balance of materials in the glaze rather than from some added opacifier such as tin.

Another opaque effect characteristic of high-fired glazes is caused by the presence of entrapped bubbles of gas in the glaze. This gives an opalescent quality to the glaze which can be very beautiful, especially when the glaze is thick. Opalescence may be induced in a glaze by adding bone ash in amounts not exceeding 10% of the glaze. Some ash glazes have this quality also, and many glazes which contain only the usual stoneware glaze ingredients will develop a cloudy opacity from entrapped bubbles.

Glazes vary widely in the smoothness of their surfaces and hence in their brightness or degree of reflectance or shine. Reflectance results from a mirror-smooth surface, and dullness or matness results from a roughness of surface. Matness may result from underfiring, or from a relative preponderance of refractory materials in the glaze. Or it may result from devitrification or the development of crystals in the glaze. Devitrification is a common cause of matness in glazes which have either a high content of silica or a high clay content. Mat glazes which have crystalline surfaces are often frosty in appearance and are pleasant to the touch.

The reaction which occurs between the body and the glaze in high-fired pottery contributes a great deal to the texture of glazes. This is true whether the effect is one of whiteness and purity, as in porcelain, or one of roughness, heavy texture, and active spotting as in some stonewares. In porcelain, the beauty of the surface resides not only in the fact that the glaze is smooth and flawless but also in the fact that there is no distinguishable dividing line between body and glaze. A unity exists between the two. In stoneware, the relatively high heat of firing makes the components of the clay body quite active and subject to reaction with the fluid glaze. If any metallic oxides are present in the body, such as iron or manganese, these will tend to boil up into the glaze, and the glaze is sure to be strongly influenced in color by the color of the body underneath, unless it is very opaque. Stoneware glazes develop a zone of reaction with the clay body which makes for quite an indistinct transition between the two, and if the glaze is thinly applied and well matured in the fire there may be no easily distinguishable line between body and glaze. This chemical union of body and glaze which is brought about by high heat makes for a unity of substance which helps to avoid the feeling that the glaze is an added and separate covering on the pot. This natural union of materials is the aesthetic *raison d'être* of stoneware.

6. Engobes for porcelain and stoneware

Many beautiful effects may be obtained through the use of engobes in high-fired wares, and the compounding and use of engobes for porcelain and stoneware is quite simple. In the case of porcelain, the best engobe is usually the clay body itself. Porcelain bodies have a relatively low shrinkage, and if a layer of slip is put on over the damp, or even over the dried clay, it is apt to adhere without checking or loosening. A satisfactory slip for porcelain can therefore be made by taking the body composition and adding coloring oxides to it for the desired color. Since the body is white, a full range of colors may be made.

For stoneware engobes, the body composition may also be used. However, the high plasticity of most stoneware bodies make such engobes useful only on the damp, freshly made pot. When used on a leather-hard piece, an engobe made from the clay body itself is apt to loosen during drying or firing because of excessive shrinkage relative to the body of the piece. However, if the engobe is applied immediately to the thrown piece before it has undergone any shrinkage, an engobe made from the clay body may be ideal. It may be colored with any coloring oxide to obtain effects darker than the clay body. Engobes may be poured or dipped onto the pots, or trailed on with a bulb. Or the engobes may be floated onto the insides of bowls, plates, or other open pieces and various colors intermingled. The engobe may be thickly applied without much danger of cracking, provided the pot is still wet from throwing.

When it is desired to apply the engobe to a leather-hard piece, or to a dry piece, an engobe composition must be devised which will have considerably less shrinkage than the clay body being used for the ware. In high-fired stoneware, simple compositions of white clays, feldspar, and flint serve very well. The following engobe composition will be found suitable for most clay bodies:

China clay	25
Ball clay	25
Feldspar	20
Flint	20
Zircopax	5
Borax	5

The zircopax is added to insure opacity, and the borax serves to give added dry strength and toughness to the engobe. If it is desired to use the engobe on dry ware rather than on damp or leather-hard clay, the amount of plastic clay in the above composition may have to be reduced. This can easily be accomplished by adding some calcined kaolin at the expense of the china clay and the ball clay. Some experimentation may be necessary to arrive at the right degree of shrinkage in the engobe for the intended application process. If the engobe is put on rather thinly, no trouble is usually encountered from cracking or loosening, but if the engobe is piled on thickly or put on in very thick ropes with a bulb, it is apt to crack unless the relative shrinkage of the clay and the engobe is carefully adjusted.

Engobes are readily colored by adding metallic oxides to the base engobe composition. If a very smooth color is desired with no specking or broken color, the engobe may be prepared by ball-milling. Usually screening is sufficient to mix the ingredients of the engobe together with the colorant. The following list suggests coloring additions to the engobe and the probable resulting color:

3%	Iron oxide	tan
7%	Iron oxide	brown
2%	Iron chromate..	medium gray
8%	Vanadium stain	yellow
1%	Cobalt oxide	blue
1%	Cobalt oxide ⎱	
2%	Iron oxide ⎰	blue-gray
3%	Manganese dioxide ⎤	
5%	Iron oxide ⎬	...... black
1%	Cobalt oxide ⎦	

Many different shades of color may be made by varying the kind and the amount of coloring oxide in the engobe. The color of the engobe is revealed in full only under a melted glaze, and the kind of glaze, its thickness, and the atmosphere of firing will naturally have a strong influence on the fired color.

In stoneware, heavily textured engobes

may be easily made by adding granular colorants to the engobe, such as ground-up red brick, shale, granular manganese, granular ilmenite, blacksmith's scale, rust, steel wool, iron, copper or brass filings, or pulverized earth.

Engobes which are saturated with coloring oxides may give beautiful surfaces in stoneware. Barnard clay is a natural material which produces this effect. It is a claylike material which is loaded with iron and manganese, and even a thin coat of it on a pot will strongly influence the glaze, giving shades of brown, reddish brown, or black. Barnard clay may be applied to either damp, dry, or bisque ware with little danger of cracking or peeling. It bleeds through most glazes, especially at temperatures of cone 10 or higher. The coloring strength of Barnard clay may be still further amplified by additions of iron or granular material. Or engobes may be prepared which are saturated with iron in amounts as high as 25%. Heavy iron slips of this sort will strongly influence any glaze applied over them.

Chapter 6

Types of High-Fired Glazes

All high-fired glazes are made up of a small number of ingredients which in combination have been found to melt to glass in the range of temperature of cone 9 to cone 14. However, in spite of the fact that not many different materials are involved, there are several distinct types of stoneware and porcelain glazes, each with its distinguishing appearance and "feel," and each with a somewhat different response to coloring oxides. The following classification of glazes refers to the base glaze alone, that is, to the glaze which is not colored by the addition of any coloring oxide or opacified by the addition of tin oxide or zirconium oxide.

1. Feldspathic glazes

Since most high-fired glazes contain considerable feldspar, usually about 40 to 50%, one could think of all high-fired glazes as being feldspathic. As we have seen, feldspar functions as the principal glaze flux at high temperatures. Glazes can be made which contain up to 90% of feldspar. Such glazes have their own particular character. For one thing, the highly feldspathic glaze crazes over most bodies, but this crazing can be made an asset rather than a liability. The so-called "fish scale" glaze is made by applying a feldspathic glaze very thickly over a flat surface, such as the inside of a plate or bowl, so that the craze lines are seen in the thick, milky glaze, giving a feeling of depth through a maze of cracks. In stoneware, where the body itself is vitreous, or nearly so, crazing is more of an aesthetic

problem than a practical one, since the well-fired stoneware pot will not leak water in any case. The tendency of high feldspar glazes to craze is caused by the relatively high content of alkali in the glaze, either soda or potash.

In appearance, the high feldspar glaze is usually milky and either opaque or semiopaque. Some of the most beautiful of the old Chinese glazes were no doubt made mostly from feldspar, and very similar-appearing glazes can be made by using a fusible feldspar with small additions of ash or lime, or of both. The cloudy depth of such glazes is exceptionally beautiful over dark clay, and their veiled opacity cannot quite be duplicated with glazes opacified with tin or with low-fired glazes. The best results are obtained from cone 10 or 11 firings. The following examples are given as suggestions for glaze compositions using a great preponderance of feldspar.

Cornwall stone	85
Whiting	15

This glaze will craze over most bodies, but it gives a smooth, semiopaque glaze of considerable depth.

Soda feldspar	80
Whiting	10
Clay	10
Bone ash	2

The bone ash in this formula acts as a flux. The glaze has a buttery, opaque quality and a smooth surface.

Interesting and varied glazes can be made by adding fluxes to feldspar, such as colemanite, volcanic ash, wood ash, red clay, alkaline frit, and whiting. In experimenting, about 80% of feldspar is a good starting point, with the remaining 20% of the glaze made up of other ingredients.

2. Clear porcelain glazes

A clear porcelain glaze is achieved by balancing the ingredients for complete fusion at the maturing temperature. Feldspar is the most important material in such glazes, and lime is always present as a flux. A high flint content and a normal amount of clay insures hardness and the proper viscosity. The beauty of this type of glaze is a clear, limpid quality and a smooth and flawless surface, unmarred by either crazing, entrapped bubbles, pinholes, or cloudiness. The following glaze matures at cone 10 or 11, and is clear and colorless.

Flint	32
Whiting	20
Potash feldspar	33
Clay	15

This glaze can be made to mature at cone 9 by substituting nepheline syenite for potash spar. The glaze can also be made opaque by the addition of about 5% of tin. If a very white color is desired and the porcelain body is somewhat gray or tan, a very white ware can be made by using a glaze similar to the one above, which is slightly opacified by the addition of 2% of tin oxide. When clear glazes are desired, a small amount of zinc is often used. Two or 3% of zinc added to a glaze will lower its maturing temperature somewhat and helps to give the glaze a longer firing range.

3. High-clay mat glazes

Mat stoneware glazes are particularly handsome, and there are several distinct types. One is the mat glaze which is achieved by using a relatively large amount of clay and a small amount of silica in the glaze. Glazes of this type are very opaque, and have a soft sheen similar to that of polished pebbles. High-clay mat glazes should be applied in a fairly thin coating, otherwise pitting or pinholing may occur. Unfortunately this type of glaze is subject to crazing because of the low silica content. However, the craze lines are not noticeable in the dull mat surface, at least not until dirt or grease gets into the cracks through use. The absence of reflectance and highlighting makes very mat glazes of this type ideal for use on sculptural forms. The glaze is not practical, however, on tableware because the surface is difficult to clean and because silver makes an unpleasant grating noise on it.

The following glaze is a typical high-clay mat glaze for firing at about cone 10:

Oxford spar	48.9
China clay	25.1
Dolomite	22.4
Whiting	3.5

4. Barium mat glazes

Barium mat glazes are similar in appearance to the high-clay mat glaze, but the presence of a large amount of barium makes some unusual colors possible which are not common to other kinds of glazes. Barium makes the glaze very opaque, and produces a frosty kind of matness which is very pleasant to the touch. Differing amounts of barium will produce glazes varying from surfaces having a satiny sheen to extremely dry, rocklike surfaces.

Barium has a pronounced effect on some coloring oxides. When copper is added to a glaze high in barium, it will produce a strong, almost ultramarine blue instead of the usual green. When used in a barium glaze, vanadium, cobalt, iron, and chrome will give brilliant colors. In reduction firing, a barium glaze with iron added tends to be yellow, rather than the expected gray or brown, and copper may give mottled tones of red and blue. If an appreciable amount of boric oxide is present in the glaze, barium may not produce the expected mat surface.

The following glaze, for firing at cone

10, produces a beautiful mat surface with subdued high lights. It should be applied rather thinly.

Barium carbonate 20
Flint 10
China clay 10
"F4" feldspar 55
Dolomite 5

5. Magnesia glazes

The magnesia type of glaze is extremely popular with stoneware potters because of its beautiful "buttery" surface, with a quality somewhere between a mat glaze and a glaze with a bright surface. At its best, the magnesia glaze has a soft feel and a lustrous appearance which can lend dignity to the most unpretentious pot. The magnesia glaze is either opaque or semiopaque, depending on the amount of magnesia in the glaze and on the thickness of application. In some examples, even though the glaze is quite opaque, it has a depth which suggests that one is looking down *into* the glaze.

Magnesia glazes are at their best in reduction firing, but handsome results can also be achieved in oxidation firing.

The glaze depends on a relatively high percentage of magnesia, enough to give opacity and density, but not enough to make the glaze really mat. Magnesia glazes are frequently made with some colemanite included in the formula, and the presence of boric oxide from this source insures smooth melting and a surface with the desired amount of reflectance. Either magnesium carbonate, dolomite, or talc may be used as a source of magnesia for the glaze, but dolomite and talc, since they contribute other oxides to the glaze besides magnesia, are perhaps preferable.

The following magnesia glaze, which should be fired to about cone 10, is typical. When applied thickly, it has an opaque quality; when applied thinly, it will reveal dark engobes.

Feldspar 45
Colemanite 13

Dolomite 7
Talc 15
China clay 5
Flint 20

6. High lime glazes

Most high-fired glazes contain a considerable percentage of lime, which is one of the principal and most reliable of the high temperature fluxes. The glaze which is given on page 82 for use where a clear porcelain glaze is desired contains 20% of whiting.

When the content of lime in a glaze is raised to a point where the glaze will no longer fuse at the working temperature to a bright glaze, the first effect is a slight dulling of the surface. If just the right amount of lime is added to a clear glaze, it will retain most of its transparency but will lose some of its shine. Such a glaze, fairly clear, but low in reflectance, is good for use over engobes or other underglaze effects. Of course, a truly mat glaze which is at the same time transparent enough to reveal slips or underglaze painting is not possible, but a glaze which is high in lime does sometimes approach that condition.

The following cone 10 glaze is a variation of the glaze already given on page 82 for use on porcelain. In this case the whiting is raised to 26%, and the other ingredients of the glaze are reduced in amount. The glaze is opaque when thickly applied, but fairly clear when thin, and with a surface having somewhat subdued high lights.

Flint 30
Whiting 26
Feldspar 31
Clay 13

7. Colemanite glazes

Colemanite is a very active flux over the whole range of temperatures used in firing pottery, and at stoneware heat it is a very potent melter and can be used in only small percentages in the glaze. High-fired glazes which rely on colemanite for flux are fluid, bright in surface, and tend to be milky and somewhat opaque in appearance. Colemanite is not only an active flux but it also gives a broken texture to the surface of the glaze. This texture may take the form of streaks on glazes which are applied to vertical surfaces, or it may be more like mottling or alligator skin on glazes which have pooled on flat surfaces, such as plates or bowls. When barium is present, very fluid melting may occur. The following glaze melts at cone 8 and is quite fluid at cone 9 or 10. It will produce a bright and smooth surface.

Whiting	10
Colemanite	12
Barium carbonate	8
Magnesium carbonate	3
Feldspar	30
Flint	32
Clay	5

8. Zinc glazes

Small amounts of zinc are useful in high-fired glazes to promote smooth melting. If the amount of zinc is more than a certain critical amount however, usually about 8%, the glaze will be rather dry and sugary in texture. Glazes which are high in zinc often have mottled surfaces with uneven color distribution. These effects can be very interesting. However, the presence of zinc in the glaze may cause pitting or pinholing, and in general, zinc glazes are not very reliable. In zinc glazes, iron produces rather dingy colors, and chrome yields brown tones rather than the usual green. For effects characteristic of zinc, additions can be made to the porcelain glaze on page 82. An addition of 15% gives a dry glaze with a broken, uneven surface.

9. Dry glazes

For very dry and earthy effects, glazes may be used which do not melt properly but which nevertheless seal the surface and give a semiglazed effect. While such glazes are obviously not suited to wares intended to be used with food, they may produce effects which are very closely integrated with the color and the texture of the clay, and which serve to enhance rather than to cover or conceal the quality of the body of the piece. A dry glaze may be readily made by adding progressively larger amounts of calcined clay to any stoneware glaze. When the amount of clay is around 30% (or three times the normal amount), the glaze remains dry and rough after firing. If dry glazes are applied very thinly, they tend to melt more completely, and usually they are best used this way—as a thin coating or "skin" over textured engobes and bodies.

There is an interesting kind of stoneware surface which is halfway between glazes and slips. The high temperatures of stoneware firing bring about a vitreous quality in most clays, and dense, tight engobes may be achieved merely by brushing or dipping one clay over another. If rough effects are desired, unglazed engobes may be used which are composed largely of fire clay, or of combinations of fire clay, kaolin, and grog. In slips of this kind, an earthy palette may be achieved by adding small amounts of iron, rutile, ilmenite or manganese, and zirconium oxide may be added for opacity. For an engobe to give a rough, unglazed surface, the following composition may be used as a starting point:

Fire clay	50
Flint	20
Feldspar	10
Fine grog	10
Zirconium oxide	10

An engobe of this type may be applied either to damp or dry clay.

Chapter 7

Color in High-Fired Glazes

The use of color in porcelain and stoneware presents a challenge and an opportunity. The opportunity consists of the possibility of great subtlety, depth, variety, and surface quality which is characteristic of high-temperature glazes at their best. But there is a definite risk of achieving, instead of subtle effects, merely dull ones, and of making glazes which are dingy and lifeless.

Higher kiln temperatures have a pronounced tendency to limit glaze color and to produce colors which are relatively not as bright as those produced in glazes fired at lower temperatures. This is hardly a limitation, since a tremendous range of color is still possible in stoneware. But certain color effects are more natural to and more effective in earthenware than in stoneware, and if the potter adopts stoneware as his mode of expression he must decide to forego these effects. For example, the luminous blue-green of copper in a highly alkaline glaze is exclusively an earthenware color. The wide range of color qualities of lead glazes are also characteristic of lower firing. These qualities can be simulated at high temperatures, but the effect is never quite the same. Brilliant yellows, scintillating blues and purples, and brilliant reds are not as easy to achieve in stoneware as in earthenware.

Whatever stoneware and porcelain glazes may lack in brilliance of color they more than make up in subtlety. High-fired glazes are ideal for producing gray, or grayed, muted colors, especially in a reducing fire. Of course, much of the attraction of stoneware glazes is in their tactile quality as well as in color. This tactile quality may take the form of dense smoothness or of rough, gritty texture, but in either case the glaze of a well-made stoneware piece can be perfectly suited to the clay body of the pot.

In planning glazes for pots, the best principle to follow is to make the most of simple means. The average student or beginner in pottery engages in a seemingly endless search for colors, textures, and effects. He usually accumulates enough of these effects in a short while to keep a creative potter busy for years, but the tendency is to push on toward more colors, new textures, and new combinations rather than to use what has already been discovered. The difficulty seems to be that there are always too many colors to choose from. It is worth remembering that the achievements of the early Chinese potters were gained by the use of only two coloring oxides, iron and copper. A few colors and a few techniques of application and decoration are enough for a great body of work. This is not to say that testing is unnecessary or that knowledge of the materials and of the possibilities of the medium is not essential. But some of the greatest pottery was made with techniques which are utterly simple and involve the use of only a few materials.

1. White and gray glazes

White glazes are achieved by adding an opacifier, either tin oxide or zirconium oxide to the base glaze. About 6% of tin oxide or about 8% of zirconium oxide will produce white in most glazes. Some glazes, as we have seen, are opaque and more or less white in color by themselves, without the addition of any opacifier. But the whitest effects are obtained by additions of opacifiers to more or less clear base glazes. White glazes fired in oxidation will have a slightly creamy or warm color while those fired in reduction will tend to be cool white or blue-white. In high firing it is difficult to prevent an interaction between the body and the glaze, and if the body of the piece is dark and contains considerable iron or other metallic oxides, these will tend to bleed out into the glaze and cause specks or discoloration in the white glaze. This will be noticed especially on edges, where the glaze tends to run thin. This tendency can be used to good effect, but if a pure white surface is desired, it is necessary to use a clay body which contains little iron or other coloring agents.

Gray glazes may be made by adding small percentages of iron chromate to the glaze. One or two per cent is sufficient for a medium dark gray. Small amounts of commercial underglaze stains may also be used, and if a warm gray is desired, small amounts of iron oxide may be added. The best grays are made by reduction firing, discussed in a later section.

2. Black glazes

Black glazes are easy to achieve. Black results from an excess or saturation of coloring oxides. Iron, copper, cobalt, and manganese are used, and about 2% of each of these oxides added to the glaze will produce a black. Black glazes may be too fluid because of the presence of so much coloring oxide. To correct this, clay may have to be added. Another problem with black is that the surface of the glaze tends to be either too bright and fluid or too dry and mat. Dryness may result from devitrification, which is very apt to occur when a glaze is saturated

with iron and copper. The correction for this is to decrease the amount of coloring oxide. Black glazes are at their best when the surface is slightly crystalline and not too shiny.

3. Red and brown glazes

True red, or bright spectrum red, cannot be made at stoneware or porcelain temperatures, and can be achieved only with cadmium-selenium glazes fired at low temperatures. Copper red, and saturated iron red, while not brilliant in hue, are interesting colors, and these are at their best at high temperatures. Both of these colors are achieved in reduction firing and are discussed in a later section.

Brown glazes are made by additions of iron oxide to the glaze. One or two per cent will give a light tan, while 4 to 6% will give browns of various depth. Rutile, which is a combination of titanium oxide and iron oxide, gives a tan or brownish tint to glazes, as does ilmenite, which is a crude titanium ore containing considerable iron oxide. Brown may also be made by additions of manganese. Manganese in low-fired glazes produces various shades of purple, but at the higher temperatures this color is very subdued, with only a slight purplish cast to the brown. Manganese is a rather weak coloring oxide, and about 5% is required to make a medium brown.

Interesting brown glazes can be made with nickel oxide, especially if the nickel is used in combination with iron, manganese, or rutile. Nickel is a rather unpredictable colorant, but in most base glazes it yields a brown or gray color. One to three per cent usually gives the best result.

If red clay is used for the clay portion of the glaze, light tan or gray colors result. Slip glazes, which are discussed later, are normally brown or black. If a percentage of some slip glaze, such as Albany slip, is added to a stoneware glaze, brown or tan colors are obtained.

(Continued on text page 143)

Portfolio of Illustrations

1. STONEWARE JAR (detail), Chinese, T'ang dynasty

The sprigged figures on this jar are applied with amazing freedom. The piece is covered with a brown slip glaze.

Courtesy, The Smithsonian Institution, Freer Gallery of Art, Washington, D.C.

2. STONEWARE VASE by Hui Ka Kwong

The richly sculptured form of this dramatic pot is covered with a blue glaze which breaks up like foam on water. The form is achieved by a combination of throwing, beating, and modeling.

1

2

3

3. STONEWARE JAR, Chinese, Han Dynasty

The sides of the jar are stamped with a coin known to have been minted in the reign of Wu Ti (140–86 B.C.). The surface variations from the stamping, together with the running and breakup of the gray ash glaze, create a fantastically rich texture.

Courtesy, The Metropolitan Museum of Art, gift of P. Jackson Higgs, 1927

4. SALT-GLAZED STONEWARE JUG, German, 17th century

The bellarmine, or jug with a bearded head modeled on the neck, was a favorite form of the German salt glaze potters. The low-relief decoration is greatly enhanced by the rich orange-peel texture of the glaze.

Courtesy, The Metropolitan Museum of Art, gift of M. Harris (of Harris and Sinclair), 1910

4

5. **STONEWARE JAR** by Marie Woo

The glaze on this piece was made from un-sieved ash, which produced the very rough, mottled, tan surface.

6. **STONEWARE BOTTLE** by Vivika and Otto Heino

The fabric-like texture of the surface is covered with a thin mat glaze.

5

6

7

7. STONEWARE POT by Peter Voulkos

Pottery form is here pushed to an extremity which creates a certain feeling of tension characteristic of much contemporary sculpture. The exaggerated ellipse of the upper part of the pot could hardly be any flatter without causing the collapse of the piece in the fire. The surface is enriched by the application of thin slabs.

8. STONEWARE VASE, Chinese, late Chou dynasty (770–256 B.C.).

The sturdy form of this pot and its freely scratched surface give the effect of immense vitality. The earthy character of the piece is amplified by the variations in the ash glaze.

Courtesy, The Metropolitan Museum of Art,
Dick Fund, 1949

8

9

9 & 10. STONEWARE BOTTLES by Paul Soldner

These massive forms are treated with a bold-ness that makes the most of the textural pos-sibilities of glaze. Here the surface is treated not as an adjunct of form but rather as a field for powerful graphic expression. The piece above is completed by attaching thin slabs to the surface. Granules of shale are imbedded in the clay and boil through the glaze. The cascading pattern on the bottle below is done in white slip, covered by a thin iron-colored glaze.

11. STONEWARE BOWL, Chinese, Chün Yao, Sung dynasty

The glaze is an opalescent grayish blue, streaked with violet and olive green. The form has the look of having come into be-ing with the utmost ease and naturalness, like a leaf or a pod. While the foot is small, it seems to generously support the swelling curve of the bowl. The small pits plainly evident in the photograph would not be con-sidered flaws by Chinese standards, which were concerned more with the total entity of the pot.

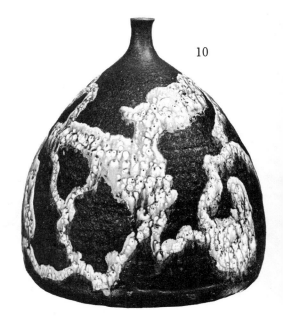

10

11

12. STONEWARE JAR by Arthur Handy

The throwing is rapid and quite casual, with fairly heavy finger marks remaining on the surface. The pot was pushed while damp into a slightly squarish form. A black and a gray slip were poured down over the shoulder, and these slips show prominently under the magnesia glaze, even though it is quite opaque. The glaze has run somewhat in the fire, forming droplets over the throwing marks. The simple direct form and the easy flow of slip and glaze combine to give the piece a fluid grace.

13. STONEWARE JAR, Chinese, pre-Han

This ancient piece seems to have been made partly by coiling, partly by throwing. The texture results from paddling with a textured beater or paddle, which also produced flattened facets in the surface. The thin glaze evidently resulted from fire flashing.

Courtesy, The Royal Ontario Museum,
Toronto, Canada

12

13

14. STONEWARE COVERED JAR by Stanley Rosen

The clay body is dark brown and shows through the opaque magnesia glaze on the high spots. The robust glaze, the incised surface variations, and the massive form of the piece combine to give a feeling of puissant vigor.

14

15

15. STONEWARE JAR by Victor Babu

The sides were deeply indented in rhythmical grooves while the pot was still damp on the wheel. The foot is modeled rather than thrown. The glaze is a rich iron red which breaks over the throwing marks. In this pot, the plasticity of the clay has been used to create a fluid, spontaneous form which, however, stops just short of being soft or mushy.

16. STONEWARE FOOTED POT by Val Cushing

While this piece is not derived from or inspired by any historical type of pottery, it nevertheless is the product of a highly developed technique and is a clarified and controlled statement of form. The foot is thrown separately, but its attachment does not interrupt the dramatic upward surge of form to the widely swelling globular body. The exterior of the pot is unglazed, with black and white engobes. The eyelike circles define flattened areas achieved by paddling the still soft form.

17. STONEWARE JAR by Peter Voulkos

Some large pots seem like ill-advised enlargements of small forms, but this piece, over 3' tall, is monumental in conception as well as execution. The exterior has been coated with a white slip, which emphasizes the cut slab relief.

17

18

18. PORCELAIN STEM CUP, Chinese, T'ang dynasty

The color of this piece is a clear ivory white. The glaze-is quite thin, and gives the effect of a polish, rather than an added coating of glaze. The form of the cup is extremely delicate and sensitive. The foot is solid and its added weight gives a feeling of stability.

Courtesy, The Royal Ontario Museum, Toronto, Canada

19. Footed Stoneware Bowl by Jack Cannon

A brown slip glaze is used inside; the outside is unglazed except for a thin coating of slip glaze over the area where the wall of the pot has been textured. This gives the effect of a slight wetting. The form of the piece is very direct and vigorous, with well-marked accents at foot and rim. Heavy grog stands out on the surface, and to some extent through the glaze.

19

20

20. Stoneware Mug, German, Seigburg ware

The piecrust foot, the widely swelling belly, the throwing marks, the boldly flaring lip, the freely attached perky handle, and the rich claylike surface with sprigged medallions all contribute to a vigorous expression of joy in the ceramic medium.

Courtesy, The Metropolitan Museum of Art,
gift of John Hemme, 1910

21. PORCELAIN CRUET by Ruth McKinley

The body of this piece is exceptionally white and the glaze is smooth and flawless. The piece was cast, yet it has a sensitivity of form usually associated with wheel work. The small lug is meant to hold a rubber or wooden stopper on a chain.

22. STONEWARE JAR, Chinese, Han dynasty

In spite of the precision and clarity of the form, this piece retains a claylike feeling. The handles are beautifully made and placed and the banding serves to relate them to the form. The ash glaze is a mottled gray-green over brown, well-vitrified clay.

Courtesy, The Smithsonian Institution, Freer Gallery of Art, Washington, D.C.

23. STONEWARE VASE by Vivika and Otto Heino

The severe verticality of this piece is emphasized by indentations which make the thrown form somewhat off-round. Linear markings boil up through the mat glaze.

24. STONEWARE VASE, Chinese, Sung dynasty, Ko ware

In some types of Sung ware the quality of the glaze seems to form the primary interest. As in this example, forms which are modest in size and shape gain, through the beauty of the glaze, the brilliance of a precious stone. The color is "claire-de-lune" blue, with brown crackle lines. The body is red-brown.

Courtesy, The Metropolitan Museum of Art, gift of Mrs. Samuel T. Peters, 1926

21

22

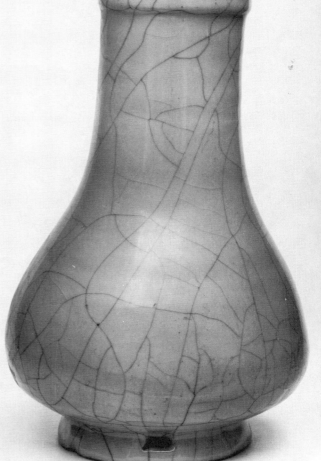

23

24

25

25. STONEWARE BOWL, Chinese, Sung dynasty, Chün Yao

The Chün glaze is indescribable, and must be seen and felt to be appreciated. On this piece, the color is a lavender-blue, with splashes of purple and crimson. The glaze is rather thickly applied over a reddish-brown clay.

Courtesy, The Metropolitan Museum of Art, gift of Mrs. Samuel T. Peters, 1926

26. STONEWARE BOWL by Karen Karnes

Although the form of this piece is very simple and would be technically well within the reach of most potters, it is distinguished by extremely subtle relationships. The trimming marks at the bottom furnish just the right accent and make a foot unnecessary. The lip is flattened into a strong bead, and just below this the sweep of the curved wall is slightly constricted. Areas of gray slip appear under the high-clay mat glaze, and granular concentrations in the slip boil out to form irregularly placed spots.

27. STONEWARE JAR by Stanley Rosen

No glaze is used on either the inside or the outside of this piece, but the surface is richly variegated with brown, black, and white slips. The form of the piece is like a narrow envelope, put together from two slabs of clay. The two facades of the pot are treated as bas-reliefs, with some clay added and some scraped away. The walls of the pot also have a quality like painting, but the color interest is held subordinate to the form. The utterly simple rectilinear silhouette gives a monumental dignity and successfully contains the rich complexity of surface modeling.

26

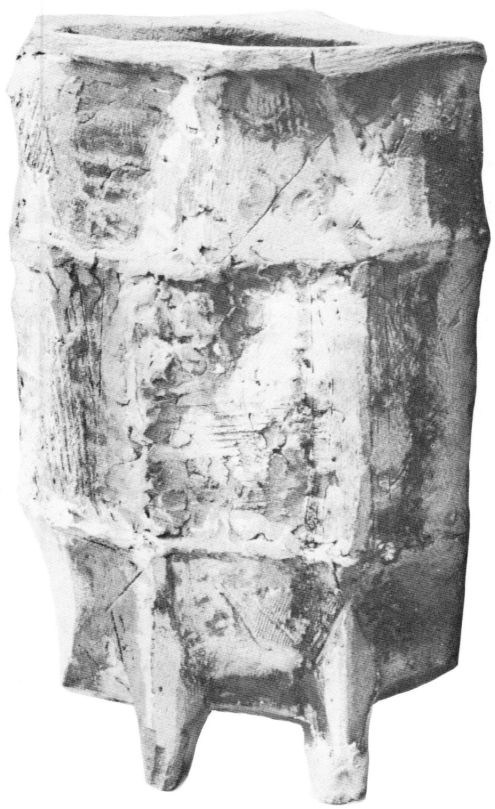

27

28. PORCELAIN BOWL, Contemporary Japanese commercial ware

Occasionally the Oriental tradition for fine and sensitive brushwork finds expression even in commercial wares. The shrimp decoration on this bowl is carried out with great verve and with an admirable economy of brush strokes.

29. STONEWARE JAR, Chinese, Sung dynasty, Tz'u Chou ware

The powerful globular form of this pot, its strong foot and neck, and its bold decoration communicate an earthy vigor. *The upper part of the piece was dipped in white engobe and glazed with a clear glaze. The brushed characters and the lower third of the form are done in a brown-black slip glaze. The close relationship between Chinese calligraphy and brushed decorations on pottery is obvious in this example.* Courtesy, The Royal Ontario Museum, Toronto, Canada

30. STONEWARE BOWL by Hui Ka Kwong

Pink and white are mingled in the mat glaze. The splashed figure in the center is gunmetal black.

29

30

34

31. STONEWARE BOWL, Chinese, Sung dynasty, Chün Yao

This piece is an example of the strength and beauty which can reside in an extremely simple form when all the elements of color, surface quality, proportion, and cross section are brought into a unified relationship. The color of the glaze is a mysterious lavender gray, somewhat darker at the rim where it has run thin. The foot is dark brown, and the glaze has gathered in a slight roll at the bottom.

Courtesy, The Smithsonian Institution, Freer Gallery of Art, Washington, D.C.

32. STONEWARE BOWL by James Secrest

The form of this piece is stated with simple clarity. The full curve of the bowl is sustained right to the foot, which forms a sturdy but beautifully proportioned base. The bowl was first covered with a dark slip and the brush strokes were reserved in wax. The glaze is a velvety brown mat. The slip showing in the brush marks and at the foot is a dense lustrous black. The inside is a grayed white.

33. STONEWARE BOWL by Robert Turner

In this piece, both the form and the glaze are managed with great authority. The subtle turn of the rim inward seems to contain the interior volume. The foot, while distinctly articulated, is very much a part of the form.

34. STONEWARE TEAPOT by Peter Voulkos

The circular wax-resist decoration repeats the roundness of the pot and the curve of the handle. The glaze is richly spotted with impurities boiling up from underneath. This piece demonstrates that strength and vitality are not inconsistent with a certain delicacy and grace, nor with the honest fulfillment of functional demands.

35

35. STONEWARE JAR by Marie Woo

Although executed with considerable freedom, the form, glaze, and surface markings
of this pot give a unified impression of vigor.
It was made in two sections, the upper part
dented and incised while still soft.

36. STONEWARE VASE, Chinese, Sung dynasty,
Tz'u Chou ware

The design is achieved by cutting away and
scratching through a white engobe. The lilt-
ing form of the piece seems to be echoed
again and again in the freely sweeping lines
of the floral pattern. The scale, proportioning, and surface texture of the neck in relation to the rest of the pot could hardly be
surpassed.

Courtesy, The Metropolitan Museum of Art,
gift of Mrs. Samuel T. Peters, 1926

36

39

37

37. Stoneware Pitcher-Vase, Japanese

The tall form of this elegant piece is accentuated by the cascade of white glaze which runs down over the black glaze on the lower part of the piece. Vertical grooves cut in the neck have made the flowing glaze gather in rivulets. In this case, as in so many fine Japanese pots, the rather erratic behavior of glazes has been put to effective use.

Courtesy, The Smithsonian Institution,
Freer Gallery of Art, Washington, D.C.

38. Stoneware Jar by Kitaōji Rosanjin, Contemporary Japanese potter

The exposed clay is red-brown. The creamy-colored ash glaze runs irregularly down the sides of the piece, collecting in green droplets. This pot has an elemental quality conveyed by its sturdy proportions, the accidental features of the glaze, and the rough treatment of the lip.

39. Stoneware Bottle by John Loree

The upper part of this piece was dipped twice in dark slip, forming an overlap at the neck. The glaze was poured on and produced three different colors: dark brown where the slip was double thick, mottled greenish brown where the slip was single thickness, and gray where there was no slip. Slip and glaze are draped over the form like a well-fitting garment.

38

40

40. STONEWARE JARS, Japanese, Seto ware, 17th–18th century.

The two little jars well illustrate the fact that there is nothing new in the use of fortuitous events in the glaze to embellish a pot. The forms are wonderfully compact and self-contained. The lids are of ivory.

Courtesy, The Metropolitan Museum of Art, gift of Mr. and Mrs. Samuel Colman, 1893

41. STONEWARE BOWL by Eunice Prieto

The flow of glaze both inside and outside forms a particularly happy decoration on this sturdy bowl.

41

42. PORCELAIN COVERED JAR by Charles Lakofsky

The body of this piece is a very dense and vitreous porcelain, slightly off-white in color. The piece was thrown, and the rather prominent throwing marks are made use of in the decoration, which consists of stripes of dark slip under the clear glaze. The color, texture, and form illustrate the possibility of porcelain which is boldly potted.

43. STONEWARE CASSEROLE by Philip Secrest

Glazed and unglazed surfaces are skillfully combined. The textured band around the piece is achieved by scraping the glaze away from an area in which the clay has been scratched and roughened. The glaze is warm gray, and the body color is burnt orange.

44. STONEWARE COVERED JAR, Chinese, Northern Celadon ware, Sung dynasty

Multi-spouted pots of this sort are quite common in old Chinese pottery, but we do not know what the function of the spouts was. Sometimes there is no opening cut through from the spout to the interior of the piece, which would indicate that the spout served some nonfunctional purpose. This pot is light and well thrown, and although the design is very complex, a sense of unity has been preserved. The incising is delicately done and is beautifully enhanced by the pooling of the gray-green celadon glaze.

Courtesy, The Royal Ontario Museum, Toronto, Canada

42

43

44

45. STONEWARE VASE, Chinese, Liao dynasty (A.D. 907–1125).

Twenty-five inches tall, this pot was thrown in sections. The very prominent throwing marks spiraling up the piece give the impression of vigorous upward thrust. The greenish glaze is applied rather unevenly by pouring, and has run somewhat to give variations in color.

Courtesy, The Royal Ontario Museum, Toronto, Canada

46. STONEWARE BOTTLE by John Tuska

The sides of this piece are deeply indented to form a shape which is reminiscent of a seed pod. The lower part is yellowish in color, and is thinly glazed, revealing the texture of the clay. The upper part is more thickly glazed, with a very mat purplish glaze which has flowed down between the indentations to form thick drops. In this pot the events of the fire have dramatically complemented and enhanced the form.

45

47

NA·2710

47. STONEWARE COVERED BOWL, Chinese, Tz'u Chou ware, Sung dynasty

The body is tan stoneware, covered with a white engobe except for the foot. The glaze is milky white, thinly applied. One could hardly imagine a more restrained color expression in pottery, but the very limitation of color in this case seems to give the pot a cool strength. This strength and simplicity is inherent in the form as well. The combined form of the pot and its lid is as compact as an acorn, and the tiny knob, freely modeled, gives a sense of scale and monumentality, even though the piece is quite modest in size—less than 7″ high.

48. STONEWARE BOWL, Chinese, Sung dynasty, Chien ware

The glaze is brown, somewhat mottled with gray-green. The spots inside are black. The rim of this piece, as is the case with many old Chinese pots, is finished with an added edge of metal. The delicately shaped lip, the exquisite rise of the form from the small foot, and the subtle changes in the glaze combine to make a work of exceptional beauty.

48

49. STONEWARE FOOTED BOWL by James Secrest

This piece was made partly by throwing, partly from slabs. The form is like a canoe, long and rather narrow. The foot and bottom of the bowl were thrown on the wheel. The slabs were pressed on a surface which gave them the raised texture, then they were joined to each other at the ends and fastened to the bottom. The textured areas are covered with a dark slip, partially rubbed off, which dramatizes the relief pattern. A strong sculptural feeling results from the relationship between the flat planes of the sides and the cylindrical foot.

49

50

50. STONEWARE JAR by Kenneth Price

The form is achieved by a combination of throwing, modeling, cutting, and beating. Its asymmetry seems related to some natural object such as a boulder, yet the piece keeps a strong identity as a pot. The sprigged-on additions, which seem more of an outgrowth of the form than a decoration, are beautifully accentuated by the greenish magnesia glaze. While traditional concepts of pottery form are not relied on, there persists that firm relationship between process and result which has characterized the best pottery of all cultures.

51. STONEWARE VASE by Peter Voulkos

If any real distinction exists between pottery and sculpture, it is blurred in this piece. Forms jut out strongly, and are freely modeled rather than achieved by any strictly pottery-making process. However, even though there is no obvious functional intent, the piece is still a pot in the sense that its suggestion of a hollow form is important to the expression.

52. COVERED STONEWARE JAR by Hui Ka Kwong

The bold figures in the glaze are done by a resist process. The colors are white, turquoise, brown, and orange. The dark knob of the lid effectively punctuates the form.

51

52

53. STONEWARE POTS by Theodore Randall

In both of these pots, pressing has been used as a creative technique. The larger piece on the left was built from slabs which were pressed out on an incised surface. The top of the piece was finished by coiling. The piece on the right was made from two identical halves which were both pressed in a clay bisque-fired mold.

54

54. STONEWARE BOTTLE, Chinese, Han dynasty

Many of the masterpieces of old Chinese pottery were constructed from slabs, rather than thrown on the wheel, or were made by a combination of throwing, pressing, and modeling. The wall of this piece was probably pressed out first on a fired clay surface which had an incised design. On the wall of the pot this appears as a design in low relief. Although this is a small piece and was evidently made rapidly, it has the character of a monument.

Courtesy, The Metropolitan Museum of Art, bequest of Mrs. H. O. Havemeyer, 1929, The H. O. Havemeyer Collection

55

55. Two Upright Stoneware Pots by Stanley Rosen

The piece on the left is glazed with a greenish colemanite glaze which reveals every minute variation of surface, including the small vertical tool marks. Three sections were combined to complete the form, and a feeling of distinct articulation remains in the finished pot. The wall is quite massive, and the effect is one of columnar strength. The pot on the right is tan-gray, and the treatment of the form and the surface have preserved a feeling of the plastic mobility of the clay, without losing a certain stony quality.

56

57

56. STONEWARE BOTTLE, Japanese, 18th century, Chikuzen Province

This piece shows many of the characteristics of the Japanese style. It is rather loose in form, with the process of making strongly expressed. Tradition is relied on only to set the general style, not the exact form or finish. "Imperfections" in glazing and firing seem to be a part of the design, and the variations in the glaze have the look of having just happened, without any exact or conscious control.

Courtesy, The Metropolitan Museum of Art, bequest of E. C. Moore, 1891

57. STONEWARE JAR, Chinese, Han dynasty

The potters of the Han period were somehow able to create forms of exceptional virility and monumentality. Pots such as this were undoubtedly intended for ceremonial use. The delicacy of the sprigged animal head holding the ring gives scale to the form.

Courtesy, The Metropolitan Museum of Art, bequest of Mrs. H. O. Havemeyer, 1929, The H. O. Havemeyer Collection

58

58. STONEWARE VASE, Chinese, Sung dynasty or later, Tz'u Chou ware

The dark brown slip glaze is cut away, revealing the body, to form a floral decoration. The technical means employed in pots of this sort are utterly simple; a quickly thrown and trimmed form, a glaze no doubt made from some local clay and then dipped on to cover the whole piece, a rapidly cut and scratched pattern, and once-firing in a neutral or reducing atmosphere.

Courtesy, The Royal Ontario Museum, Toronto, Canada

59. Detail of Decoration on Piece in Illus. 58

59

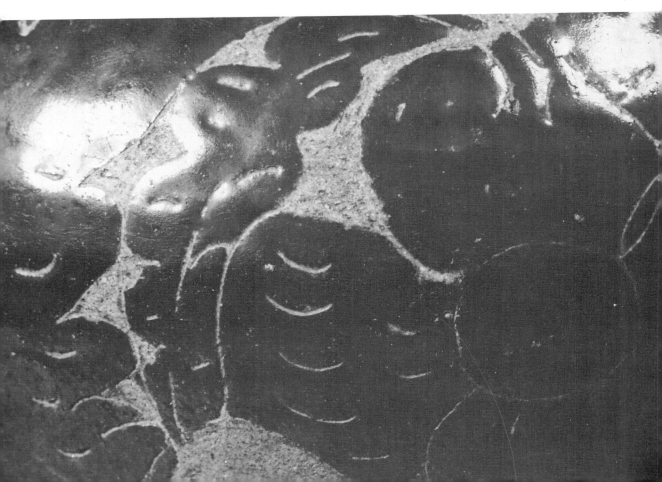

60. STONEWARE PITCHER by David Shaner

The body is a very light gray clay, salt glazed.
The lower part was covered with a stoneware
glaze before salting, with the circular mark
done in wax resist. The functional parts of
the pitcher are well articulated and the handle well placed in relationship to the weight
of the pitcher when full.

61. STONEWARE BOWL by Warren and Alix Mac-
Kenzie

Oatmeal and rust glazes are combined to form
a handsome pattern.

60

61

62

62. STONEWARE JAR, Chinese Late Chou dynasty (770–256 B.C.)

The sure, clarified form, the orderly scaling of detail, and the reliance on natural materials and process are evident even in this early expression of the Chinese genius for pottery. The rings on the shoulder seem to indicate that the form derived from a bronze prototype. There is some glaze on the shoulder, no doubt from ash.

Courtesy, The Metropolitan Museum of Art,
Dick Fund, 1950

63. PORCELAIN BOTTLE by Elena Netherby

The glaze is an ox-blood red, with subtle gradations from the lip downward.

64. STONEWARE BOTTLES by James Secrest

These pieces were thrown as tall cylinders, open at the top, and pressed into oval shapes. The tops and necks were made separately and luted on. The two bottles at the left are unglazed except for the upper part, and the bottle on the right has a gray glaze with dark brown stripes. The potting is very clean and sure, and the handles seem in perfect scale to the forms.

63

64

65, 66 & 67. STONEWARE FLOOR VASES by Paul Soldner

These pots are gigantic in scale, 42″ to 51″ tall, yet they are masterful and sure in form. The actual size of pottery has been traditionally limited by the processes involved, by the difficulties of firing, and by functional considerations. Many contemporary potters have refused to be bound by size limitations and have worked out methods of forming and have acquired kilns capable of producing large work. This tendency parallels the appearance of very large formats in contemporary painting.

65

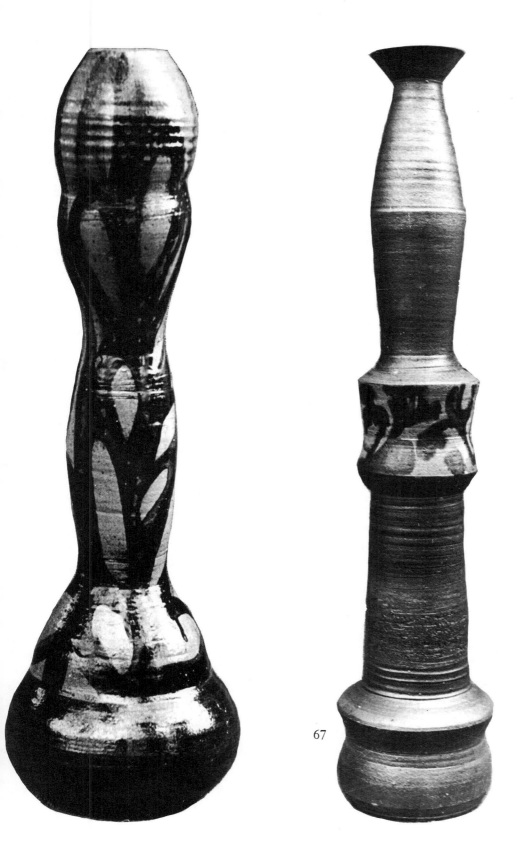

67

68. STONEWARE BOTTLE, Chinese, Sung dynasty, Tz'u Chou

The form is wonderfully sure and full, and seems almost distended from pressure inside. The roundness of the pot is accentuated by the slight reverse curve at the foot and by the neck. The brush strokes, which seem to reach around the pot, are rust color on a rich black slip glaze.

Courtesy, The Smithsonian Institution,
Freer Gallery of Art, Washington, D.C.

69. STONEWARE JAR by Marie Woo

The form of this pot is full of vitality and strength. The upper part is glazed with a rust-colored glaze with circular areas of yellow.

70. STONEWARE VASES AND BOWL by Charles Fergus Binns

The forms are controlled toward an ultimate refinement of shape and proportion. The glazes, in subtle colors of brown, black, ocher, and gray, are flawless in surface.

68

69

70

71. STONEWARE BOWL, Chinese, Sung dynasty, Yüeh ware

The dragon pattern on this bowl is typical of the Yüeh style which persisted in China for hundreds of years. The body is dense, smooth, and vitrified. The pooled celadon glaze reveals every nuance of the incised design.

Courtesy, The Metropolitan Museum of Art, Rogers Fund, 1917

72. STONEWARE POT by Peter Voulkos

Most pottery, probably influenced by coiling and throwing techniques, has been compact and centered about an interior point. In this piece, however, the forms break into the surrounding space with explosive force.

71

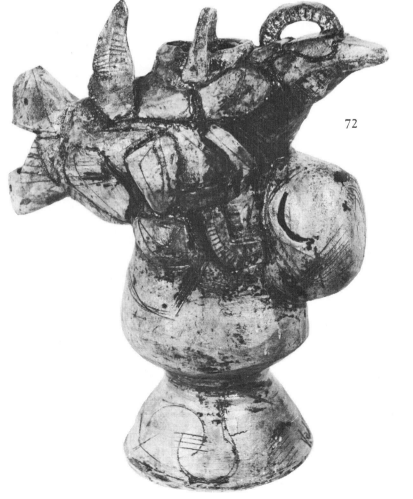

72

73

73. STONEWARE JAR, Chinese, six dynasties (A.D. 265–617)

The full swelling of this monumental piece is wonderfully accented by the banding in relief, and by the freely modeled lugs. Rhythmically incised birds in the upper band and clouds in the middle band show through the thin ash glaze.

Courtesy, The Metropolitan Museum of Art, Rogers Fund, 1917

74. STONEWARE BOWL by Vivika and Otto Heino

The exciting surface of this piece is achieved by a very simple process. The stiff glaze is scratched through with a sharp point before firing. In the fire the scratched lines create a pattern which is in effect a series of crawls, more or less under control, but having also many accidental dimensions.

74

75

76

77

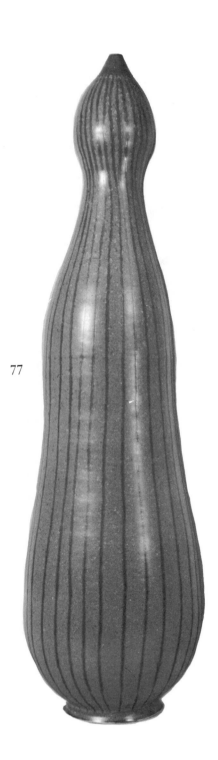

75. STONEWARE BOTTLE by Ruth McKinley

The lower part of this piece is glazed with a subtle gray glaze which breaks over the throwing marks, emphasizing the rhythmical surface striations which are most prominent just above the middle of the form. The upper part of the bottle is glazed with an iron red. The form is essentially simple, but the slight swelling of the sides, the curving inward at the top, and the neck with its accenting rim are stated with sure clarity.

76. STONEWARE VASE, Chinese, Sung dynasty, Tz'u Chou ware

The pattern is carried out in sgraffito through a white engobe, and the whole pot is covered with a thin, transparent glaze. In Western ceramics, floral patterns are usually an expression of the decorative and tend toward prettiness, but in old Chinese pots, especially the Tz'u Chou wares, flower and leaf forms are often the vehicle for surface embellishment of great virility and dignity.

Courtesy, The Metropolitan Museum of Art, gift of Mrs. Samuel T. Peters, 1926

77. PORCELAIN BOTTLE by Antonio Prieto

The sinuous form is controlled with sensitivity and skill, and the scratch lines through the glaze give the piece a gourdlike quality.

78. STONEWARE BOWL, Chinese, Kuan Yao type, Sung dynasty

The utterly simple form of this piece gives prominence to the spectacular crackle pattern in the glaze. This pot has an ultimate refinement and subtlety of both form and surface which brings to mind certain works of modern sculpture, such as the polished marble forms of Brancusi.

Courtesy, The Metropolitan Museum of Art, Rogers Fund, 1917

78

80

79

79. PORCELAIN VASE by Theodore Randall

The body of this piece is a very dense, gray, vitrified clay. The fluid shape is thrown with great sensitivity, and enhanced by the variations in the poured glaze, which varies from deep rich browns and black to grayed yellow.

80. STONEWARE VASE, Chinese, Tz'u Chou type, Sung dynasty

The ripened tradition of Sung times enabled potters to state forms with unequivocal strength. The least slackening in the curve of this piece, especially toward the bottom, might result in a soft and floppy contour. The pot was made in two sections, and evidence of the joint may be seen near the point of widest swelling. The buff body is coated with white slip, and glazed with a transparent green glaze.

Courtesy, The Metropolitan Museum of Art, gift of Mrs. Samuel T. Peters, 1926

81. STONEWARE VASE by Peter Voulkos

The huge scale of this pot, almost 40" high, and its incorporation of two poised horizontal forms reaching out laterally, create a dramatic effect rare in pottery. While the intent is sculptural, there is still the strong feeling for the enclosed volume, for the air inside the pot, which is expressed by the swelling slabs, and even by the "stitching" marks in the clay, which bring to mind sewn canvas or leather.

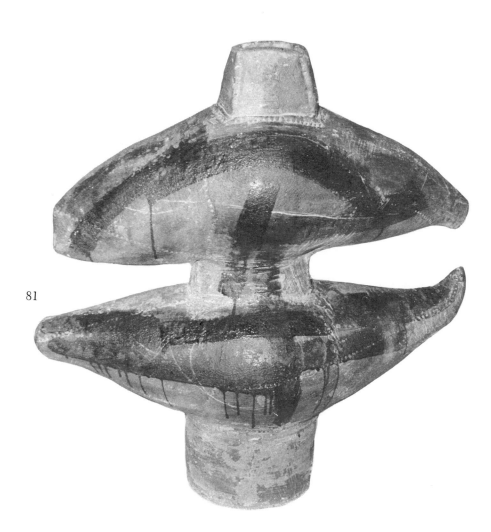

81

82

82. STONEWARE BOTTLE, Chinese, Sung dynasty, Ting ware

Few modern potters would be content with the limited range of color and texture typical of the Ting wares. A light porcelanous body is covered with a clear, thin, smooth glaze giving a surface not unlike ivory. The body is not highly translucent, and the color does not approach the bleached white of the perfected porcelains of later times, yet the substance of the Ting ware is elegant, refined, subtle, and inviting to the touch. This piece was evidently made in a mold, or made by combining slabs which had been pressed out on an incised surface.

Courtesy, The Metropolitan Museum of Art, bequest of Mrs. H. O. Havemeyer, 1929, The H. O. Havemeyer Collection

(Continued from text page 86)

4. Yellow glazes

Yellow glazes are made by additions of vanadium stain. About 6 to 8% is required to make a strong yellow. Warm yellows may be produced by additions of vanadium and small amounts of iron or rutile, and yellow-greens may result from combinations of vanadium and copper oxide. Vanadium stain contains considerable tin oxide and will opacify the glaze. For this reason it is best used in base glazes which are fairly fluid. Vanadium stain does not yield any color in reduction firing. Subdued yellows, even in reduction, can be obtained in high barium base glazes with small amounts of iron oxide added.

5. Green glazes

Celadon glazes, which are light gray-green or olive-green glazes obtained by the reduction firing of glaze bases containing small amounts of iron, are discussed in a later section. In oxidation, various shades of green may be obtained with copper oxide and chromium oxide. Two to five per cent of copper will give a pronounced green or blue-green color. In high fire, more copper must be used to produce a given shade of green than in low-fired glazes because the copper tends to volatilize and to be lost from the glaze. The color from copper in high-fired glazes is considerably more subdued than in low-fired glazes, especially in the case of stoneware, where there is apt to be some influence from a dark body. Chrome gives a heavier shade of green than copper, and it must be used in small amounts to avoid an excessively pasty color. Base glazes containing zinc oxide will be brown when colored by chrome, rather than green. Chromium oxide and cobalt oxide together make a very subtle blue-green color. Both oxides should be added in small quantities, one half of 1% or less.

6. Blue glazes

Cobalt oxide can be relied on to produce blue glazes at all temperatures and kiln atmospheres. It is a very powerful colorant, and less than 1% is required in a glaze to produce a strong color. If a smooth blue is wanted, glazes colored with cobalt must be thoroughly mixed or milled.

While cobalt blues are very reliable and easy to produce, there is something about the color which does not wear well, and most potters seem to avoid making blue pottery. Although it is true that a glaze colored only with cobalt is strongly reminiscent of the cheap type of ware sold at roadside stands, cobalt, when combined with other colorants, will produce very beautiful and subtle blues of many different sorts. Cobalt should be tried out with iron, iron chromate, vanadium, manganese, chrome, nickel, rutile, and copper in various percentages, and with combinations of two or more of these, and with or without tin oxide. Also, a cobalt glaze which may be garish by itself can be very beautiful when applied over slips which influence it toward brown or gray.

Following is a list of likely combinations of coloring oxides and the probable resultant color, and a list of the usual amounts of coloring oxides which are added to glazes.

Iron +
$\begin{cases} \text{cobalt—gray-blue} \\ \text{copper—warm green, metallic green, black} \\ \text{manganese—brown} \\ \text{vanadium—ocher} \\ \text{rutile—ocher, brown} \\ \text{nickel—brown to gray} \\ \text{chrome—blackish green} \end{cases}$

Copper +
- cobalt—blue-green
- manganese—brown, black
- vanadium—yellow-green
- rutile—warm or textured green
- nickel—gray-green
- chrome—green

Manganese +
- vanadium—yellowish brown
- nickel—gray or brown
- rutile—brown
- cobalt—blue-purple
- chrome—brown

Nickel +
- vanadium—gray, brown
- rutile—brown
- cobalt—gray-blue
- chrome—brown

Cobalt +
- vanadium—grayed yellow or mustard
- rutile—textured warm blue or gray-blue
- chrome—blue-green

Rutile +
- vanadium—ocherish yellow
- chrome—warm green

Chrome +
- vanadium—yellow-green

Suggested Additions of Coloring Oxides to Oxidation Glazes

Cobalt carbonate	½%	medium blue
Cobalt carbonate	1%	strong blue
Copper carbonate	2%	light green
Copper carbonate	4%	strong green
Iron oxide	2%	tan
Iron oxide	4%	medium brown
Iron oxide	6%	dark brown
Manganese carbonate	4%	medium purple
Manganese carbonate	6%	dark purple
Chrome oxide	2%	green
Rutile	5%	tan
Nickel oxide	2%	gray or brown
Iron chromate	2%	gray
Vanadium stain	6%	medium yellow
Cobalt carbonate Iron oxide	½% 2%	gray-blue
Cobalt carbonate Manganese carbonate	½% 5%	purple-blue
Cobalt carbonate Copper carbonate	½% 2%	blue-green
Copper carbonate Iron oxide	2% 2%	warm green
Copper carbonate Vanadium stain	3% 3%	yellow-green
Copper carbonate Rutile	3% 3%	warm green
Cobalt carbonate Rutile	½% 3%	warm blue
Vanadium stain Rutile	5% 4%	warm ocher

Cobalt carbonate	½%	medium blue
Cobalt carbonate	¼%	light blue
Cobalt carbonate	½%	turquoise
Chrome oxide	1%	
Cobalt carbonate	½%	warm textured blue
Rutile	3%	
Cobalt carbonate	½%	gray-blue
Nickel oxide	1%	
Nickel oxide	1%	gray or gray-brown
Manganese carbonate	4%	brown
Manganese carbonate	4%	textured brown
Rutile	4%	
Ilmenite	3%	spotty brown
Ilmenite	2%	textured yellow-brown
Rutile	2%	
Iron	1%	celadon
Iron	2%	dark olive celadon
Iron	4%	mottled green or brown
Iron	10%	saturated iron red
Copper	½%	copper red
Copper	1%	deep copper red
Copper	3%	red to black
Cobalt	1%	black
Iron	8%	
Manganese	3%	

The permanence and beauty of colored glazes is certainly one of the features of pottery which have distinguished it. In no other medium is a similar range of color and texture possible. Glazes, besides being so various in color, have the advantage of being controllable in transparency, so that a glaze may be made either clear and transparent, semiopaque, or opaque. This makes it possible to reveal all, some, or none of the clay body or slip beneath the glaze. Thus in ceramics we are able to make use of the depth of the glaze coating, and various layers may contribute to the total color effect. Color may be in the clay body, in the engobe, in the underglaze painting, in the glaze, or over the glaze in majolica style. This wealth of effects presents an opportunity for richness, depth, and variety of surface. All too often one is tempted to go too far, to become involved with surface at the expense of other qualities. In pottery, painting and sculpture meet; and it is perhaps best if, in each particular work, either painting or sculpture, form or surface, plays the leading part, rather than vying with each other.

The potter who is intensely interested in color or in glaze texture usually holds form under certain restraints so that the glaze may speak with full effect; on the other hand, one who is interested primarily in form and who thinks of pottery as a sculptural expression may be reluctant to use brilliant glazes or glazes of high reflectance. However, there are many valid statements which have been made that give free rein to both color and form.

Contemporary stonewares and porcelains are sometimes said to be lacking in color. While there may be some truth to this, it would be a mistake to equate color in ceramics merely with brilliance of hue. More important to expressive power is the relationship which exists between colors, and the relationship between color and texture. For example, while gray or black could hardly be considered strong "colors," it is possible to make gray and black glazes with such depth, variety of surface, and tactile quality that the effect is one of colorfulness. Color harmony or tension, the play of warm or cool tones, sharp contrasts of values or textures—all of these contribute to color expression. Some of the most "colorful" pots are those which make the most of a definitely limited range of hues, and many a brilliantly colored pot proves to be tiresome.

The following procedure is suggested as a way of making full use of the range of color in high-fired pottery: What is needed is a vocabulary of color. Tests should first be made to give a wide selection of glazes from which to choose. It is desirable to limit the number of base glazes to a very few—only using those which have been proved reliable at the intended temperature, firing cycle, and atmosphere. Variations of all sorts should be made on the chosen base glazes —many different combinations of coloring oxides in various percentages should be tried out, and the glazes should be applied thickly, thinly, over engobes, and over textured areas in the clay. If the testing is directed toward the development of a great variety of color rather than toward a few specific colors, it will give more to choose from. Testing should continue until there seems to be a wealth of different hues and textures.

The next step, the evaluation of the colors, is the hardest and the most important of all. Many of the tests, of course, will be eliminated at once for various reasons. From those which remain, *only a very few* should be chosen for use on pots. In the group chosen for use, it is well to have some glazes which are very light in value, some which are very dark. Some should be warm in hue, and some should be cool. Some should be textured, and some smooth. These opposite qualities enable the introduction of contrast, variation, and tension into the work. Choice will be determined by the kind of pottery which is intended and by one's feeling about the colors, the textures, and the potential of each test in terms of finished work.

Before new glazes and new colors are tried out on pots, it is a good idea to test the glaze on fairly large tiles or curved slabs. The appearance of the color on a surface larger than a test tile will tell a great deal about its potential for color, texture, and surface quality. Also, the various glaze flaws are much more apt to show up in a larger trial. Once a group of glazes has been selected and thoroughly tested, finished pottery can be visualized and planned.

If only a relatively few colors and decorative processes are being used at any one time, the potter has a chance to exploit to the full the means at hand. He can prepare his glazes in large quantities and thus facilitate glazing by dipping and pouring. He can use one glaze over another, or glaze the outside of one piece with one color, the inside with another. It is remarkable how many and how varied can be the effects secured with only a few glazes. And when a considerable number of pieces have been fired, the potter will begin to really understand his glazes; how thickly they should be applied, how much they run, which colors work well together, which glazes can be used over each other, which glazes work well with engobes of various colors, how the various glazes behave in different parts of the kiln, how much variation occurs between different firings, what the effect of overlapping and of varying thickness will be, the sensitivity of glazes to oxidation or reduction, the tendency toward flaws such as pitting or crazing, the relationships of the colors to the fired color of the clay body being used, and a "feel" for the right combinations of color, texture, tone, and accents. When true familiarity with a group of glazes has been gained, the real work of creating pottery can begin. Unfortunately, the more usual procedure is to glaze each new pot with a new and relatively untried glaze. This way of working forever prevents the potter from achieving that freedom which grows out of control over the materials.

146

Chapter 8

Firing

Firing stoneware and porcelain is dramatic, exciting, and endlessly fascinating. The suspense is heightened by the uncertainties which attend the process, and by the possibility of happy as well as unfortunate accidents. And all potters come to a philosophical acceptance of the fact that firing may result in failure, discouragement, and disappointment. In some ways, firing high-temperature wares is simpler than firing earthenware. The glazes tend to have a longer range, which lessens the danger of overfiring or underfiring, and the action of the heat and flame on the pots frequently bestows a bonus of color nuance or variation having a natural sort of beauty which could never be achieved by plan. On the other hand, the high temperature also increases the likelihood of kiln mishaps, such as pots sticking to shelves, kiln crumbs falling onto and marring the glazes, shelves and supports giving way, or of pots slumping and warping out of shape. As in all other kinds of pottery making, stoneware and porcelain require careful and expert firing. The cycle of firing is the heart of the whole process of pottery making. Stoneware, and more particularly porcelain, requires special firing procedures because of the degree of softening which occurs in the clay during the high maturing heat of firing.

1. Kiln setting

No matter how inspired or insightful a pot is in concept and design, or how beautifully made it is, a pot may be lost from improper setting in the kiln. There is no escape from thorough craftsmanship here. The first essential in firing is a certain cleanliness and order about the process. Kilns have a tendency to become surrounded by broken and discarded refractories, bits of discarded clay, used cone plaques, broken or abandoned pots, and other debris. Worse still is disorder inside the kiln—broken bits of shelves or supports, crumbs of clay or chips of broken pots, and loose crumbs on the walls and crown. All this confusion should be kept under reasonable control. It is especially important to clean out the kiln after firing, and to sweep loose bits off the inside of the kiln to prevent their falling or blowing onto the glazes during firing.

The best kiln shelves are those made from silicon carbide. These are expensive, but outlast the clay refractory shelves by many times. They are very resistant to the fatigue which results from repeated heating and cooling and will bear great loads, even at high temperatures. New shelves should be lightly washed with a mixture of kaolin and flint in about equal amount. It is not good to allow too great a thickness of kiln wash to build up on the shelves because this causes an uneven and rough surface. After each firing, the shelves should be inspected, and if any bits of glaze have fallen onto the shelves they should be chipped off, and some kiln wash brushed on the area. Shelves should be carefully stored in wooden racks. More kiln shelves are usually lost from being kicked over onto the floor and broken than from wear and tear in the kiln.

Before setting the kiln, it is a good idea to assemble on a large table all the pots which are ready to be fired. They should be carefully checked to see that there is no glaze on the bottoms, and that no glaze has chipped or been rubbed off rims or sides. If the pots are arranged in groups according to size, it is much easier to select pieces for shelves of certain heights. It is a considerable help to kiln setting if there are a good many more glazed pots on hand than will fit into the kiln—this gives a greater variety of size and shape to choose from and permits closer stacking. If the kiln fires unevenly, certain glazes may be best put in certain parts of the kiln which are either hotter or colder than the nominal firing temperature.

Starting at the back of the kiln, shelf supports are set up and the pots are placed on the first shelf. It is best to arrange the pots as close together as possible, leaving only a quarter of an inch or so of space between pieces. The more closely packed the pots are in the kiln, the better it will fire, and the more chance there will be for radiation of heat inside the kiln, which tends to even out the temperature. When one shelf of pots is set, the next shelf is carefully lowered onto the supports. There should be three bearing supports for each shelf. Three are better than four because three supports preclude teetering. Supports should be arranged in similar positions for each succeeding shelf. Pots can be set safely to within a half an inch of the crown. It is best to reserve the top shelf for the tallest pieces.

A space should be provided for the cone plaque which is not too near the door, or in any other spot which is apt to be either abnormally hot or cold. Space must be allowed for the cones to bend and fall without touching any piece. The cone plaque must be level, and must be very plainly visible from the spy-hole. At cone 9 or more, the color inside the kiln is a blinding yellow and the visibility of the objects as seen through the spy-hole is very poor.

In placing both stoneware and porcelain in the kiln, it is important that the actual shelf surface on which the pieces rest be smooth and level. If the foot of a piece is set on an uneven surface, warping of the whole piece is apt to occur. This is, of course, more particularly the case with porcelain, where the body becomes very soft and subject to uneven settling or subsiding. When the kiln shelves have become roughened or warped from use, it may be necessary to set the pots on smaller, smooth, and level pieces of shelf which are laid over the uneven shelves. Large pieces, especially if they have high thrown feet, may need special shrinkage "platforms" under them to prevent warpage. These are smooth slabs, or cookies, which are made of the same clay as the pot, and which shrink to the same extent as the pot.

A thin layer of silica sand should be placed between the shrinkage platform and the shelf. This enables the clay platform to shrink freely without sticking to the shelf. Larger stoneware pots, particularly those with foot rings, should be placed on a thin layer of sand. Care must be taken not to let the sand fall onto glazed pots below.

Porcelain must be set in the kiln with great care. In large-scale production, special kiln furniture is made to permit piles or bungs of plates, saucers, bowls, or other flat pieces to be set in the kiln; these setters provide a smooth and protected setting for each piece besides enabling a maximum number of pieces to be set in the space. Provision must be made for a large shrinkage, and often fine sand is spread over the shelf to enable the pieces to shrink inward without catching on any irregularity on the shelf. Porcelain must be protected from any direct impingement of the flame, as this is very apt to cause slight unevenness of shrinkage and thus warping. The difficulty of firing porcelain varies greatly with the shape of the piece. Closed-in shapes such as vases, teapots, or pitchers are relatively easy to fire because their compact forms have a structural resistance to warping. But all flat porcelain pieces, such as plates, are extremely difficult to make and to fire. The rims of plates slump down considerably during the firing, and unless the plate is perfectly made and evenly fired on a very level surface it is sure to warp. Open forms, such as cups and bowls, are also very subject to warping. These are usually fired boxed, rim to rim, which holds them in shape. Boxing makes it necessary to leave the rim unglazed, but in vitrified porcelain this is barely noticeable. Cups are stuck together with "cup stick," a mixture of wheat paste, calcined alumina, and a little kaolin. This not only glues the cups together for ease of placing in the kiln, but prevents them from becoming stuck to each other in firing. The "cup stick" is painted on a piece of glass and the rim of the cup is touched on to it to receive a coating of the mixture on the very edge.

In spite of every precaution in both making, setting, and firing, a certain percentage of porcelain pieces will warp, especially if they are thinly potted. The high percentage of wasters and seconds in commercial porcelain manufacture adds greatly to the cost of the ware. However, it is the traditional tableware shapes —such as plates, saucers, low bowls, platters, oval platters, tureen and casserole lids—which cause the greatest trouble in firing. If studio production is concentrated on upright forms, or accessory forms which are cast fairly thickly, losses need not be abnormally great.

True porcelain tableware has never been made to any extent in the United States. Fine tableware in this country, the so-called "china," is made by a process which is a modification of porcelain making and which eliminates most of the uncertainties of the process and greatly lessens the percentage of losses in firing. In china manufacture, the body composition is not unlike that of porcelain, although the maturing temperature is usually somewhat lower than the European porcelain fire—cone 9 or 10, instead of cone 12 to 14. The ware is given a high maturing bisque fire which renders it nonabsorbent, hard, and translucent. Since no glaze is applied in this fire, the ware can be supported to prevent warping. Flatware, such as plates, saucers, soup plates, and low bowls, may be fired upside down on refractory setters which are made in the shape of the inside of the piece. The plate in this case shrinks on the setter, supported at all times, and when it becomes soft at the height of the fire, it settles against the refractory support like a limp pancake. The setters are made of refractory material and are used over and over again. They are covered with a thin wash of alumina, flint, and china clay to prevent the piece from sticking, and are shaped in a way which permits piles or bungs of setters being placed in the kiln for the most economical use of the space. The design of these setters presents a difficult problem because the setter must accommodate the raw plate and at the same time must permit the plate to shrink to its final shape. Cups and bowls are fired boxed or paired together in a manner similar to porcelain. Thicker china plates, or other heavy flatware such as that made for restaurant use, are commonly fired in stacks of twelve or more, with a mixture of pure silica sand or calcined kaolin and sand-packed between the pieces. This loose mixture supports the plates and prevents them from slumping down or warping. The bottom plate is held rigid in a refractory setter. Although this method has the advantage of permitting many plates to be fired in a small amount of kiln space, it necessitates some cleaning process to remove the sand or clay from the bisque prior to glazing. Plates are sometimes tumbled with pebbles in revolving wooden scrubbers, which effectively remove every trace of the setting sand or clay. These methods of giving the china a vitrifying fire without warpage or deformation require very careful control and are not accomplished without difficulty, but the process is more economical of kiln space and more certain of results than is the porcelain glost fire.

In making china, the glaze fire is carried out at a much lower temperature than the bisque, usually at about cone 4 or 5. The vitrified, cleaned bisque is thinly glazed with a lead borosilicate glaze made up largely of fritted ingredients. Glazes of this type have been developed which are remarkably smooth, flawless, and trouble-free. Since the ware has already been vitrified at a higher temperature, there is no tendency for it to warp or slump in the lower glaze fire, and this enables the glazed ware to be supported on pins in racks or saggers. When the pieces are supported in this fashion, the kiln can be very economically packed, and the foot rims of the plates may be glazed. The small scars left in the glaze by the setting pins are easily ground smooth, and are noticeable in the finished ware only as three slight scars on the back of the plate.

While china is similar to porcelain as far as the body is concerned, it is definitely inferior in glaze. The lower-fired glaze is softer and more subject to abrasion in use than the harder porcelain glaze. Lacking also is the beautiful unity between body and glaze which characterizes true porcelains. Another difference between the European porcelain and American china or English bone china is that the porcelains are fired in a reducing atmosphere which makes them blue-white in color, whereas china is fired in a strictly oxidizing atmosphere in both the bisque and glaze fire, and consequently has a creamy or warm white color.

Methods of setting and firing the kiln are determined by the kind of pottery which is being made. The manufacture

of china and porcelain calls for the most exact control over every detail of the process, because the standards for such wares require exact uniformity and flawless perfection. The more rough and casual kinds of ware, such as commercial stoneware, have a different standard, and the personal production of the individual potter may have a still different criterion of what is acceptable. What is a flaw in one connection may be an accepted feature of process and expression in another.

2. The bisque fire

Since the bisque firing temperature for stoneware and porcelains is normally far below that of the maturing glaze fire, there is little danger of warping, and the pots can be stacked in the kiln rather casually, with smaller pieces placed inside larger ones, flat pieces stacked one on top of the other, or pieces placed upside down.

In firing bisque, the main problem is firing slowly enough at the beginning of the cycle to avoid breaking the ware. The firing must proceed very slowly, especially at the very first when the last of the moisture in the pots is being driven off. Another danger point occurs with the first appearance of color in the kiln, and this period should also be gone through very slowly to prevent cracking the pots. Beyond red heat, the firing may safely proceed at a much faster rate. About 100°C per hour is not too rapid. Firing should be strictly oxidizing.

The temperature of the bisque fire should be sufficiently high to harden the ware so it can be glazed and handled without undue breakage, yet not so high that it becomes too dense and nonabsorbent for easy glazing. Cone 04 is usually a practical bisquing temperature for both stoneware and porcelain. If the bisque fire is too low and the ware remains very soft, it may not be sufficiently strong to withstand the strains of cooling. One frequent cause of cracks in finished glazed ware is the occurrence of hairline cracks in the pots during the bisque fire. These cracks may not be noticed during the process of glazing and may show up only when the ware is taken from the glaze fire. Another common cause of cracks is subjecting very soft bisque to too rapid an increase of heat during the early stages of the glaze fire. In almost every case it will be found advantageous to bisque-fire pottery rather than to once-fire. Bisquing not only greatly decreases the chance of glaze flaws of various sorts, but it enables the use of many glazing techniques which are difficult or impossible on the raw, unfired piece. However, if all the procedures of glazing and decorating are planned for a once-fire process, it may work out very successfully.

3. The oxidizing glaze fire

In any discussion of firing, a distinction must be made between electric firing and other types of firing. The electric kiln utilizes the radiant heat that develops in an electrical element which offers resistance to the flow of electrical current. In the electric kiln there is no movement of air or gas through the kiln, and the heat is generated in a way which does not affect the atmosphere inside the firing chamber. Unless carbon is introduced into the firing chamber during the fire, the atmosphere of the electric kiln is oxidizing, and the potter need not concern himself with it. Since all electric firings are oxidizing, there is little variation between firings (except perhaps in temperature), and for this reason the results from firing in electric kilns are more uniform and certain than results obtained in kilns which burn fuel. This uniformity is certainly an advantage in many situations.

In kilns which burn fuel, whether it be gas, oil, coal, or wood, the heat is generated by a combustion process which involves air and the passage of hot gas through the chamber of the kiln. Combustion is a chemical reaction between the carbon in the fuel and the oxygen in the atmosphere. When the fuel is subjected to heat it reaches its "kindling temperature" and a sustaining reaction is begun which involves the combination of carbon and oxygen into a new compound, carbon dioxide. This reaction liberates energy in the form of heat. Nitrogen, which makes up a substantial part of the atmosphere, does not enter into this reaction, but in the process of burning it becomes heated and travels through the kiln together with the carbon dioxide. Oil and gas are made up of carbohydrates which, when dissociated by combustion, result also in water vapor (steam), and this moves through the kiln together with the other hot gases.

In oxidation firing, it is essential to maintain at all times enough air entering the burners to insure that the fuel is consumed and that a minimum of unburned fuel in the form of carbon or carbon monoxide is being allowed to pass through the kiln. However, if too much air is allowed to enter the burners, combustion becomes inefficient, because quantities of air, including nitrogen, are being heated and put through the kiln but are not entering into the combustion process.

It is quite easy to tell whether a kiln is oxidizing. When it is, the atmosphere inside the kiln will appear to be clear and the objects inside the kiln can be seen sharply and clearly. At the burners, the flame will show a blue cone near the burner, turning to orange or white in the combustion chambers. When the spy-hole is open, there should be a slight draft or suction into the kiln rather than any back pressure which is expelling air at this point. This can easily be determined by holding up a lighted cigarette or burning a scrap of paper just in front of the spy-hole and seeing whether the smoke is drawn into the kiln or blown away from it. At the entrance to the flue or chimney of the kiln there should be no visible flame. One symptom of too much air being admitted to the burners is the failure of the kiln to advance in temperature.

Oxidation glaze firing involves only the proper setting of the burners to maintain the desired rate of climb, and a clean oxidizing fire throughout. The proper rate of temperature advance in glaze firing depends not only on the kind of ware being fired but also on the size of the kiln. Small kilns can be fired quite rapidly without becoming uneven in temperature, but a larger kiln usually has to be fired quite slowly to allow for an even distribution of heat throughout. The temperature inside a kiln evens out largely by radiation from one part of the kiln to the other and by radiation between the ware and the kiln furniture. The evening effect of radiation requires time, and too fast an advance of temperature usually results in cold areas near the flue or exit region of the firing chamber. Large or thick pieces must be fired more slowly than small and thin ones. The usual rate of advance for a glaze firing is between 50° and 100°C per hour, but in a kiln of over 50 cubic feet capacity an advance of 50°C per hour may be much too fast.

For the proper maturation of glazes and bodies, plenty of time should be allowed at the height of firing. Usually, in high firing, the kiln will have a natural tendency to slow down its rate of climb as it reaches cone 8 or 9. During the final stage of firing, when the cones are going down, the rate of advance should be slowed to permit at least 20 minutes, and preferably a half hour or even longer to elapse between the bending of each cone. A soaking period at the end, during which the temperature neither advances nor decreases, is very desirable for the best firing of glazes. This soaking period should last at least a half hour.

The cooling period also should not be hurried. Any well-insulated kiln will cool slowly enough if the damper is closed and the openings around the burners are shut after the firing ceases. When a kiln is shut off there is usually quite a rapid drop in temperature immediately. One hundred degrees of temperature may be lost during the first half hour. This rapid decrease in temperature does not seem to harm glazes. When the heat has diminished to a dull red heat, care must be taken not to let the cooling proceed too rapidly, because it is at this point that dunting is most likely to occur.

4. Reduction glaze firing

In reduction firing, a cloudy, smoky atmosphere is used rather than the clear, clean fire of oxidation. This is accomplished by limiting the amount of air which enters the burners, thus permitting a certain amount of unburned carbon and carbon monoxide to pass through the setting in the kiln. In kilns which burn fuel, creating a reducing atmosphere presents no difficulty; in fact, many kilns are very prone to reduce even when this condition is not wanted, especially if the chimney is not high and the draft not too lively. Reduction firing should not be thought of as something which is difficult to do—on the contrary it is quite simple. In primitive kilns with imperfect arrangements for burning the fuel, reduction is the normal rather than the exceptional condition, and in primitive firings carried out in earth pits with an open fire, reduction usually blackens the pots. Burners for gas or oil have some mechanism for admitting air and for mixing it with the fuel. In the case of atmospheric gas burners, the air is entrained with the gas as the gas emerges from a small orifice and the gas and air are mixed together as they travel through a venturi tube. Burning occurs as the mixed gas and air leave the end of the burner. In burners of this type, the air can be adjusted by a device which opens or closes the opening through which it enters the burner. In forced-air gas burners, the air is supplied by a motor-driven blower. The supply of air may be decreased by closing a valve in the air line. Oil burners atomize the oil and mix it with air supplied by a motor-driven blower. As in the case of forced-air gas burners, the quantity of air is easily controlled by a valve. Where the burner enters the kiln, more air is usually allowed to mix with the flame; this is called the secondary air supply. To bring about reduction, the primary air, or the supply of air at the burner itself, is cut back until the flame assumes a yellowish cast and there is little or no blue flame. At the same time, the damper of the kiln is closed somewhat until there is a back pressure in the kiln sufficient to cause some flame to emerge from the spy-holes. When a kiln is reducing, flames may be observed at the point where the hot gases passing through the kiln enter the flue. In heavy reduction, smoke will be observed at the spy-holes and also coming from the chimney.

In reduction firing, the question is not so much whether reduction can be accomplished as *how much* reduction is taking place. The exact degree of reduction is hard to control, and it is this factor which introduces uncertainty into the process. In commercial work, where the exact duplication of colors and textures is a necessity, reduction firing is not a very practical method of firing because results are certain to vary somewhat from firing to firing. This variety, which must be considered detrimental to certain kinds of production, is a distinct advantage where the aim is to make very individual, personal, or one-of-a-kind pottery. But even in reduction firing, variables from one firing to the next can be brought under a reasonable degree of control. If the potter knows his kiln well, and follows a set firing procedure each time, there is no reason why the results should not be quite consistent over many firings.

In a reduction glaze fire, the firing is started in the usual manner, and the kiln is kept oxidizing until about 800°C. At this point some reduction is begun. If reduction is commenced at a fairly early stage of the firing, the clay of the ware is still open and porous, and some car-bon will penetrate the ware from the smoky atmosphere. The presence of this carbon in the pores of the clay will affect the final color of any ware which contains an appreciable amount of iron, causing it to burn dark, usually a warm reddish brown or gray. This period of "body reduction" may be continued for an hour or so. In firing porcelain, it is not necessary to begin reduction during the early stages of the firing, and the fire can be kept oxidizing until about 1100°C is reached.

In reduction firing it is very helpful to use a pyrometer to indicate the advance of temperature. When reduction is heavy and there is considerable cloudiness in the kiln with some smoke coming from the chimney, it will be noted that the temperature does not advance, or may even decrease. This is because of the quantity of unburned fuel which is passing through the kiln. If the temperature actually falls, it is an indication that the reduction is unnecessarily heavy and more air should be allowed to enter the burners until the pyrometer indicates, over a period of a half hour or so, some advance in heat. For most reduction effects, very heavy reduction is not necessary, and may actually be harmful to the ware. It has been found that a light reduction continued throughout the latter part of the firing is enough for all the usual colors such as copper red, celadon, and saturated iron, and that such a fire is much more efficient, rapid, and convenient than alternating periods of very heavy reduction and oxidation. A light reduction is indicated by a normal rise in the temperature of the kiln, a yellow color in the flame at the burners, a moderate back pressure at the spy-holes with perhaps some flame showing when the spy-hole plug is taken out (but no smoke), a yellow flame at the flue, and a slightly cloudy but not murky atmosphere inside the kiln.

The following procedure is recommended for reduction firing: An oxidizing fire is maintained until the temperature reaches 800°C, with a normal advance of temperature of about 100°C per hour. At this point, light reduction is begun and the temperature advance is slowed down slightly. Light reduction is continued until the cones begin to bend. At this point the air supply is cut back somewhat and the damper closed a bit until the back pressure in the kiln is increased. The increased reduction slows the advance of temperature, giving a period of at least a half hour between the bending of each cone. The advance of temperature in the kiln, in other words, is slowed down by an increase in reduction. When the last cone is down and after a period of soaking, the kiln is shut off and the damper closed. The secondary air ports, spy-holes, and any cracks in the door should be closed to prevent too rapid cooling.

When reduction is too heavy, particularly during the early stages of the fire, an excess of carbon is deposited in the open pores of the ware. If the later stages of firing are also heavily reducing, this carbon remains in the clay and may swell and bloat the body of the ware. This happens when the clay body reaches maturity and becomes dense and impervious, thus sealing off the carbon in the pores of the clay. This type of bloating is more apt to occur if the latter stages of the firing are rapid. Another effect of too much carbon in the pores of the ware is to cause pitting and pinholing in the glazes. This is apparently caused by the escape of carbon dioxide through the viscous glaze. Very heavy reduction at the end of a firing has no damaging effect on either the body of the ware or on the glaze, but it is doubtful if it has any desirable effect either; besides, quantities of fuel are wasted.

It is certainly true that reduction firing remains very much of an art, rather than a science. One reason for this is that each individual kiln will have its own peculiarities, such as the amount of

gas pressure, the kind of burners, the strength of draft, and above all, size. The size of the kiln has an important effect on the degree of reduction which is effected by a given amount of flame. A small kiln may reduce heavily with hardly any flame being visible beyond the burners, while a large kiln may require what seems like a great deal more reduction to accomplish the same results. The problem of when to reduce a kiln and how much to reduce it can be solved only by trial and error with a particular kiln and a particular kind of ware, and with a certain group of glazes and glaze colors. The important thing is to establish a satisfactory routine of firing and to stick to it until the necessity for some change is clearly indicated. Reasonably uniform results from one firing to the next can be achieved only by very careful management of the kiln, and a very close observation of such factors as draft, conditions at the spy-holes, amount of flame at the flues, rate of temperature advance, and the "look" of the firing chamber. One variable which the potter must look out for while firing is the weather. When the barometric pressure is rising, the draft will be more lively; when the weather is damp and stormy, the firing is usually slowed down. If the air is supplied by a blower, the weather will have less effect on the firing, but no matter what equipment is used, it is commonly noticed that there is a marked change in the behavior of a kiln as a result of differing weather conditions, and this is particularly the case with reduction firing.

It is very desirable to keep a careful log or record of all firings. The most useful kind of kiln log is a graph which indicates the rise of temperature hour by hour. This type of record necessitates a pyrometer. Once a desirable and economical firing schedule has been arrived at, it is helpful to be able to repeat the schedule more or less exactly. This, in addition to giving predictable results, prevents the waste of fuel which is apt to occur if the firing does not advance efficiently.

Reduction firing is best accomplished in a kiln burning either gas, oil, or wood. Muffle kilns, where the ware is protected from the direct impingement of the flames from the burners, are not satisfactory. Some muffle kilns have been successfully adapted for reduction by removing part of the muffle, thus permitting the flame to enter the ware chamber. Pots may be placed in saggers for reduction firing, but this is not really necessary except in the case of firing with solid fuel, such as wood or coal, where a certain amount of ash may reach the ware. Where the setting is completely open and the flames from the burners are led directly through the setting, some of the pots are apt to get flashed and a variation in color from one side to the other develops, but this is more often pleasant than not.

There is little use in attempting to approximate reduction effects in the electric kiln, although this can be done by adding carbonaceous solids to the chamber of the kiln during firing. Moth balls, charcoal, oil-soaked bandages, and the like have been used. The results achieved by such methods never seem to equal those achieved in kilns burning fuel, and if the potter is really interested in reduction ware he should try to obtain a suitable kiln for the purpose. Even with the best of equipment, there are plenty of difficulties in pottery processes.

5. Surface characteristics of oxidation and reduction pottery

Oxidation and reduction firing produce characteristic colors and qualities, and both methods of firing have certain advantages and disadvantages.

Oxidation has the advantage of making possible a reasonably exact control of the firing, and therefore more uniform results from one firing to another. In oxidation firing, a great variety of surfaces and colors are possible, enough to satisfy almost any conceivable practical need or creative urge. Clay bodies may be white, black, gray, brown, smooth, rough-textured, or plain, or any of the stages between. Glazes may be clear, opaque, mat, or bright, and of innumerable hues. Oxidation firing can be carried out in either gas or oil-burning kilns, or in electric kilns. The firing tends to be shorter and the consumption of fuel considerably less than in reduction firing.

Reduction firing, while it has some disadvantages of a practical sort, offers the potter a palette of color and a kind of surface quality not possible in oxidation. Reduction makes possible two glaze types which are unique in ceramics: the class of gray or greenish glazes known as celadon, and the red colors derived from copper. Both of these colors are discussed in a later section. Also unique to reduction firing is a crystalline reddish brown resulting from iron in the glaze, although a somewhat related color tending more toward brown can be achieved in an oxidizing fire. More important, perhaps, than these unique reduction colors, is the surface quality and over-all color character of reduction glazes.

In surface quality, reduction glazes tend to be softer, more lustrous, and more pleasant to the touch than oxidation glazes, especially when the glaze is mat. It is hard to account for the differences between the surfaces of oxidation and reduction glazes, but it may have something to do with length of firing as well as with chemical reactions in the glaze. This difference in the "feel" of reduction glazes is difficult to describe but is obvious to anyone who has made a direct comparison. Here we are speaking, of course, of reduction glazes at their best. It is certainly true that harsh, garish and unattractive glazes can be produced in reduction firing. Reduction, in other words, is no guarantee of success in the production of beautiful glazes, but the fire does seem to be working for one a little bit more than in the case of oxidation firing.

In color, reduction glazes tend to relate rather closely to each other. This is in part the result of a more limited range of possible color in reduction but also seems to be the result of a grayness or a brownish quality which suffuses all the colors. Reduction firing also seems to favor the interaction between the layers of body, engobe, and glaze; as a result, the glazes tend to be more textured and more spotted with impurities. Reduction firing is perhaps most effective in the production of gray glazes. In oxidation, gray is not an easy color to achieve and is apt to be harsh. In reduction, gray of various sorts occurs whenever some iron is present, and when small amounts of iron are used in the glaze together with other coloring oxides, gray colors result which may be extremely varied and subtle.

Prior to about 1930, reduction firing was very little used by studio potters as a firing method in the United States; in fact, only a very few potters were aware of the possibilities in reduction glazes. An interest in reduction firing has grown along with the renewal of interest in the accomplishments of the early Chinese potters. Of course, 30 years ago there were only a handful of people making high-fired pottery, aside from the commercial production of utilitarian stoneware and tableware. In recent years reduction firing has come to be a very common rather than an exceptional method of firing practiced by the individual artist-potter. Potters have found in reduced wares a way of satisfying their desire to make the utmost use of natural effects, and of expressing their conception of the earthy nature of the ceramic medium. Enthusiasm for reduction glazes has grown until nearly every showing of pottery now includes stoneware glazed in the subtle colors characteristic of this method of firing.

Chapter 9

Natural Glazes

One of the best features of high firing is the ease with which various materials melt to form glazes. In low-fired pottery, the glaze maker must always use one of the active fluxes, such as lead, sodium, potassium, or boron to achieve a glassy melt. But at temperatures in excess of cone 8, many natural minerals will melt. This opens up the possibility of making glazes from natural materials rather than from prepared materials. Historically, potters have, of course, had to depend on glaze materials which were readily obtained rather than those which were the result of involved chemical or mechanical processing. As has already been noted in Chapter 5, feldspar alone will form an acceptable glaze, and simple combinations of feldspar, limestone, flint, and clay, all of which are available as natural minerals in most localities, will form beautiful and practical glazes. It should not be thought that there is anything superior in a hand-picked specimen of feldspar or limestone as compared to the ground and prepared feldspar or whiting which one would buy from a supplier. The commercial materials, in fact, have the definite advantage of uniformity of chemical composition and fineness of grind. However, for the potter who is interested in personal and individual achievement in ceramics, the use of selected local materials has the advantage of encouraging a reliance on essentially simple and direct means, and of bringing about a firsthand and intimate knowledge of the materials involved.

Perhaps one of the best reasons for working with natural glaze materials is that the limitations which the use of such materials impose requires sensitive and skillful potting which does not rely on the spectacular, or on virtuosity of glaze surface. Anyone who has done even a small amount of work with glazes will realize that the problem is not so much one of finding beautiful or interesting surfaces, as it is the difficulty of making choices, of using surface color and texture in ways which are appropriate to the form of the pots, and in avoiding complexities and involvements of surface which tend to become ends in themselves rather than part of a unified expression. At any firing temperature, thousands of colors and textures are possible, in fact, are very easily achieved. The temptation is always to try to use too many different glazes at once, and to inflict too much of surface interest on each defenseless pot. Most pots of great beauty, interest, or utility will be found to be quite simple, in the sense that all parts work together in creating a unity.

1. Slip glazes

Slip glazes are glazes composed largely or entirely of clay. Most common clays which contain considerable iron and other impurities, mature to a tight and hard body at about cone 04 or less, and firing in excess of about cone 4 causes such clays to vitrify and finally to melt. Relatively few clays will withstand temperatures of cone 9 or more, only, in fact, stoneware clays, fire clay, and kaolins. Most surface clays melt to a brown or black glass at about cone 10. When a red clay is melted, it first vitrifies into a dense mass, and then, as the heat advances, it begins to bloat. Bloating is followed by a boiling of more or less intensity, and finally, the melted material settles down into a smooth puddle of glass. The degree of boiling seems to vary with the composition of the clay, and clays which are high in sulfur or which contain bits of gypsum or limestone boil more than those which contain few impurities other than iron.

Clays which melt completely at cone 10 or 11 may be used effectively as glazes on stoneware. Such clays may require no additions of any kind and may form a satisfactory glaze from the utilitarian point of view—smooth, and free from crawling, crazing, or pitting. To test a clay for possible usefulness as a slip glaze, it is only necessary to place a small sample of the dried clay on a firebrick or a bit of broken kiln shelf, and to fire it to the regular stoneware glaze temperature. If the clay melts to a smooth puddle of glass, it is a likely material for glazes. If the clay remains full of bubbles or pits, the chances are that a higher temperature is necessary to make a good glaze. For satisfactory slip glazes made from clay alone, a firing temperature of at least cone 10 is desirable, and cone 11 or 12 will give the best results.

In using slip glazes, the potter is pretty much dependent on the behavior of the clay which is available. With the exception of Albany slip, no glazing clays are marketed commercially, and the potter must dig or find his own. Common surface clays dug out of banks or streams, or clay used for the manufacture of common red bricks are possible sources for slip glazes. The clays found along the Hudson River in New York make beautiful slip glazes, and in most localities suitable clay can be found.

If the available clay does not melt suf- ficiently to make a good smooth glaze, or if the temperature available in the kiln is not quite hot enough, fluxes may be added. Colemanite, borax, or a fusible frit used in amounts up to about 20% will render most slip clays quite fluid, even at cone 8. The results from such doctored-up slip glazes are in no way inferior to those obtained with the clay used by itself with no additions.

The application of slip glazes presents a special problem. Unlike most glaze mixtures, slip glazes have a very high shrinkage, and if they are applied thickly, they will crack and fall off the ware. One way out of this difficulty is to glaze the ware when it is leather-hard, allowing the glaze and body to shrink together. This works well for small pieces, but may be awkward for larger or more complicated shapes. A better system, perhaps, is to calcine all or part of the slip glaze before using it. A light firing to red heat will complete the shrinkage of the clay and make it behave like any other powdered glaze material. The raw clay can be placed in a sagger for firing, or on the shelves of the kiln. Calcination at about 800°C should be sufficient. After calcining, the clay may need to be ground to reduce it again to a fine powder and to break up any lumps which may have formed during firing. It may then be mixed with water to form the glaze slip. An addition of the raw clay should be used to improve the strength of the raw glaze coat. Slip glaze prepared in this way may be used over dry ware or over bisqued pots in the same way as any other kind of glaze.

Slip glazes have a very narrow range of color, being always tan, brown, or black. These various shades of brown, however, may have considerable surface texture and interest. The old Chinese pottery will no doubt always serve as a model of beautiful slip glazing. The unpretentious yet dignified slip glazes of the Honan and Tz'u Chou pottery made in Sung times have never been surpassed.

The subtlety of color and texture of these wares, and their perfectly integrated surface variations, make them an inspiration for any potter.

The hare's fur, or Temmoku type of slip glaze is characterized by streaks of brown or tan mingled with black which run down from the lip of the pot toward the foot. This effect depends on just the right amount of fluidity in the glaze. If the glaze does not run sufficiently, it may be marked with brown or tan spots rather than streaks. If, on the other hand, the glaze is too fluid, the streaks will disappear and the glaze will have a tendency to run off the pot at the foot. Careful firing is therefore necessary for just the desired texture in the glaze. The so-called partridge feather glaze is a slip glaze characterized by pronounced spots or splotches of tan or brown on a black glaze. The spots may be rather regularly spaced and each spot of a complexity which suggests the markings on feathers. This type of spot in a slip glaze indicates the subsidence of craters and blisters which occur in the glaze during heating. The thin film of glaze which is raised into a blister or bubble becomes more oxidized than the mass of the glaze, and is thus more tan or brown in color when it flattens out toward the end of the fire. The bubbling and boiling, and consequent color variation which makes the hare's-fur and partridge-feather effects in slip glazes results from the presence of impurities in the slip clay, particularly sulfur or lime. Many clays will give results similar to the hare's-fur glaze with no adjustments or additions. It is rather difficult to induce the effect by adding materials to a clay, but some success has been obtained by additions of granules of gypsum.

The oil spot glaze is usually black with rather uniformly spaced spots of a lighter color. The spots may be silvery or iridescent. Oil spot glazes are actually rather difficult to achieve. They develop best in oxidation firing at temperatures in excess of cone 10. The trick seems to be to get the right clay, one which tends to form spots without requiring any additions. Successful oil spots have been produced, however, by making additions of iron, rutile, spodumene, and whiting to Albany slip clay or other similar slip clays. To develop oil spotting, a slip glaze must be quite fluid, and should contain a high percentage of iron, either as part of the composition of the clay or as an addition to it.

Reddish slip glazes are especially interesting. To produce reddish-brown colors, a heavily reducing atmosphere is needed, and the slip clay must contain considerable iron. Adding a flux such as nepheline syenite may favor the development of red or russet color. Another color which is characteristic of slip glazes is a rich shiny black, the "mirror black" of old Chinese stonewares. This color is relatively easy to obtain—the glaze slip is darkened by the addition of 10 or 15% of iron and perhaps a small amount of copper or cobalt, and the firing carried out in oxidation to a heat sufficient to mature the glaze to a smooth bright surface.

Slip glazes are sometimes radically different in color, depending on the thickness of application. Thus a glaze may be a light tan color when thinly applied and black where it is thick. This difference makes it possible to introduce variations in the glaze of a pot merely by controlling the thickness. A pot may be thinly glazed and a design made by removing all the glaze from certain areas. Then the pot is dipped into the glaze again, giving two different thicknesses which develop into two colors in the fire. Or, wax-resist processes may be used to achieve different thicknesses. Various techniques of dipping and pouring may give variations in thickness which are more or less controlled.

Slip glazes may be applied over or under glazes which are composed of the usual materials. When a slip glaze and some other type of glaze mingle, the result may be a mottled or broken texture, and the brown of the slip glaze can easily be modified in color by thin coatings of regular glaze. Slip glazes applied either over or under magnesia glaze will give mottled colors ranging from light tan to black. Much of the Japanese stoneware is glazed in this manner, with bold patterns created by the flow of glaze and slip in application, or by double dipping. A favorite type of Japanese glaze known as *kaki* is a slip glaze which is applied very thinly, giving a light brown or tan color having a burnished or lustrous quality.

Slip glazes seem to work well in a once-fire process, and if the ware is glazed raw there is the possibility of cutting through the glaze into the body to form incised designs or patterns. This technique gives particularly happy results when the body is a fairly light sand or toast color and the glaze is a darker red-brown or black. It is possible to glaze the pot while it is leather-hard and then to scratch or cut through the glaze with great freedom.

The use of slip glazes presents a challenge to the potter. The quiet browns and tans of slip glazes are of no great interest in themselves, and the beauty of the pot must come from the skill and sensitivity with which color, texture, form, and surface variety are brought together rather than on any spectacular quality in the glaze itself. The danger is, of course, that slip-glazed wares will be dull and dingy. They need not be. The earthy colors of natural glazes, with proper management, can be made as lively as any blue or green, and much more expressive of the nature of the materials of pottery and its maturing in the fire. In using slip glazes, the potter should look for lively contrasts between body and glaze, for a good relationship between the size and shape of glazed and unglazed areas, and for strong contrasts between glazes which are used inside and outside the piece. Such contrasts can be used to relieve the possible monotony of a uniformly brownish glaze.

2. Ash glazes

Another natural glaze material which has tempting possibilities is the ash of wood or other vegetable matter. Ashes contain alkalies in more or less soluble form together with silica, alumina, and small percentages of other elements. The composition of ashes varies widely, depending on the source. Some ashes are composed almost entirely of silica, and contain very little soda, potash, or other elements, rice hull ash, for example. Some ashes are quite fusible and others are refractory and difficult to melt, and this variation makes the use of ash in glazes dependent on careful testing. An ash with the right melting characteristics makes a valuable and often very beautiful stoneware glaze material.

Actually ashes contain no elements which are not easily obtained in commercially available raw materials, such as feldspar and frit of various sorts. But it is true that glazes made with ash have a distinctive quality and appearance which is hard to reproduce with other materials. Colemanite comes nearer to ash, perhaps, than any other material in its effects in a glaze. Ash glazes tend to be rather fluid, and broken in texture. The presence of small amounts of iron and other metallic oxides usually gives to ash glazes a spotted and somewhat grayed quality.

The selection, procuring, and preparation of ashes for use in glazes presents unusual difficulties. Some source for ash must be found which will furnish large enough quantities of the material for extended use. Of course it is possible to burn material especially for the purpose of making glaze material, but large quantities of wood or other material must be burned to obtain even a small amount of ash, and it is more practical to find a source of ash resulting from some commercial or agricultural process. One likely source is the ash which results from burning scrap at sawmills or woodworking factories. Another possibility is the ash from the burning of agricultural wastes such as corn cobs, fruit pits, and the like. Small batches of ash may also be collected from the fireplace or from the burning of grass or brush, enough to make a few pounds of glaze, but rather extensive testing is necessary to arrive at good glazes from such small batches, and when the glaze has been used up one must start all over again with some other material. The Chinese and Japanese had a ready source of ash from the burning of wood or brush in the kiln, and if the same kind of wood was always used such ash must have been quite uniform in composition.

One way of gathering ash for glazes is to keep a large receptacle, such as a galvanized iron covered can, and to collect in it ash of various sorts until quite a quantity has been secured. The ash can then be prepared and tested and a large supply of glaze made up. When this is exhausted, another batch of ash is collected. I know of one potter who collected over one hundred pounds of ash from the debris of a barn which had burned. When this ash was prepared and tested it proved to have specks of iron in it, probably from nails, which gave a reddish-brown spot, and the ash combined with nepheline syenite produced a glaze of unusual beauty. When the supply was exhausted, the glaze could never be made again. It will be seen that the use of ash glazes can develop into an extensive, and time-consuming study, but one which is well worth-while in terms of the beautiful glazes which can be achieved.

To prepare ash for use in glazes, it should first be screened dry through a coarse screen to remove bits of charcoal and other unburned material. The ash is then mixed with water to form a thin slip and passed through a fine screen, about 60 mesh. The slip is then allowed to settle, and the excess water is decanted.

Several days may be required for settling. The remaining sludge is then dried out (it can be placed on top of the kiln during firing) and is ready for use. After only one such washing, quite a bit of soluble potash is apt to be still left in the ash, and sometimes it is advisable to wash the ash a second time. However, each washing removes alkalies from the ash, and the more thoroughly washed the ash is the less fusible it will be in the glaze. The soluble potash which remains in the ash makes it caustic and the solution, in fact, contains lye. It is advisable to wear rubber gloves when washing and straining the ash.

It is possible to use ash in glazes without any washing. The ash is merely sifted through a 30-mesh screen to remove lumpy material, and then weighed out directly for the glaze. Glazes made this way, if they contain a high percentage of ash, are caustic, and must be handled with care to prevent skin irritation.

The composition of ash glazes must be determined by experimentation, since the exact composition of each batch of ash is an unknown quantity, chemically. Some ash by itself will form a glaze of sorts when fired to cone 9 or higher, and the first step in formulating an ash glaze is to fire the ash on a bit of tile and then decide what additions are needed. The ash may not in itself be fusible, but may form, with the alumina and silica of the clay, compounds which melt at the glaze temperature. Ash is commonly used as a flux, rather than as the major constituent of the glaze. If tests show the ash to be fluid and thoroughly melted at the glazing temperature, some trials may be made using 50% of ash in the glaze, and making up the rest with clay, flint, and feldspar. Combinations of feldspar and ash in about equal proportions may be found to produce handsome glazes, although such a composition is likely to craze. It is very difficult to give specific recommendations for ash glaze compositions, because of the uncertain fusion point of ash, and in this type of glaze making the potter is definitely dependent on his own ingenuity in testing and formulation.

One approach to the use of ash in stoneware glaze is to use the ash as an addition to glazes which are in themselves more or less fusible at the glaze temperature. For instance, one can take a very dry glaze and add a percentage of ash to it. The result will be a new glaze, perhaps semiopaque, with a character which derives from the ash, even though only 25 or 30% of ash may be present. Glazes made with ash may be colored with coloring oxides in the usual manner.

Ash glazes should be tried in both oxidation and reduction firing. In oxidation most glazes made with ash will tend to be somewhat tan in color, due to the small amounts of iron normally present in the ash. In reduction the prevailing color will be gray or gray-green. The subtle texture and surface quality of the ash glaze seems to be favored by a reducing fire. Small percentages of zinc, rutile, ilmenite, nickel, tin, and red clay should be tried with ash glazes for interesting variations of color and texture.

Like slip glazes, ash glazes are quiet, and differ from ordinary glazes only in the most subtle ways. Mastering the use of ash is rewarding, not so much because startlingly different effects are obtained but because of the satisfaction of having made something beautiful from common, everyday material, and of learning to control the glaze by personal experimentation rather than relying in any way on formulas originated by others.

3. Vapor glazing

Salt glazing and glazing which results from ash from the fuel of the kiln offer possibilities in stoneware which cannot be achieved in any other way.

Salt glazing requires a special kiln which can be used for no other purpose (see later section on kilns), and this makes the process impractical for most potters, who are lucky if they have the use of one good high-temperature kiln, to say nothing of an extra one which is used only occasionally. Since the effects obtainable in the salt kiln are limited in range of color and texture, most potters would not be satisfied to work exclusively with salt glaze.

For a description of the chemical reactions which take place in salt glazing and of the procedures involved, see the author's book, *Clay and Glazes for the Potter*, page 183.

Salt glaze is always transparent and colorless, and the color of the salt-glazed pot must depend on the color of the clay body or of the engobe. Salt glaze is also shiny, and it is not possible to make mat glaze except by glazing very thinly. The charm of salt glaze is in its texture, and in the way in which it accentuates the surface modeling of the clay. The salt glaze, especially on a body which contains some iron, develops a mottled and slightly bumpy surface—the orange-peel look. There is certainly a rough and earthy sort of charm in this surface, and it conceals the character of the clay less than most other kinds of glaze.

There are some difficulties in firing salt-glazed ware. For one thing, it is very difficult to repeat effects exactly because the color of the glaze is extremely sensitive to atmosphere, and it may not be possible to control this sufficiently to obtain uniform results. If unique pots are the aim, this may not be a real disadvantage. Another difficulty is that the shelves and props in the salt-glaze kiln become glazed, and with repeated firings may become useless. The build-up of glaze on the kiln furniture may be partially prevented by washing it with a slip of aluminum oxide before each firing, but at best, the wear and tear on the kiln furniture, and on the kiln itself, is severe. The salt vapors have a very corrosive action on the kiln, and around the burners where the salt is introduced, the refractories become eaten away and repairs must be made much more frequently than with regular firing. Still another difficulty in salt glazing is that the vapor does not get inside the pots sufficiently to form a glaze, and some sort of regular glaze must be used. The behavior of the glazes used on the insides of pots may be quite erratic because of the influence of the salt vapors. If a shop is regularly producing salt-glazed ware, these shortcomings in the process may be overcome, or allowed for, but for the occasional producer, salt glazing is apt to result in ware which is, on the whole, less satisfactory than that achieved by regular glazing processes.

When the kiln is fired with wood, a natural glaze may appear on the pots as a result of ash being carried through the kiln with the draft. The glaze is thin, barely wetting the shoulders and the tops of the pots, but it gives somewhat the effect of a true glaze. Such glazing varies greatly with the position of the ware in the kiln and with the manner of stoking and raking out the ashes during firing. The Japanese Bizen ware is glazed in this manner. Sometimes the Japanese potters put additional ash on the pots before putting them in the kiln to enhance or supplement the effects of natural fire glazing. One possibility, where wood is used as a fuel, is to finish each firing with a small amount of salt introduced into the firebox to enrich the ash vapor glaze. The combination of ash and salt glaze will give very beautiful color and textural variations.

4. Celadon and copper-red glazes

So much has been written on the celadon and the copper-red glazes that a detailed description seems hardly necessary here. The reader is urged to refer to A. L. Heatherington's excellent book, *Chinese Ceramic Glazes*, which contains a detailed technical account of the two colors and how they are achieved.

Celadon, or variations of the color, occur very naturally in any reduction firing, and it must not be thought that the color is particularly difficult or elusive. Small amounts of iron in either body or glaze are bound to result in gray or gray-green colors when the fire is reducing, and it is actually rather difficult to make reduction ware which does not tend toward the gray. Certainly the color at its best is very attractive, and has a subtle and mysterious depth.

Copper red is more difficult to produce than celadon, and is apt to vary in color rather widely from firing to firing. There is a certain romance about copper red which stems no doubt from the time, about a hundred years ago, when the secret of how to make the color was not known in the West. Many potters have devoted countless hours to the testing and firing of copper red. However, if the color is looked at honestly, most will agree that it is not particularly beautiful, being either rather dirty and brown, or rather garish and liver-colored. There seems to have been some critical opinion in China which despised the color when it first came into use in Ming times. The color is, after all, just one of the many possible ceramic glaze colors, and the expenditure of excessive time and effort to track down some certain shade of red, or some exact firing procedure for a particular color may hardly be justified by the end results.

For a discussion of the materials and firing procedures for celadon and for copper red, together with suitable glaze formulas, refer to the author's book, *Clay and Glazes for the Potter*, pages 173–177.

Chapter 10

Stoneware—Forms and Surfaces

Stoneware is the medium par excellence for the expression of form in pottery. The sturdy substance of the material, and the beauty of the clay itself, entirely aside from any embellishment of glaze or slip, seems ideal for the embodiment of distinct and strongly stated pottery shapes. Stoneware clay may also be highly plastic, with scarcely any limitations in wheelwork or in any other forming process.

Historically, stoneware had its beginnings in styles which were functional, down to earth, and more concerned with easy and rapid production and with natural and readily performed glazing techniques, than they were with decoration, refinement, symbolism, or naturalistic representation. The old stonewares of the Han period in China, the strong earthy everyday wares of the Sung and T'ang periods, the free, imaginative, and untamed stonewares of the Koreans, the flowing forms and uninhibited techniques of Japanese stoneware, the strong shapes and surfaces of old Rhenish salt-glazed stoneware, and the sturdy, unassuming, yet beautifully shaped wares of the 19th century stoneware potters; all of these have in common a union of means and ends, and an honest strength of statement which is inspiring for the present-day potter, and which furnishes a basic and continuing standard. Without such wares we might not be aware of the sculptural poetry which can exist in pots. The challenge is to state our own insights into the potential of the medium, both as to the technical possibilities of material and process and the creative potential of form and surface, with equal vigor and truth.

1. Throwing

Throwing is a process of forming which is unique to pottery, and which differs from shaping operations employed with any other material. It is a process which requires no tools other than the hands (and the revolving wheel) and which enables the potter to create form directly, swiftly, and out of a material which in itself has no form and no particular character except that which is given it by the processes and procedures chosen by the potter. In this sense, the thrown pot is *entirely* the creation of the potter, and every feature of it—its shape, weight, form, character, color, texture, feel—is his doing and his responsibility. All other materials with which man makes objects (with the possible exception of plastics) have a quality of substance which is *given*, and the maker, while he may create a new object full of individuality, is limited to what he finds already in the material. Objects made of wood or metal remain wood or metal and the designer accommodates himself to the texture, the hardness, the color, and the working properties of the wood or the metal. In a sense, potters create their own material. We are revealed for what we are in our pots, and cannot rely on the natural beauty of an already formed material.

Throwing is a discipline and a skill which is not easy to acquire. It is one process in pottery which marks the serious worker from the dilettante, and which may give to forms the authority of highly developed craftsmanship. It is also a process which enables us to put our signature into the very shape of the pot so that none will be needed on the bottom, for each thrower develops his own distinctive style, a style which may be almost as easily recognized as his handwriting.

As a production process, throwing has long since been superseded by the plaster mold, the jigger and the jolly, and by the hydraulic press. But there are probably many more individuals today who can throw pots than there ever were before in history; and skill on the wheel, far from being in danger of dying out, is becoming more widespread than ever before. It is as foolish to worry about throwing being an anachronistic or vestigial method of making pots as it would be to predict the end of walking because of the automobile, or the end of handwriting because of the typewriter. If one must seek a practical justification for the potter's wheel, the ease with which it enables designers to project shapes would be enough. Potters will love the wheel for itself.

Learning to throw can be a very difficult, even an agonizing process. Perhaps one should not even attempt to learn unless one is willing to devote considerable time to the wheel over an extended period. Throwing, like learning to play a musical instrument, is a discipline requiring almost daily practice, with gradual but steady improvement as the only hope of eventual mastery and ease of performance.

The first essential in skillful throwing is a good wheel. It is surprising, considering all the designs which have been made for throwing wheels, and also considering the simplicity and antiquity of the device, that so many bad wheels are in use. The wheel should be so designed that it permits one to work while comfortably seated, rather than requiring one to stand. Some potters prefer a molded seat, such as an agricultural implement seat, while others prefer to sit on a flat plank. The seat should be no more than a few inches below the level of the wheel head and should incline slightly forward rather than backward. The wheel head should be near the seat so that one works close to the pot. If the wheel is foot propelled, the type which is operated by kicking directly on a heavy flywheel is to be preferred to the treadle bar. The flywheel should weigh between 60 and 100 pounds, and the shaft should be sturdy and secured at two points by good ball bearings. The wheel should start easily and should run noiselessly and with good momentum. The head may be a disk of metal or wood, or removable plaster heads may be used. If the pots are to be cut off the wheel directly after throwing, a metal or wooden head is best, but if the work is to be lifted off without cutting, some sort of removable plaster bat is necessary. A wheel head of plaster has some disadvantages: it may become soaked with water, in which case the clay will not stick to it; or, on the other hand, if it is too dry, the bottom of the pot becomes stiff and unresponsive to the pressures of throwing. Also, it is difficult to cut the pots off with a wire from a plaster head. One practical solution is to provide the wheel with a metal or wooden head for general throwing and trimming, and to provide also some disks of asbestos-cement board to use when the pot is to be lifted off the wheel without cutting. The cement-board disks are easily stuck onto the wheel head with a bit of slip, and if they are exactly the same size as the head itself, it is not difficult to recenter a disk on the wheel if further work is to be done on a pot at a later time. Many wheels are designed with a recessed type of head meant to receive a removable plaster bat. After each pot is finished, it is removed from the wheel while still on the bat, and another bat inserted for the next pot. This system works well, but the wheel should also be provided with a wooden bat to use when the pots are to be cut and lifted off the wheel.

While the foot-powered wheel has the advantage of easy and direct control of speed, the motorized wheel has the definite advantage of conserving the energy which is otherwise expended in kicking, and for large shapes, the power wheel is almost indispensable. It is necessary, however, to have a very sensitive control of the speed of the wheel. The most desirable type of wheel is one which works either by kicking or by a motor when power is needed. With a wheel of this type, operations such as trimming or banding, which do not require much momentum, can be done by foot power, while the motor is used for throwing large shapes.

Another essential to wheel throwing is good clay, suitably prepared. Much of the difficulty experienced by beginners can be traced to poor clay or clay which has not been properly wedged. Clay bodies for throwing have been discussed in a previous section. It should be added that the clay bodies which are prepared and sold commercially for use in schools and by craftsmen are seldom really suitable for wheel work. Most of these bodies are designed for earthenware and contain a high percentage of nonplastic material, usually talc, and little or no coarse material. While clays of this kind are suitable for modeling small shapes, and perhaps for making pots by coiling or slab building, they do not work well on the wheel.

Preliminary study in wheel work should consist more of wedging than of throwing, until the art of thoroughly kneading the clay is mastered. This is not as easy as it looks. Proper wedging requires a certain vigor and strength as well as skill. Also required is some judgment as to when the clay is ready for use. It must be smooth, free from lumps or air pockets, and of the right degree of softness. Knowing when the clay is ready is a matter of experience. It is true that most beginners go to the wheel with clay that the most skillful thrower would find impossible to manage, and an important part of learning to throw is to learn also how to mix, temper, age, and wedge the clay so that it can be shaped and controlled with relative ease. All this must be done with great care, and no matter how spontaneous or offhand the style of work, there is no escaping a craftsmanlike approach to the preparation of the material. The more skilled a potter becomes, the more exacting he is apt to be regarding the condition of his clay, and technical mastery does not in any way free the potter from attention to such details, any more than the violinist is freed by his skill from the necessity of tuning his instrument.

Wedging should be first practiced by simply combining and recombining fistfuls of clay about the size of baseballs. A round wad of clay is grasped in each hand and the two combined forcefully. The combined mass is then torn in two with a twisting motion, and after slightly shifting the position of the ball in the right hand the two are again smashed together. For this kind of hand wedging, the clay should be soft, but not quite soft enough to stick to the hands. The operation can be done in a rapid and rhythmic sequence. Another technique which should be practiced is to take a piece of clay about the size of a loaf of bread and throw it down on the wedge table so that half of it is overhanging the edge. This half is then broken off and thrown with some force on the top of the other. The whole piece is then picked up, given a quarter turn, and the operation repeated. Quite large lumps of clay can be wedged in this manner. Cutting the loaf of clay on a wire and recombining the halves is an excellent way to wedge, but perhaps the best technique is spiral wedging, which mixes and de-airs the clay rapidly. In spiral wedging the ball of clay is squeezed near its middle by pushing with the heel of the left hand. The ball is then given a quarter twist with the right hand, and squeezed again. If the operation is rapidly repeated and the clay pressed and turned correctly, the clay is forced into a spiral movement.

For making small shapes the clay should be rather soft, almost soft enough to stick to the hands, and beginners who are still working toward accuracy and speed should use very soft clay. Larger and more extreme shapes require as stiff a consistency as it is possible to center on the wheel.

To learn to throw well it is necessary to practice on exercises of gradually increasing difficulty. The first objective, of course, is to learn to center. To practice centering it is best to use very soft clay at first, clay which is really too soft to make into much of a pot. This makes centering very much easier, and enables one to learn the knack of it much more quickly. Learning to center is actually more a matter of acquiring a "feeling" for center than of any difficult manual operation. To center, it is necessary only to press the clay firmly and relentlessly between the steadied hands as it revolves. But some experience will be required to enable the student to know if the clay is truly running on center.

After centering is beginning to come fairly easily, a small pot can be attempted. A good shape to try for at first is a small jar about 3 or 4 inches in diameter and about 3 inches high, with sides which slope outward slightly. To make a modest pot of this sort cleanly, rapidly, and well is no mean accomplishment, and many an alleged potter who has been attempting forms on the wheel for a long time has not acquired the skill and discipline needed for making even such an easy shape with assurance. It is very helpful if each attempt is made with a similar sized ball of clay, and if the general proportion and size of each pot is kept the same.

After the completion of each little pot, it should be released from the wheel by passing a flexible brass wire, held tautly between the thumbs, under the pot, and the piece should then be gently lifted between the palms of the hands onto a ware board. This process of cutting off is important, and it should be practiced with the very first exercises on the wheel and not deferred until some later time. It requires considerable skill to lift a wet, soft pot from the wheel, but overcoming the fear of distorting or ruining the pot is half the battle. To lift off a pot, the hands should be damp, but not covered with slurry. The pot is grasped near its base, using the palms and heel of the hand. The ware board should be close to the wheel head to make the carrying distance as short as possible. Some distortion is inevitable in lifting a freshly thrown pot, but such irregularities are easily straightened out when the piece has stiffened a bit. If a pot is to be lifted successfully, it must not be too soft or covered with too much soft slurry. Cutting and lifting off the work can only be successful if the throwing has been fairly rapid and the pot has not become too wet and soft.

When practicing, each pot should be cut in two with a knife or wire to study its cross section. The important points to be looked for are:

1. The bottom should be about the same thickness as the side walls of the pot.
2. The walls of the pot should be uniform with no thicker part near the bottom.
3. The bottom, inside, should be level and smooth.
4. The upper edge or lip should be level, smooth, and accented by a slight thickening.
5. Both the exterior and the interior of the pot should be free from deep or erratic finger marks. Such finger marks as are left on the piece should be regular, rhythmic, and in scale with the size of the form.

Many people who are seriously interested in making pottery look with horror on the idea of making two or more things alike, or at anything having to do with repetition or drill. But in throwing, true freedom can come only with skill and competence, and these can be won only by disciplined practice. The skill which enables one to make two forms alike is also the skill which enables one to make each form different *according to intent rather than accident*. Of course, gaining technical mastery over the wheel is no assurance of an ability to create forms of meaning, but lack of mastery only puts one at the mercy of the clay. In practicing, the aim should be to work within a definite limitation of shape and size, but within that limit to refine and to enliven the form to the greatest possible extent. It is surprising how much can be projected into a small pot, how much life and feeling of plasticity and form, even though the shape be of the utmost simplicity. It is this principle of *much from little* which is the fundamental lesson in pottery. There is room in pottery for the expressionist, even the exhibitionist statement, and there are times when large size, complexity of shape or surface, and extremities of form are appropriate. But such extremes should be ventured only after the potter has the process well under control.

When some control has been won over small, open forms, cylinders should be attempted. A good form to practice on is a drum shape about 4 inches in diameter and at least 4 inches high. As skill increases, higher cylinders can be made until a form like a mug or beaker is perfected. The straight cylinder is a basic form in pottery, the one from which most other forms grow, and it is worth a great deal of work in perfecting. Practice should be directed toward getting the bottom smooth inside, the wall straight and with little variation in thickness, the bottom as thin as the wall, and the lip true, and fattened into a slight bead. It

may be necessary to clean off a little excess clay at the bottom of the form by scraping with a pointed stick as the wheel revolves. Each piece should be cut free from the wheel head with the wire, and lifted off onto the ware board.

The student should practice making cylinders of increasing size, always working toward an even wall section, a clean profile without accidental undulations or unevenness, and an increase of height relative to width. As skill increases, the cylinder can be made with fewer "pulls" and the operation of centering, hollowing out, and raising the form should blend into a continuous, smooth, and efficient operation. The object of such practice is not so much to make pottery of a precise and controlled character as it is to gain control over the process of throwing, to make it more free of frustration and struggle. Throwing becomes a really worth-while method of making pots only when it can be perfected to the point where the thrower can forget his technique and allow his intention to flow into the pot without hindrance. This sensation of effortlessness, of the ability to concentrate on the pot rather than on the process, will occur first on small modest shapes which are relatively easy to make, and as skill increases, on larger and more complex forms.

Once the cylinder has been mastered, no great difficulty will be experienced in making forms which swell out into jars or bowls, which spread out to plate or platter shapes, or which are constricted at the top to form bottle shapes. Thinning and extending the form may be accomplished by starting either at the top of the form or at the bottom. The wheel is turned rather slowly at this stage of throwing, and the degree of pressure on the wall of the pot must be very carefully controlled to avoid producing irregular or exaggerated bulges which weaken the form. The art of throwing consists mainly in gauging the effect of pressure on the soft clay, and of being able to subtly guide the form by applying just the right amount of "squeeze" between the fingers. Each pot will have a limit beyond which its form cannot be extended without the whole shape collapsing, and the knowledge of how far a particular curve can be pushed, or of how broadly a bowl form can be made to extend, comes only from the experience gained through many failures.

Forms are contracted, narrowed, or enclosed by applying a gentle pressure inward with the fingers. This operation must be done more slowly than the process of swelling or extending the form. In "collaring in," the danger is the development of wrinkles or irregularities in the wall of the pot, but with just the right amount of pressure applied to the outside of the spinning form, narrow necks can be formed at the top of very wide shapes, and such forms as narrow spouts can be made.

In throwing, the tempo of the work is of great importance. Due to the nature of the process involving the manipulation of plastic clay which becomes increasingly soft as the work progresses, throwing must be direct and quite rapid. Otherwise the clay becomes soft, tired, formless, and tends to sag. When a form is completed on the wheel, its surface should be relatively dry and free from loose slurry, and it should still be stiff enough to pick up without serious distortion. The best forms result when the work goes forward swiftly, surely, and without groping.

While throwing requires very few and simple tools, some tools will greatly help to achieve and to clarify certain forms. A sharpened bamboo stick is excellent for cleaning the excess clay away from the bottom of the pot where it meets the wheel head. A wooden rib firmly held against the outside of the pot when it is being drawn up into a cylinder keeps the form controlled and straight. Ribs are small flat tools made of wood or metal which are held between the fingers and pressed against the revolving pot as an aid either to pulling it up into a cylinder or in shaping. Final shaping may be done with thin flexible metal ribs rather than with the fingers, one rib held inside the pot and another held against the outside. The use of ribs gives a precision to the form which is difficult to achieve with the fingers. Ribs also make more extreme forms possible since, when the rib is used, no further water need be added for lubrication, and the shape may be further developed without the clay getting soft and slumping. When finger marks are to be left on the walls of the pot or when a more casual sense of form is sought, ribs had probably best be avoided and the final shaping done with the fingers.

While trimming is not nearly as difficult as throwing, it too demands exacting craftsmanship. Most important is to trim when the clay is exactly the right degree of stiffness. Thrown pots should either be cut and lifted off the wheel, or released from their bats immediately after throwing by passing the wire under them, and when they have stiffened a little they should be turned over on a smooth dry surface so the bottoms can begin to dry. When the bottom of a pot begins to stiffen, but can still easily be indented with the thumbnail, it is ready for trimming. The pot is then centered on a dry, level wheel head by tapping or bumping it gently as it slowly revolves, thus coaxing it toward center. Concentric lines drawn or scratched on the wheel head help in the centering process. When the piece is running true it is anchored down with three soft clay wads, or a rope of clay pressed around the lip. For trimming, the wheel should run at a brisk speed. Tools for trimming, either a hooked knife, or metal angles, should be kept very sharp. The Japanese use sharpened bamboo sticks as well as metal tools for trimming.

First the bottom of the pot is leveled off. The clay should come from the tool in long ribbons—if the scrap is crumbly, this is an indication that the pot is too dry, and if the clay balls up on the tool, the pot is too wet. If the pot is to have a foot, the inside of the foot ring is cut into the clay until the bottom of the pot just yields to the pressure of the finger. The outside of the ring is then shaped and any excess clay cut from the wall of the pot near the bottom. The texture and striations of the trimming tool can be as beautiful as the throwing marks, and can relate in scale to the texture of the pot as a whole.

Pots which have been cut from the wheel with a twisted wire will have a sworl on the bottom. If the bottom is not too thick, this often very beautiful mark may be left undisturbed, and only the sides of the pot trimmed. The bottom may be tapped to arch it upward slightly and to make the pot stand securely. Trimming is not always necessary to finish off a pot satisfactorily at the bottom. If the throwing is skillfully done, and if no great excess of clay has been left at the bottom, the pot may be cut from the wheel a finished shape. The bottom edge can be finished merely by rolling it on a table or by rubbing it around with the finger. It is never good to depend too much on trimming to achieve a finished thrown shape, and as nearly as possible, wheel-made shapes should be completed on the wheel in a single operation. Pots which are trimmed too much have a mechanical, almost lathe-cut character rather than the plastic fluidity which is the beauty of thrown forms.

Numerous pots may be thrown from one large centered lump of clay. A small ball is drawn up at the top of a large centered mass of clay on the wheel head. From this the pot is shaped in the usual fashion. Then, with the wheel revolving slowly, the pot is cut off with a string, and lifted to the ware board. This method is good for producing numerous small shapes at a single sitting, and saves the work of preparing separate balls of clay

for each piece and of centering for each.

Making large shapes on the wheel presents a challenge. Cylinders more than about 14 inches in height are actually very difficult to make, no matter how large a lump of clay is used. For large pieces, the clay must be very plastic, yet contain enough coarse material to prevent slumping. Wedging and centering must be properly done, and the throwing in the early stages of hollowing out and pulling up must be very accurate. A very rapid wheel speed will help in mastering large lumps of clay. Another great help is to center the lump of clay as nearly as possible by patting and slapping it as the wheel slowly revolves before the actual throwing process begins. The tall cylinder must be pulled up energetically and rapidly, for too many separate pulls and too much wetting will soften the clay and make finishing impossible. Shapes higher than about 14 inches must be somewhat thick at the bottom to prevent slumping, and it is almost impossible to make very large shapes without having to do, later, some trimming and thinning in the leather-hard stage. A large pot must be started as a very narrow cylinder and expanded out into a wider form only at the end of the throwing process, because on a large scale only the straight cylinder will withstand the strain of pulling up and thinning.

Very large pots are best made in sections, or by a process which combines coiling and throwing. In making a sectional pot, the bottom part is thrown first, great care being taken to provide a level, true-running upper edge. The next section is thrown upside down on another bat, and its upper edge is made exactly the same thickness and the same diameter as the upper edge of the bottom section. When these two pieces have stiffened somewhat, the second section is cut off the bat with a wire, inverted, and luted to the bottom section with slip. After the joint has set, throwing is begun again, and the top of the second section, which will be somewhat thick, is pulled up for additional height. After some dampening with a sponge, the whole form can be shaped to a certain extent, but there is a limit to the changes that can be made in the lower first section. Any number of sections can be added in this manner, but the more sections added, the more chance there is for the pot to become too wobbly and uneven to work on. Making large sectional pots demands a great deal of skill and patience, and also practiced judgment as to when the various parts are of the right degree of stiffness for assembly.

In many ways a technique which combines coiling and throwing is a better method of making very large pots than making them in separate sections. In this method the bottom part of the pot is thrown in the usual manner, and as large as can be readily made. This bottom section is allowed to dry a bit until the upper edge is stiffened, then a fat coil is made and fastened to the edge with slip. The wheel is then spun again and the clay which has been added as a coil is trued up, and thrown to form an addition onto the pot. As many coils can be added as desired, and theoretically, there is no limit to the height or diameter of a pot which can be made in this way. The coils may be rolled out with a rolling pin between wooden guides to insure uniform thickness; this helps to keep the pot from becoming wobbly or off-center. Each coil must be carefully made, attached, and joined at the ends to keep the pot from developing irregularities. Coiling and throwing, while not a rapid way of making pots, enables a firm control over the shape. Time is saved by making two or more pots at a time with this method. While a coil is being added to one pot, the others are drying. The Korean potters, who make jars 3 or 4 feet high, use a small oil lamp suspended inside the pot with a string to hasten the stiffening of the pot so that coiling and throwing can proceed rapidly. An infrared heat lamp may be used in this manner.

Handles, lids, knobs, and other appendages are difficult to add without giving the effect that the pot is an assemblage of parts rather than a unified, single, whole. In general, the appendages are best made strictly subordinate to the body of the piece. Beginners commonly make handles which are much too big and too thick, and lids, with their knobs, have a way of overwhelming the pot beneath them.

Many variations of thrown forms can be made which depart more or less radically from perfectly round and symmetrical shapes. The pot may be squeezed or coaxed into squarish, oval, or triangular shapes soon after throwing. Or indentations may be made in the walls of the pot and irregular swellings produced by pressure of the finger inside the damp piece. Variations of this sort capitalize on the very plastic nature of soft clay. If carried to excess, however, deformations of the thrown form may result in a feeling that structure is lacking, and that the final form is untrue to the hard, rocklike quality of fired clay.

While it might be possible to learn to throw from written instructions and perhaps from action photographs, it is certainly much better to work with a good teacher, someone who throws well and understands the problems. Watching good throwers work is a great help, and the most rapid progress will result from daily practice, coupled with observation of pots being competently made and trimmed. From this, the student gains a firsthand knowledge of the right rhythms of work and of the spirit of pleasurable craft.

2. Thrown forms

Not only is throwing an intriguing process, but the thrown pot has some qualities not found in any other man-made objects. The wheel-made piece of pottery is uniquely the product of the hand. Its character is determined solely by the potter as he interprets the potential of clay and process.

Pots begin as formless lumps of clay, a raw material which, although full of possibilities, is in itself nearly nothing. As the wheel spins, the potter forces a kind of order on the clay, he controls it first toward a smoothly running, centered ball, compact and ready to be opened out into a shape. From the low formless lump, the pot grows upward like a plant. If the potter is skillful, the preliminary shapes which appear at first foreshadow the final flowering of the form, and the final shape should emerge surely and rhythmically. The pot may express an upward thrust in its beginnings at the foot, in its fullest distention at the belly or shoulder, and in the terminating accent at the lip or neck or mouth. The best pots seem to have grown swiftly, and as naturally as a mushroom.

Whereas most objects are made either by a process of addition or subtraction (carving, modeling, assembling, casting, weaving, pressing), pots are achieved by a process of *growth from the inside*. At the very beginning of the process of throwing, the hand establishes the preliminary hollow, and throughout the process the hand inside the pot is the active influence in guiding the changing shape, while the hand on the outside counters, constrains, and controls the growth of form. As a Chinese philosopher has said, it is the *inside* of the pot which is important, and in the well-thrown piece one feels the inside, the unseen hollow, as the essence of the design. Pottery shapes are amazingly like the growing forms of nature—like the root vegetables which achieve their compact, firm, sculptured forms by pushing from within against the constraining earth, or like pods and husks, which grow outward, cell by cell, to form a container for the precious seed within.

Like the forms which are achieved in nature by processes of growth, the parts of the pot may relate organically to form

an indivisible whole. As the human form, though made up of parts—torso, limbs, head—presents a unity and a miracle of co-ordination, so the parts of a pot—foot, body, handles, spout, neck, shoulder, lip, or lid—may belong together and form a unified expression. This unification of parts to form a whole by no means precludes relationships which are unexpected, extreme, or whimsical.

The idea and the fact of containment have been the primary significance of pottery from the beginning, and the pots of all ages and peoples, even when their ostensible function was ceremonial or symbolical, have expressed, by their generous swelling volumes, the potential of holding things of vital importance to man—food, liquid, or the furnishings of the grave. This idea of holding and containment can find embodiment in the pot through the expression of positive volume or outward distention which forms the dominant theme, and such distentions and swellings may be countered, emphasized, controlled, or given contrast by constrictions, narrowings, and concavities. It is in the play of these two forces, one, the tendency to extend outward (which coincides with the centrifugal forces of the wheel), and the other, the constraining forces working inward toward the axis of the form, that the vitality of the pot originates. Even though a form may be small in scale, simple in shape, and perhaps made up of predominately straight lines, it may nevertheless be generous and full in proportion. Many pots, although large and pretentious, are mean and pinched in form.

Some of the most exciting pottery forms have the look of containing a slight pressure within, as if they were puffed out like a balloon. An interesting experiment is to throw on the wheel a bottle shape with a very small neck. Immediately after throwing, the potter places his lips on the opening at the neck, and the pot is blown full of air until it distends slightly from interior pressure. The effect on the form is miraculous—the walls of the pot swell with a sureness very difficult to achieve in throwing.

Pots are accented by the foot, by surface textures or throwing marks, by sudden turns of shape, by constrictions, and by the lip, spout, lid, or knob. These accents, if well managed, seem to emphasize or punctuate the flow of form upward from the foot. Accents may give the form a sense of a beginning, a point of farthest extension or development, and a termination. Straight line and curve, roundness or squareness, rough or smooth, convex or concave, inward or outward, quick and slow—all these qualities of form may find resolution or create tension in the shape of a thrown pot.

The smallest pot may have a monumental dignity, while the largest may be a banal magnification of a puny shape. While the nature of pottery processes and usage have resulted, for the most part, in forms which are hand size, or which can be easily picked up, some expressions in pottery certainly do demand monumental scale. Granted that size alone is no virtue, scale is nevertheless one of the important factors in our reaction to a pot, and, as Henry Moore has said of sculpture, there does seem to be a right scale for every idea. No less important than scale is the weight of pots, especially those which are meant to be picked up during use, such as plates, bowls, pitchers, and teapots. A pot which is too heavy impresses us as being awkward and lumpy, while those which are too light seem brittle and overly fragile.

The forms of pots are infinitely various, and no rules governing their shapes can begin to explain the life in existing ones or to prescribe for those to come. More important than any turn of form or any specific relationship is a feeling of plastic flow, a feeling that the pot came into being effortlessly and naturally. There is a mysterious property about pots which defies analysis, yet which is real to all who know them well. It is the property of vitality, and it seems to flow directly into the form without the intervention of either thought or effort.

In the final analysis, it is probably the quality of the person who is making the pot which is all that really matters, and technique means nothing except as it enables the authentic statement of the potter himself. The real adventure of making pots can begin only when discipline, skill, control, and science have become intuitive and can be subordinated to the creative insights.

3. Impressed textures

Plastic clay is such a soft and impressionable material that it is almost impossible to avoid impressing some sort of texture into it during the course of work. Thus coiled pots will show the remains of the coil and of the pressings of the fingers which secured the coils to each other; and the thrown pot, unless it is later carefully shaved down, will show the rhythmic striations given to the surface by the fingers as they thinned and guided the form. The accumulations of texture may tell much about the sureness and craftsmanship (or lack of it) of the potter. The surface impressions may also reflect and extend the whole spirit of the pot—a sturdy and rough-hewn form may have a craggy texture, and thinly drawn porcelain may have a lightly engraved texture expressive of the fineness of its material. The texture of any object is often a kind of visible history of the events which shaped it—sea-worn pebbles are smooth and round, igneous rocks in the mountains are sharp and jagged. And the surface of living organisms expresses the processes of growth and development of which they are the result. "The skin fits." The skin may also express function—the cactus, the armadillo, the furred or feathered animal, or the fish, for example.

Throwing marks occur naturally and easily when the throwing goes well. Without conscious effort on the part of the potter they express the force and pressure of the knuckle in pulling the soft clay up into a cylinder and the gentle and delicate fingering which defines the shape of a neck or a lip. The points of accent in a pot, such as sudden turnings of form, or the transition from one curve to another, are often points where the throwing marks change from broad to delicate or from rough to smooth. Throwing marks should be in scale with the pot and should be expressive of the process. The throwing marks should belong on the pot. If they are excessively prominent they may destroy or obscure the form. Although tool marks have a beauty of their own, the imitation throwing mark which is trimmed into the surface with a tool seldom has the fluid grace of finger marks in the wet clay.

Trimming textures may be very smooth, like tooled leather, or rough and sandy, depending on the coarseness of the body and the handling of the trimming tool. The texture produced by a sharp trimming tool on the rapidly turning groggy clay seems to enhance perfectly the pleasantly gritty material. If trimming is done at just the right stage of dryness, the work can be rapid and free, and the surfaces, while having a cut or shaved look, will still have a feeling of plasticity.

Many tools may be used to achieve texture in the thrown pot. When textures are made in the clay while it is still very soft (during or immediately after throwing), a very fresh and wet-looking kind of surface results. When the clay is tooled or incised in the leather-hard stage of drying, the texture is apt to be much more precise. Still another kind of surface texture may be achieved by scratching or scraping the bone-dry clay. For freshly thrown pots, combs and brushes offer many possibilities for surface variation. An ordinary hair comb with widely spaced teeth may be used. It can be held against the rotating pot or used like a brush to give sweeping striations in different directions. A piece broken from the comb and measuring about 2 inches long is a useful size. For some kinds of combing, a coarser tooth is preferable. Wonderful combs for pottery may be made by cutting teeth in thin pieces of hardwood. The teeth need not be long, not more than half an inch. If the comb is wielded with confidence on a damp pot, very free and racy textures may be achieved. An effect similar to combing can be done with a wire brush. A wire brush, such as that made for cleaning pots and pans, gives a very rich texture, not quite so precise as the comb.

When the pot has dried and stiffened a bit, it may be altered in both shape and texture with the beater. By tapping the pot with a beater, it may be coaxed into a squarish form or one in which flat planes break into the spherical shape. If the beater is textured, it will leave imprints on the pot. For beaters, ordinary sticks or paddles of soft wood may be used. These may be carved on the surface, roughly or precisely, in various patterns. Or, the beater may be wrapped with burlap or other coarse-textured fabric. Still another texture results from wrapping the beater with cord or twine. Old-fashioned butter paddles make excellent pot beaters. Beating can give a pot a delightful off-round and casual quality, and the textural possibilities are endless.

The roulette is a small wheel which is held against the revolving damp pot to give continuous bands of texture or pattern. Roulettes may be carved from wood, made from wooden spools, or from the rubber wheels of discarded toys. The design of roulette wheels must be quite simple to avoid clogging with the damp clay, especially if they are used for wet, freshly thrown pots. All sorts of patterns are possible—impressed dots, groups of bars, dents in the shape of the letter *s*, or free and nongeometrical patterns. The roulette must be used with a certain restraint, however, or the pottery takes on

174

the look of pie crust or tooled leather. There are many inspiring models from the past of beautiful roulette patterns, particularly among the stonewares of the Han period in China.

A tremendous variety of textures and patterns may be achieved with stamps. Stamps may be made from wood, plaster, or clay, or various "found" objects and tools which come to hand may be used. To make wooden stamps, soft pine may be carved in various ways with wood carving or engraving tools. Carved blocks of wood may be used both as beaters and as stamps and may be carved in different ways on their several sides and ends. Plaster stamps are very easy to make and wear well enough for most uses. To make a plaster stamp, a slab of clay is rolled out, and various stamp designs are made in it—with the fingers or with various tools—just as they might appear on the walls of a pot. Dozens of designs can be quickly made in the soft clay. The best designs are then cut out of the slab and a little dam of clay made around them. The cavity so formed is then filled with plaster of Paris, and when this has set and the clay model removed, the stamp is ready for use. To make a fired clay stamp, the design is first made on a soft or leather-hard clay surface and this is allowed to dry. Using very soft clay, an impression is made of the design by pressing. This impression is dried, trimmed to suitable size and shape, and is fired. It should be fired sufficiently hard to wear well, but should still be open and porous. Or, clay stamps may be carved directly in soft or leather-hard clay and then fired. Stamps made in this way usually have designs or patterns made up of lines or depressions carved, scratched, or dug into the clay; when the stamp is used, these depressions produce raised or relief textures.

Ordinary tools and objects are often surprisingly effective as stamps. Files, rasps, nail or screw heads, the threads of large screws or bolts, bits of wood or bark, stones and pebbles, shells—all these and innumerable other easily obtained objects may be used. With them, patterns of great precision and regularity, or textures of a free and wayward sort, may be quickly built up. All types of stamps, both those made for the purpose and those which are found, work best when the clay is stiffened but not dried quite to the leather-hard stage. The stamp will leave an impression of great sharpness if the clay is just right, and if the clay is not too soft, it will not stick to the tool or the stamp. Sprigs are additions made onto the surface of the damp clay. These may be modeled or formed in molds, or formed with the aid of stamps. The effect is that of low relief. Perhaps the best known examples of the sprig technique are the decorative wares of Wedgwood, which often incorporate elaborately molded sprigs in white clay on a body of blue clay. In this case the sprigs, almost paper thin in places, were formed by pressing in shallow molds, then lifted out and carefully luted onto the body of the vase. Sprigs need not be delicate; they can be thick, freely modeled or stamped, and of more or less irregular shape.

If pots are built of slabs rather than thrown, some interesting textural possibilities are opened up. The slabs may be rolled or beaten with tools which impart texture before the pot is assembled. Or the slabs may be formed by rolling out clay onto textured surfaces—such as fabric, string or cord laid out in random or regular pattern, on carved plaster surfaces, or on surfaces of dried or fired clay which have been previously given some texture.

Stamps, combs, beaters, and other tools used to give an impressed design or texture all result in surfaces of some precision. This precise or regular quality usually results from the repetition of a motif of some sort—even a very freely contrived stamp which in itself has no symmetry or precision of design will, when repeated, give a controlled pattern. For completely free texture, the pot may be attacked directly with various tools to give a carved, scratched, striated, or roughened surface. Very spontaneous and rapidly done patterns may be made on the walls of a pot while it is still soft, or while it is still turning slowly on the potter's wheel. In the leather-hard stage the pot may be shaved, giving the effect of planes, or cut, scratched, or carved. Carving in leather-hard clay with a sharp tool leaves impressions of great crispness and clarity. Whereas textures done on the soft clay are easy, fluid, and rapidly done, textures imparted to the completely dried clay are apt to be rather harsh, crumbly, and dry. But there are possibilities in carving or scratching the dry pot too—a certain eroded, rough, and earthy surface can be achieved that is especially effective if a very groggy clay is used.

The textural potential of clay is very great, and the problem may be more one of holding to a certain restraint in the use of texture and pattern than it is of searching for methods of elaborating the surface. The softness and impressionability of the clay make it a telltale medium, one which reveals accurately the skill and sureness of intention of the potter. Also revealed is his sense of the fitness of things, and his ability to express the wholeness, health, and unity of the pot. The management of surface is perhaps the most difficult part of such an expression.

All sorts of surface variations on the walls of pots are amplified and often enhanced by the effect of glaze. Glazes will run and pool and settle into low spots, so that a scratch in the clay which is barely visible in the raw can become quite prominent when glazed. Usually a glaze which is semiopaque and rather thinly applied is the most flattering to surface texture; if the glaze is too thick it will, of course, minimize or obscure the texture.

4. Engobe treatments

Engobe or slip treatments of all sorts seem right for stoneware. The colors and textures of body, slips and glazes in stoneware can be made to melt together, to fuse and mingle so as to be almost indistinguishable from one another and to function together to create surfaces which are all of a piece with the clay and the form. In high firing, the uneven and sometimes accidental effects of the fire such as flashing, burning dark where coatings are thin, the roll or movement of glaze, the boiling through of granular impurities, or the subtle changes of color from one side of a piece to the other as a result of the way the fire impinged on it—all these serve to give an interest and a look of naturalness or inevitability to slips as well as to glazes. And for an additional repertoire of surface change, slips may be used in various ways with impressed or low relief textures in the clay.

The simplest engobe treatment is the covering of all or most of a pot with some slip, the glaze appearing over it and gaining its color chiefly from the slip. For example, a leather-hard pot may be dipped in slip, either immersed entirely or partially covered, and if the slip is adjusted to the right thickness, and the pot is neither too damp nor too dry, a very even and smooth coating of slip may be achieved. Slip may also be sprayed onto the pot, but with this method it is more difficult to achieve a perfectly smooth and even application. An over-all engobe treatment has the effect of changing the color of the body of the pot, so that if a pot is covered with white engobe and then given a clear glaze, the result is a white piece.

A very direct approach to slip decorating is the application of slips to the wet pot immediately after throwing. For this, a slip of high shrinkage is required. The clay body itself, colored with oxides, may be used. The slip should be very thick, and is applied with a bulb or with broad brushes. An old shaving brush works very well, or homemade brushes made from broom straw. The rough, free slip decoration on the old Korean pottery known as "Hakeme" was applied with some such coarse brush. Slip may be applied to the slowly turning pot to form bands or striations, or different colored slips may be flooded inside open forms, such as bowls or plates, to form more or less fortuitous patterns. Very broad effects are most suitable for slip work on damp pots, and the brush marks are apt to show prominently.

Pots which are to be dipped in slip or are to have slip poured over them should be leather-hard, or even approaching dryness. The slip has to be exactly the right consistency, or it will either build up on the piece too thickly or will be too thin for dipping and pouring. It is best to have a generous amount of slip on hand—a large panful or a tub of slip will enable rapid and easy application. If enough slip is on hand, the ware may be lowered into it up to the desired point and then quickly withdrawn. Or the piece may be dipped in at an angle, or panels of slip may be formed by lowering the pot in at different angles. Or the piece may be dipped in several times to form overlapping panels or areas. All these ways of dipping have the possibility of emphasizing or accentuating the form of the pot. For pouring slip, a pitcher with a broad spout is needed. As in the case of dipping, the consistency of the slip must be carefully adjusted to achieve the right thickness. The slip may be poured onto the pot in more or less regular panels or areas, or it may be quickly flooded on and made to cascade in irregular curtains, runs, or drips, down the walls of the pot. Combinations of dipping and pouring, and the use of two or more colors of slip can result in fantastically rich variations of color, especially when a glaze is used which adds its own variations of color and texture. In both dipping and pouring, the tendency of the slip to follow the form of the piece can be capitalized on. Pouring techniques can be used to give a fluid, spontaneous, and casual feeling to the pot. But the distinction between true spontaneity, verve, daring, and love of the natural and easy effect, and mere sloppiness is sometimes a fine one. It will usually be found that the "freest" surface is the product of a hand well in command of the situation.

Sgraffito is a technique of carving or scratching through a slip coating, thus revealing the clay beneath. It is best carried out on the leather-hard piece which has been evenly dipped in slip. Various tools may be used, such as knives, nails, dentist's tools, or a nut pick—any sharp, pointed tool. If the clay is still damp, the tool glides easily over the surface, biting more or less deeply into the body and producing lines of varying widths. It is best not to make the lines too deep or too narrow, as this may prevent the glaze from covering properly. The sgraffito line has a quality of its own. It is like drawing and like engraving or etching, but it has a peculiarly free character, and the ease with which lines of different depths and thicknesses may be made, and the change of thickness as lines change direction, may give it the look of having been rapidly done. Linear patterns or textures in sgraffito may be varied or alternated with areas in which the slip is cut away to reveal broad areas of clay body. Or different colored slips may be used, combining the effects of dipping and pouring with sgraffito lines.

Normally, a more or less transparent glaze is used over sgraffito, one which will clearly reveal the scratched lines and the dark color of the body. In stoneware, sgraffito is usually done through a light slip into a darker body, but the scheme can be reversed, and a dark slip used over a light body. The glaze, while transparent, can be colored, and this may give a mysterious depth to the line as it is seen beneath a more or less thick layer or pool of colored glaze. As in most ceramic processes, effects can be multiplied almost endlessly, and one process combined with another until extraordinarily complex surfaces result. For example, in a single pot one might combine various engobe techniques, such as dipped or poured panels of colored slip which are treated with both brushwork and sgraffito.

Brush designs in slip call for considerable skill, or at least considerable nerve. For brushing, the slip needs to be quite thick and heavy, almost pudding-like in consistency. Fat brushes work well, and anything from small sable brushes to shaving brushes or even whisk brooms, will give characteristic and perhaps useful kinds of brush strokes in slip. Brush strokes are best laid on with rapidity and sureness, and it is best not to go over the strokes a second time. The thin places where the bristles of the brush drag through the slip usually show up quite prominently when glazed, and reveal the pace and direction of the stroke. In brushing slip, it is wise to accommodate oneself to the character of stroke peculiar to any one brush, and not to fight the brush and try to make it do things it does not want to do. To brush on the slip confidently requires a relaxed state of readiness which is not easy to achieve, especially if one feels that there is danger of wrecking a piece which cost considerable effort to make. The best slip work is apt to occur on work which the potter regards as expendable. In the old days when pottery was more of a group effort, the man who did the decoration was seldom the same as the one who made the pots, and he could feel casual about them. This fact alone may go far toward explaining the wonderful freedom in the decorations on some of the old Korean and Japanese pots.

Slip trailing and the use of the slip bulb is almost an art in itself, and effects can be achieved by this technique which are more or less unique to pottery. The slip-trailed line is not only linear, it also has dimension and may give almost the effect of low relief. Moreover, it can readily be controlled as to thickness of line and may be used to give hatchings, dots, parallel lines, sinuous, freely swinging lines, or blobs and blots. Slip trailing may be done with a variety of tools.

The easiest to come by is a rubber syringe, such as is sold for medical use. An ear syringe is about the right size. Slip is sucked up into it, and the line is made by drawing the nose of the syringe across the clay surface and at the same time squeezing the bulb slightly to give just the right flow of slip. Bulbs with smaller openings may be made by inserting a short length of glass tube in the end of the syringe. The glass can be drawn out to any fineness of opening by heating over a Bunsen burner. Or, instead of glass, goose or turkey quills may be used. In the past, quills were always used for slip work. The membrane inside the dried quill must be poked out first, then the quill is cut to proper length and inserted in the rubber bulb. Quills make excellent trailers, but they do wear out rather rapidly. This is no great disadvantage, however, since they are easy to obtain.

While the bulb works well for trailing slip, it does have a tendency to spit out too much slip at times, and, if not skillfully managed, to give a somewhat uneven or unsure line. The gravity type of trailer requires a little more practice to use, but is perhaps better. A small cup is made of clay, of a size convenient to hold in the hand. It is open at the top, and on the side, toward the bottom, it has a small opening for the quill. It is fired and glazed. A cork is inserted in the lower opening, and the quill is slipped into a small hole in the cork. The little vessel is filled with slip. To trail a line it is merely tilted a bit until the slip flows out of the quill. A variation of this trailer is one which has a fairly narrow opening at the top which can be covered with the thumb. To stop the flow of slip the thumb is placed over this hole. Or, tandem trailers may be made by having two quills spaced at any desired distance apart—this device permits the trailing of two perfectly parallel lines at once. Two or more colors can be trailed at once by having separate compartments for each color, each having its own quill and all arranged side by side. Trailers of the gravity type can be modeled by hand and made to fit nicely into the particular sized hand of the potter.

The slip trailer produces a very fluid and sinuous line. Although lines can be made rapidly, controlling them is rather difficult and requires considerable practice. The slip has a way of flowing from the bulb when it is not wanted, and of refusing to flow when it is. The slip must be absolutely free of lumps and of exactly the right consistency to work well. Trailing is easier on flat forms, such as plates, and much more difficult on the walls of upright pots. Since slip trailing produces a line of considerable body which stands out from the surface, sometimes the lines have a tendency to loosen and to fall off when dry. This can be prevented by using a slip of the right shrinkage, and applying it to ware which is in just the right stage of dryness. A slip with a fairly low shrinkage, applied to the body when it is a little dryer than leather-hard usually adheres well.

Slip combing is a technique closely related to slip trailing. It is familiar in examples of old Staffordshire slip ware and in some Pennsylvania Dutch wares. The general effect of slip combing is of bands of slip which are crossed and penetrated by lines, causing a wavering, over-all pattern, not unlike the patterns sometimes seen inside the covers of old books. If one did not know how such combing was done, one would be mystified at its minutely perfect pattern. Slip combing is usually carried out on damp slabs of plastic clay which are later pressed over molds to form plates, bowls, or platters. Or, the jigger mold may be used to form the piece. The success of the method depends on applying the decoration to clay which is in a very soft, plastic condition. The clay is rolled out on a slab of plaster or on a worktable which has been lightly dusted with grog. A slab roughly the shape of the intended piece, but somewhat larger, is cut out. Then thick bands

of slip are laid across the slab with a bulb or a trailer. The slip must be quite fluid and is put on so that each band is adjacent to the next, with no clay showing between. To get fairly even bands of slip of different or alternating colors, all touching, all fluid, and not slopping over into one another takes a good deal of skill with the bulb. As soon as the slip is laid on, and before it has had the slightest chance to dry or stiffen, a point such as a pin or an awl is gingerly drawn across the bands, dragging the slip from one band slightly into the next. The point may be drawn through in regular intervals, or in irregular spacing, and the direction may be alternated if desired. The end of a feather is sometimes used rather than a point. The decorated slab is allowed to dry for an hour or two, or until the various slips are no longer fluid. Then it is turned over and pressed onto the plaster or clay mold, decorated side down. Whatever relief or bumpiness exists in the decorated design is thus pressed flat. The "points and brackets" of slip combing, while very intriguing in themselves, are always much the same in general character, and the method, while interesting, certainly has its limitations. However, combinations of combing with other freer methods of application have great possibilities which have hardly been explored as yet. Slip combing has been associated traditionally with earthenwares, but actually the technique produces very beautiful surfaces in stoneware material and firing, and there is no reason why combing, as well as other slip techniques, should not be fully exploited in high-temperature ware.

Inlaid slip, sometimes known by the Japanese term *mishima*, is achieved by cutting or scratching a pattern into the surface clay, then inlaying the lines with slip and scraping away the excess to leave a more or less precise linear pattern. The method was used with great effect by the old Korean potters; in fact, Korean wares seem to be the first historical examples

179

of slip inlays. The process is an essentially simple one. A pattern is scratched into the clay, either in the leather-hard state or when dry. For very precise or for regular lines and patterns a smooth clay should be used, but if rougher lines are acceptable, a clay with considerable grog works as well. The scratches or lines need not be deep. When a suitable network of lines has been developed on the pot, slip is freely worked into the lines with a coarse brush. Then, using a scraping tool, or flexible steel rib, the excess clay is scraped off the surface leaving the slip-filled lines standing distinct in the body. Two or more colors of slip may be used, or a pattern may be made in one color, scraped down, and accents or an amplification of the pattern may be added in another color. Lines may vary in width, and dots, patches, or areas used in addition to lines.

Inlaid slip has a somewhat dry character, compared to most other slip techniques, but it need not be geometrical or precise. The advantage of inlay is in the rather careful control which is possible—lines may be placed with deliberation, and the wall of a pot built up with linear accents and direction in an almost architectural way. Furthermore, inlays can be used for building up textures of great depth and complexity.

Resist techniques offer still another way of decorating with slip. Patterns or shapes may be cut out of paper and stuck to the leather-hard pot with water, and the slip poured or dipped on. The wet paper is then pulled off, leaving a bare area of clay. Green leaves may be used the same way for naturalistic profiles. String or twine can be wrapped around the pot, and then the slip poured on. When the string is pulled off, a swirling pattern of line is left. Or resist patterns may be carried out in wax or wax emulsion. The use of wax for resist is described more fully in the next section.

A simple palette of colors is all that one needs for colorful work in stoneware, and slip colors seem more natural and right if an earthy range of color is adhered to rather than too many cool colors. A good white, a rich black, gray, brown, ocher, and perhaps a textured gray-blue are enough, especially when all these slip colors can be varied by the use of different covering glazes.

5. Resist techniques

Resists may be used with either slips or glazes. The technique is based on the fact that any watery medium, such as a glaze or a slip, is repelled by a waxy surface. Thus, when part of a surface is covered with wax, glaze will not adhere to it but will run off, leaving the waxed surface clean of glaze. Wax, being an organic substance, burns off in the fire, leaving no trace on the finished piece.

Resist may be done with beeswax or paraffin. The wax is heated sufficiently to melt it to a liquid and then applied to the pot by dipping or brushing. The foot of the pot may be dipped in wax, which prevents the glaze from sticking to it and makes it unnecessary to clean glaze from the foot before the piece is set in the kiln. Or any other part of the pot which is intended to be free of glaze can first be coated with wax. For brushing, the pure wax may be somewhat too stiff, and a mixture of wax and turpentine makes for a better consistency. (Wax, especially when mixed with turpentine is flammable and care must be used in heating it.) Brush strokes made with wax are rather hard to control, and the method works best either for very precise areas which can be carefully built up with wax, using a small brush, or for very bold brush strokes which are somewhat shaggy.

Pots which have been treated with wax for resist patterns should be glazed by dipping. Spraying does not work well, because droplets of glaze light on the waxed areas and must be laboriously cleaned off. But when the ware is dipped, the glaze will run freely off the waxed portion. If it does not, the wax coat has been put on too thinly. The virtue of wax resist is that it enables the potter to reserve clean bare clay body wherever he wishes on the pot, and if the relationship between the color and the texture of the body and the glaze is right, beautiful contrasts may be achieved.

Wax emulsions may be used, rather than the pure wax or paraffin. Wax emulsions contain water, and are therefore thin and fluid and require no heating before use. They brush on much more easily than wax, but must be allowed to dry before the glazing is done. When an emulsion is used, there is more likelihood of getting a coat of wax which is too thin to shed the glaze properly. But in general, the emulsions have proved to be superior to pure wax for most resist processes. The use of emulsions enables the sweeping and rapid use of the brush to achieve patterns of great energy and spontaneity. A favorite technique in recent years has been to brush a pattern on the raw, dried pot with a wax emulsion, using a large brush. The pot is then placed on the banding wheel, and a thin slip of Barnard clay is brushed over the whole pot—except for the waxed areas, which repel the slip. Only a thin coating of Barnard is required. The piece is then bisque-fired, glazed with a magnesia glaze, and fired in reduction. The parts which were covered with the Barnard slip will be a rich reddish-brown or black, depending on the thickness of the slip, and the parts which were waxed will be gray or textured gray, depending on the amount of iron or speck-producing materials in the clay body. If the application of wax has been sure and masterful, the contrast between the two colors may be very dramatic.

Wax may be used not only to reveal the bare clay, or to control the areas of slip or engobe, but it may also be used between coats of glaze to make patterns or color changes. For example, a pot may be dipped in one glaze for an all-over coat, then certain parts of the piece may be dipped or brushed with wax, and the whole glazed with another color. The waxed parts will then appear as a distinct area of a different color. There are many variations of this procedure. Three or more coats of thin glaze may be applied, with wax-resist areas added between each coat, giving patterns as complex as a patchwork quilt. Or a pot may be glazed, given a brush or scratch pattern which is then covered with a patch or panel of wax. When the pot is then dipped in another glaze, the brush pattern may appear on an area or panel of a color different than that of the rest of the pot.

Another medium which is sometimes used for resist processes is liquid latex. This material can be brushed on in much the same fashion as wax or wax emulsion, and has the advantage that it can be pulled or rubbed off like rubber cement. Thus a pattern can be made in latex rubber, the piece glazed, and then the latex removed and another area painted in. It will be seen that the use of latex enables the production of freely overlapping effects. If the latex is to be pulled off a coating of raw glaze, however, it may be necessary to use glazes which contain some gum so that they dry in a very tough coat.

The success of all resist processes depends not only on the skill and feeling with which the patterns are done but also equally important, on the color and texture relationships between the clay and the glaze or between the various colors which are used. The danger is a jumpy, uneven surface having violent contrasts of color or value which destroy or work against the form of the piece. If properly used, it is just these contrasts which can be made to contribute to the full expression of the character of the materials in stoneware—the rough against the smooth, the warm against the cool, clay against glaze, and color against color.

6. Underglaze and overglaze processes

Even if no textural variations were possible in the surface of pottery, and if engobe techniques were ruled out, the possibilities in underglaze treatments and in the management of the glaze itself offer such riches that no potter would feel seriously deprived of ways of carrying out his creative ideas.

Underglaze painting is usually associated with earthenware, but there seems little reason for this, since the method has been beautifully used on stoneware. It is true that the available palette of underglaze colors is considerably lessened at the higher temperatures, but a wealth of color is possible nonetheless.

Rather than the prepared commercial underglaze stains the coloring oxides, such as iron oxide, copper oxide, or manganese dioxide may be brushed directly on the bisqued pot, using only a little water for a medium, and the glaze applied over the painting. Or mixtures such as iron and granular manganese may be used to give a textured color. Effects are limited only by the imagination of the potter, for many colors and textures are possible, depending on the selection of pigments and glazes and on the manner of firing. Some of the most dramatic pots made by Sam Haile, the English stoneware potter, were decorated by a few broad and masterful strokes of an impure oxide of iron, which, under a simple semiopaque gray glaze, became a miraculously rich and mysterious red-brown, infused with subtle variations.

If the underglaze painting is to serve as an important feature of the pot, it may be carried out over panels of white slip or over a surface, say of a plate or bowl, which is completely covered with a light-colored engobe. Or linear patterns may be made in sgraffito in the slip and then color washed on with underglaze pigments before glazing. The stoneware potter who is interested in underglaze painting should test various commercial underglaze colors at his firing temperature and under various glazes. Some of the colors may not turn out in the high fire anything like the shade intended by the color manufacturer, but they may be very beautiful nevertheless. Some colors, of course, are fugitive above about cone 7 and may disappear entirely in high fire. No elaborate mediums or oils are ordinarily necessary for underglaze painting —the colors may be brushed on with water in a manner very similar to watercolor technique. The potter with painterly inclinations will wish to explore the possibilities in combining various slips and glazes with underglaze colors. In spite of the fact that all the basic techniques of painting on pottery have been known and used for over a thousand years, so many nuances of color and texture are possible that each potter can discover technical resources which seem to have been designed for him.

Glazing should not be thought of as a process which merely gives the pot an over-all, uniform coating of glaze, although it may be that, among other things. The application of the glaze, the use of one glaze over another, the control over the thickness of the glaze, and the color accents which can be applied over the glaze; all of these constitute a family of effects quite distinct from other kinds of pottery decoration. The actual procedure of glazing is not only fraught with hazards such as getting the glaze on too thick or too thin, or of producing a confused, sloppy, and uneven surface, but also has the possibility of greatly enhancing the pot through changes of thickness and hence of color, and through the right relationships between glazed areas and between the glaze and the exposed clay body. In most cases the best way to glaze pots is by dipping. This method is fast, economical of glaze, and makes possible many "events" in the glaze which would never occur if the glaze is

182

sprayed. For rapid glazing, and to make the most of glazing as a part of the whole design of the pot, ample quantities of glaze must be provided. For small pieces a gallon of glaze may be sufficient, but for larger shapes, a reserve of two or three gallons is needed. The glaze may be kept in covered enamel pails or in wooden buckets with wooden lids. While it is quite expensive to make up some glazes in large quantity, this does not affect the total cost of making pottery if a limited number of glazes are used—and it is always advisable to limit the number of glazes in use at any one time.

To glaze a stoneware pot, the glaze slip must first be adjusted as to water content so that a properly thick coating will build up on the bisque. (Bisque firing should always be at the same temperature so that the ware will always be of the same absorbency for glazing.) A small shard of broken bisque can be dipped into the tub of glaze as a test for thickness. The glaze is kept thoroughly stirred with a paddle, and the pot is quickly lowered into the glaze, pulled out, given a shake, and allowed to drain. In the case of bowls with feet, the piece is held by the foot as it is dipped, and the inside of the pot may be glazed by giving the pot a quick jerk when it is in the glaze, thus splashing the glaze up into the inside. Or by using a pitcher, the inside of pieces may be poured full of glaze, then immediately dumped out, and the outside quickly glazed by dipping. When a bowl is lowered into the glaze, the amount of bare clay which is left at the foot will have an important effect on the proportion and the character of the piece.

For contrasts of double and single thickness of glaze, the piece may be dipped into the glaze several times at different angles, or the glaze may be poured onto the piece with a pitcher in overlapping cascades. Some glazes differ a great deal, depending on their thickness, and may be either white, gray, or brown over the body when applied thick, medium, or thin. Another possibility with poured glaze is the use of freely flowing streams, stripes, curtains, or drips of glaze. When glazes are allowed to run rather freely in this way, the effect may be one of great spontaneity and gusto. On the other hand, poured glaze can easily result in surfaces which are merely sloppy and uncontrolled, and which actually detract from the pot rather than add to its effectiveness. To glaze pots beautifully, the potter must first train himself in the techniques required for even, flawless coatings of controlled thickness and area. This requires considerable skill. Once he has the process well under control, his more spontaneous glazing will have a fitness for the pot which is utterly beyond the reach of the clumsy. Another inescapable requirement for successful glazing is experience with the fired effects of the particular glazes which are being used. One must build up some experience with the glaze as to its optimum thicknesses, effects of overlap, and relationship of glaze to body color before one can glaze with any understanding of the probable actual finished appearance of the work. Of course, one can glaze pots without knowing exactly what the results will be and can discover exciting things that way, but if one is entirely at the mercy of accident, whatever good results will be purely fortuitous.

Aside from the accents which originate in the actual glazing process itself, the surface may be enriched by the use of one glaze over another, either as an overspray or an underspray, by dipping one glaze on top of another, or by trailing, or brushing one glaze over another. All of these methods depend on the selection of the right glazes for the intended results, and on the use of judgment as to the thicknesses of the various coatings. Sprayed effects are very easy to do, but they are all too likely to have an airbrush look reminiscent of the cheapest sort of commercial artwares. For an underspray, a layer or veil of one color glaze is sprayed on all or part of the piece, then the glazing is done in the usual manner with another color. In the fire, the two colors mingle, and may give broken or textured colors as a result. Oversprays are done in a similar manner; the glazed piece is sprayed in certain parts with a different color glaze, giving a change of color and texture, perhaps on rims or edges.

When one glaze is dipped on over another (this process sometimes results in very unusual colors and textures), it is best if the first coating is quite thin. If the first coating is heavy, any subsequent glazing by dipping is apt to result in the loosening and cracking of the glaze coat. A pot may be only partially covered in the first color, on the rim for example, or on the inside only, and then glazed in the second color. By using double glazing, a few glazes can be made to yield a great many different colors; if, in addition, some of the bisque is wholly or partially coated with slip, the possible effects are still further multiplied.

Glazes as well as slips may be applied with the bulb or slip trailer. One possibility is to trail a design in glaze, for example, a very dark glaze such as black or brown, directly on the bisqued pot, and then to glaze the piece all over in the usual way. The trailed design will bleed through in the fire, giving a linear effect of more or less definition, depending on the fusion characteristics of the glazes used. Or the pot may be glazed all over with a gray or colored glaze, and a pattern trailed on top of this in some contrasting color. Designs done in this way often fuse together when the glaze melts, giving slightly out-of-focus edges which can enhance the effectiveness of whatever motif is used.

It is very difficult to do brushed patterns in glazes, majolica style, and it is hard to see any reason for treating pots this way since there are so many other possibilities less dependent on the va-

garies of the material. To brush glaze on glaze successfully, it is necessary to make the cover or over-all glaze somewhat nonabsorbent; otherwise the dry, dusty, fragile surface grabs the juice out of the brush and makes any sort of flowing line or brush stroke impossible. Of course, one can make the best of it and build up patterns in dots or small dabs. But for work which has the character of the brush, the surface must be coated over with a glue solution, or the glaze must be compounded in the first place with some sort of gum to make smoother sledding for the brush. Brushwork very similar to majolica can be done by painting on the surface of a glazed pot with underglaze colors which have simply been diluted with water and a small amount of glaze. Such a mixture may be very thin and fluid, yet of sufficient tinting strength to give a strong color; in fact, the danger is always the likelihood that the brushwork will be too much in contrast to the color of the glaze and that it will tend to jump off the pot. Still another method of doing brushwork over the glaze is to use soluble metallic salts. Iron chloride, copper sulfate, and the like are liquids no different than water in brushing consistency, yet they yield the color which one could expect from the elements present in them. The difficulty is that it is hard to know how much soluble salt to brush on; after firing one may be surprised to find no brushwork appearing on the pots; on the other hand (and usually worse!), the brushwork may be much too dark and prominent. One way around this is to tint the soluble salts with vegetable dyes which burn out in the fire and do not affect the color but which darken the salts and make them more prominent in the raw state, thus making each brush stroke more apparent as it is put on.

An interesting method of decorating in the glaze is the pin scratch. The pot is glazed in the usual way; then the design is scratched through the glaze with a sharp point. The kind of glaze used is all-important in this technique. In the raw, the glaze must have enough clay in it to be fairly tough and thus not flake away or crumble when the point is drawn through it. When fired, the glaze should hold its position without running, but if the glaze is too dry and is even slightly susceptible to crawling, this defect will be accentuated by the lines of the scratched design. A light glaze over a dark body is usually used, but the reverse color scheme works as well. Volatilization of the melting glaze at stoneware temperatures will usually cause the scratched lines to become thinly glazed. In pin scratching through the glaze, the lines must not be too close together or the glaze will tend to flake off between, and the places where lines cross or join must be rather carefully done to prevent flaking. Pin scratching is at its best in a style reminiscent of etching, where the line is incisive yet free. It is no medium for the timid, because no changes can be made in the design as it develops. For an effect that may resemble a drawing tinted with water color, pin scratches may be used as accentuating lines for patterns brushed in with soluble salts.

7. Unglazed surfaces

Most of the decorative processes described so far involve the use of glaze, but there is a whole galaxy of color and surface quality which can be achieved without using glaze. Of course, glazes are not only handsome but highly practical as well, and glazed surfaces are a necessity for any pottery which is to be used in the kitchen or on the table. To abandon glazes entirely would be to turn back the clock on ceramic history. But at the same time, it is true that many pots, from a utilitarian point of view, do not need a glaze, especially on the outside, and that unglazed surfaces can be just as beautiful, and for certain pots just as useful, as those which are glazed. And in stoneware especially, where the color of the clay body and of unglazed slips and coatings may be extremely beautiful in itself, it is certainly not always necessary to completely cover up the pot with glaze.

If less reliance than usual is to be put on glazes, the clay bodies in use should be beautiful in color and texture. This does not mean that the body needs to be very dark or spotty, but it should be a color for which the potter, if no one else, feels sympathetic. If this is the case, pots which are textured by the processes of making, or by the use of tools, sprigs, stamps, or by the fingers, may be handsome if well fired without any glaze, or with glaze on the inside only. Stoneware bodies, especially dark ones, can be given a slight patina by rubbing them with a mixture of china clay and flint or by making a slip of china clay and flint, painting the clay with this, and then removing most of it with a sponge. The effect of this is not unlike the color which is frequently seen on the walls and the shelves of kilns which have been washed with kiln wash.

In a previous section, methods of making dry glazes and earthy slip coatings have been given. Many ways of using such slips will occur to the potter—brushings, scratching, trailing, scumbling one coat over another, dipping on patches or areas, spattering or splashing, banding, sgraffito patterns, rubbing through one coat into another, inlays, and resists. These various methods of handling unglazed pots, especially when enhanced by the natural events of the fire such as flashing and uneven burning, make the possibilities for claylike surfaces very great.

The almost unlimited opportunity in stoneware for surface complexity and involvement creates a problem for the potter. Which of these tempting processes is the one to follow? How can they all be mastered so the work can flow smoothly, naturally, and with a minimum of failures and ineptitudes? How can the potter avoid becoming so obsessed with the surfaces of his pots that the forms, perhaps the very meaning of the pots, is lost in decoration? The fact is that pottery surfaces are so various and temperamental, and the possible colors and textures and forms are so numerous, that many potters become lost in a wilderness of materials and techniques and never succeed in making any statement of clarity. Any contemporary pottery exhibit reveals the seemingly passionate preoccupation of potters with decorative process, with glazes, with slips, with "effects," and although many of these decorations are carried out with skill, too few have a look of inevitability or suitability for the pot.

It is obvious that no potter can practice all the methods of slipping and glazing and coloring simultaneously. Of the many possible technical approaches to the art, he must select only a few, and try to develop these to his utmost capacity. Actually, the simplest techniques, if fully understood and used, can serve as the vehicle for mature, even profound expressions. The history of ceramics proves that, if it proves nothing else. The ceramic art of the past also demonstrates that the most involved and skillful techniques will be of no avail and will succeed only in producing pretentious, false, and empty work if the intelligence and drive behind the work is pretentious, false, or empty. Having selected an approach to the method of making and finishing his pots, the potter should stick to this with perseverance until he begins to feel at home with his techniques and feels that he is using various processes, not for themselves or out of curiosity, but because he feels that they are inseparable from the meaning and scope of his work.

Most contemporary pottery is overdecorated. Most of it displays a tendency toward too many techniques of surface employed on one pot, and fails in making a coherent, unified statement. Surface accents and qualities should grow naturally and surely on the pots, like the ripening skin of an apple.

Chapter 11

Porcelain–Forms and Surfaces

Much that has been said of the forms and surfaces of stoneware applies equally to porcelain. In this chapter, the points of difference will be stressed, as well as those qualities of form and glaze which are peculiarly suitable to porcelain.

1. Thrown porcelain forms

The range of forms which can be achieved in porcelain by plastic shaping is rather severely limited by the non-plastic character of porcelain bodies. Yet within that range, pottery of a sensitive beauty of shape can be made. As described in an earlier section, the preparation of porcelain bodies must be done with a great deal of care. And especially if the body is to be used on the wheel, it must be carefully aged and wedged.

The potter who is throwing with a porcelain clay must be reconciled to the fact that only forms of modest size can be made on the wheel. It is extremely difficult to pull up any cylinder higher than about 8 inches. It may be wondered how the large porcelain jars originating in China during Ming times were made. The clay from which they were made was, no doubt, unusually plastic, perhaps better for wheel work than any porcelain body available to us. The jars were made in parts, and probably a combination of coiling and throwing was used. However, much as we may admire the skill which went into the making of these monumental porcelain pots, they do seem out of scale for the material

used, and porcelain by its nature is more suitable for small forms. It is refined, smooth, dense, transparent, and glasslike, and its semiprecious feel is not very adaptable to great size.

Not only is the size of porcelain pieces limited by the material, but the shapes are also limited by both the lack of plasticity in the clay and by the inability of the clay to withstand beyond a certain point the tendency toward slumping and deformation when it is softened by the maturing fire. Porcelain must adhere to a rather strict architecture of form to survive the process which makes it what it is. Porcelain bowls or plates cannot be thrown with extreme overhangs. Pieces with widely swelling bellies are difficult to make, and the clay cannot be collared in easily to form very narrow necks on wide bottle shapes. The clay resists all of these maneuvers on the wheel by slumping down into a heap. For this reason, the free, and sometimes exaggerated shapes of stoneware, are not for porcelain. But what can be made is still considerable—bowls of all sorts, jars, plates, covered pieces, closed-in bottle-like forms (on a modest scale), cylindrical forms, and functional things like pitchers or teapots. But the beauty of the forms must reside in grace, proportion, and refinement, rather than in strength, ruggedness, or extremes of conformation.

Since porcelain is difficult to throw, more is usually left to the trimming than is usual in stoneware making. Thus bowls are made with considerable clay left about the foot, and this additional thickness makes slumping less likely and permits more latitude in design. The pots may be shaved to the desired thinness when leather-hard, and the trimming may include not only the region of the foot, as is usually done in stoneware, but the whole wall of the piece. If a piece is to be finished by trimming, certain exactitudes in the whole process must be observed. For one thing, centering and throwing must be very exact, and the rim of the pot must be perfectly true. When plates and bowls are drying after throwing, they should be turned over as soon as possible on a perfectly level plaster surface to prevent warping. When the piece is trimmed it must be very accurately centered. Trimming should be done at a brisk wheel speed and with sharp tools.

As in the case of stoneware, the danger of leaving too much of the shaping to the trimming process is that the forms will appear to be stiff and carved, rather than plastic and claylike. In porcelain, this difficulty must be allowed for by carefully planning the shape while throwing, making due allowances for the changes planned during trimming, and by trimming in such a way that the grace and flow of the form is not destroyed. The inside and the outside of the piece must relate to bring about a cross section of the desired thickness and strength at points of stress. If translucent ware is desired, the walls of the piece are thinned to a sixteenth of an inch or less. Shaving down a form to this thickness is actually very hard to do without developing unequal thicknesses, chatter marks, or unwanted ridges. It is usually necessary to remove the piece from the wheel several times to check its thickness, and each time it must be carefully recentered for further trimming.

As a result of the working characteristics of the material, of the throwing and trimming process, and of the exigencies of the fire, thrown porcelain forms are usually marked by restraint and simplicity. Out of these very limitations may come a quality of directness, of control, of limited but succinct statement which may be extremely satisfying in all its aspects, visual and tactile.

Since the porcelain form is usually wrought by a process of both throwing and trimming, the typical surface quality of thrown stonewares or earthenwares, which is marked by prominent throwing ridges or finger marks, is unnatural to it. A perfectly smooth surface usually seems right, and such a surface is apt to make more prominent the subtle qualities of profile, of accent at the foot or rim, and of the quality of thickness and thinness as experienced tactilely rather than visually.

2. Cast porcelains

Casting makes possible many designs in porcelain which would be difficult or impossible to make by other methods, and it has the further advantage of enabling the easy production of very thin and consequently translucent pieces. However, for the individual potter who is interested in making one-of-a-kind pottery and is not interested in producing ware in quantity, casting may not be a feasible method of shaping. The use of molds ties one's efforts to a given set of forms, which can be changed only by the laborious addition of more molds and the discarding of old ones. This puts pottery making on an entirely different basis than the making of individual forms on the wheel or by modeling. Not only does the use of molds severely limit the number of shapes which the potter can make at any one time, it also changes radically the pattern of creative work in the shop. When pots are made by hand or on the wheel, each one is a separate individual creation and the making of each piece requires choice, judgment, planning, and critical appraisal. On the other hand, when pots are molded, the making of them becomes a matter of repetitious workmanship; and while the work may be exacting and demand skill and craftsmanship, it does not directly involve creative ability. The creative part of pottery, when molds are used, is in the preliminary planning, in the model making which establishes the form, and in the choice of colors and surfaces. While molded wares as such are in no way inferior to thrown or modeled ware (and in fact, they may be superior to badly made wheel pots), the process of designing them and the manner of work which goes into the making of them is radically different. Before embarking on a project in molded porcelain, the potter should ask himself if production with molds, and all that this involves in determining the character of the pottery and the character of the actual work of potting, fits in with his real aims and desires in ceramics. If pots are to be made primarily for sale, there are very real advantages in molded production as against handwork—the pots are uniform, rapidly produced, and can be made to sell for a lower price than strictly individual pots. All modern retailing and selling is based on standardization, and marketing one-of-a-kind objects entails a break with all the usual procedures of ordering, pricing, packaging, and selling.

For the studio potter there is the possibility of combining hand and wheel production with some molded pieces. There is also the possibility of combining molded and handmade or wheel-made parts on one piece, thus leaving open the chance to make each piece different in some way. There is no reason why pieces made on the jigger wheel cannot be finished and made individual by the addition of thrown feet, knobs, lids, or by the addition of textures and surfaces which are the product of the hand rather than the machine. The potter who wishes to work out his ideas in porcelain may decide that the use of molds, at least for part of his work, will give him a control over shape, a refinement of cross section,

and a designed and premeditated quality that he desires.

The present work is hardly the place for a detailed description of model-making and mold-making techniques, but perhaps a few words about these processes will clarify for some the nature of the effort which is necessary. All molds start with a model of some sort, a prototype of the shape to be made. In pottery, models are usually made from plaster. Clay models are very unsatisfactory because of the difficulty of giving them the necessary refinement of surface and perfect symmetry which is required. To make models of rounded forms which are symmetrical about an axis, a turning wheel or an upright lathe is used. The plaster is cast on the wheel head into a cylindrical blank, using cardboard or linoleum as a form, and the shape is quickly roughed out while the plaster is setting and is still very soft. As the plaster hardens, the form is shaved as it turns with very sharp scraping tools. Shapes of great smoothness and accuracy can be cut quite rapidly in this manner, and if one shape is not quite satisfactory for any reason, it can be discarded and another made. Considerable skill and experience is required to properly mix and cast plaster, to turn models rapidly and accurately, and to develop shapes from preliminary drawings or templates. If asymmetrical models are being made, such as free-form or sculptural shapes, the original model is usually roughed out in clay. A waste mold is made of plaster around this clay model, and the model is cast in plaster for final shaping and finishing. Plaster models may be shaped with scrapers, rasps, or sandpaper, and may be polished to a very smooth surface by rubbing with pieces of felt or with sections of horsetail reeds. Each step in the making of a model in plaster must be carried out with great care and exactitude, and clumsy or badly planned work will result in models which are uneven and full of imperfections, such as pits and roughnesses, and which are generally unsuitable for use in making molds.

The models for handles, spouts, and other appendages are usually made separately by carving them in plaster. Rounded forms, such as plates, bowls, and the like, can be made with metal templates which rotate about an axis forming the model from soft, setting plaster. Models made by the use of hand-spun templates, however, are seldom as accurate as the ones which are turned on the power wheel.

After the plaster model for a piece is finished, the mold is made. Allowance must be made in the model for the shrinkage of the clay in drying and firing, and for any expected change in the form resulting from slumping or subsidence in the fire. Pottery molds are made from plaster of Paris. The model is surfaced with soft soap, and dams of clay or plaster are made along the lines where the mold must separate. The different parts of the mold are then cast against the model and are prevented from sticking to it by the coating of soap. When the mold has set, it is taken off the model. The mold is, in effect, a negative of the pottery form to be cast. After the mold is thoroughly dry it is ready for use in casting clay pieces.

If more than one mold of a particular shape is wanted, and this is usually the case, master molds, or "molds for molds," must be made. A master mold is made by pouring plaster against each piece of the mold, thus making a negative shape of the mold. From these "blocks," more molds can be made. The various parts of the mold are keyed together with notches so they will always fit together in the same way when they are assembled for casting.

Mold and model making is a separate craft in itself, and one not easy to master. The skill which goes into plaster work is exact and painstaking, quite different from the more relaxed and easygoing craft of the potter. It is true that most pot-ters who have a high degree of feeling for, and skill with, the plastic clay make very poor mold makers. The opposite is also true—few good mold makers are capable of the offhand intuitive kind of craftsmanship indispensable for the best work in clay.

Although the process of casting clay pots in molds is an essentially simple one, it is not without its difficulties, especially if the relatively nonplastic porcelain slips are being used. The clay, deflocculated and made into a smoothly flowing slip containing about 40% of water, is poured into the plaster mold, filling the cavity. The absorbent surface of the mold immediately begins to draw water out of the slip, and a layer of clay particles builds up on the mold and forms the wall of the pot. When this wall has built up to sufficient thickness, the clay slip is emptied from the mold, leaving the hollow piece inside. When the piece has dried enough to be able to stand by itself, the mold is removed from it. The process of casting may take anywhere from about eight minutes up to half an hour, depending on the condition of the mold and on the size and thickness of the piece being cast. When only one surface of the piece is molded, the process is called hollow casting, or drain casting; if both the inside and the outside surfaces of the piece are controlled by the mold, it is called solid casting. Solid casting is limited to the making of open pieces, such as trays, platters, and the like, where the mold can be made to part from the piece on both sides.

In casting porcelain, trouble may be expected from the tendency of the clay piece to cast too fast and to crack from shrinkage before it can be taken from the mold. This is particularly true of clay bodies which are short and contain little or no ball clay. Difficulty may also be encountered in trimming off the spare or extra part at the mouth of the mold, without making a ragged and torn edge. Sometimes the trimming is left until the piece is bone-dry, and sandpaper is used for finishing. After the molds have been broken in by casting a few dozen pieces, and the slip is perfectly adjusted as to water content and plasticity, no great difficulty should be encountered in casting porcelain.

The cast green ware is very fragile, and in some cases it may be better to leave the final finishing of the piece until after it has been bisque-fired. If the bisque fire is not too high in temperature and the ware is soft, the piece may be scraped and sanded to remove the marks where the mold parted, and to finish edges, spouts, and the joints where handles were put on. If perfectly finished ware is the objective, this finishing may be a rather time-consuming process, but if it is not done well, the porcelain will have a rather shabby look, no matter how fine its substance and glaze. Mold seams will require especially careful finishing if they are not to show up under the glaze. In porcelain the glaze has a way of revealing rather than concealing any flaws in the finish of the piece.

Porcelain cast in molds may assume a tremendous variety of shape, and except for the limitations of the parting of the molds, and of the ability of the shape to stand up during the softening which occurs during the height of the fire, almost any form can be made. This freedom has resulted in the design of many monstrosities in porcelain, but it also creates an opportunity for the potter to seek out forms which, while they are beyond the reach of the potter's wheel, are nevertheless expressive of the materials, of the nature of pottery functions and meanings, and of his own sculptural insight.

It is difficult to make any generalization as to what forms are most suitable for porcelain, but an assessment of the virtues (and defects) of the material may give some broad indications. For one thing, porcelain *looks* more fragile than either earthenware or stoneware, even though it may not be so in fact. This

being the case, forms which have thin projections and other extremes of shape, may be less suitable than those of a more compact sort. Of course, there are many examples of pottery which were intended by their makers to look fragile and which derive part of their value from this—bowls or plates made in imitation of woven baskets, for example. On the other hand, since one of the unique features of porcelain is its translucency, most porcelain designs have contrived to exhibit this quality in some way—by thin cross section or through parts of the design which are drawn out to thinness. Translucency inevitably means fragility.

Porcelain is valued most for the substance itself, although the substance must be given suitable form. For this reason the most successful porcelains seem to be rather modest both in form and in any surface interest which might detract from the beauty of the body and the glaze. Here is perhaps the key to appropriate porcelain forms—a reliance on subtlety rather than on overstatement or flamboyance, a quietness or dignity rather than extremes of contrast, and a finely drawn rather than a casual shape.

3. Porcelain textures and surfaces

Most of the textural and surface treatments described in the section dealing with stoneware surfaces can be carried out in porcelain. The clay may be modeled, scratched, carved, and otherwise textured, and it may be enriched by the use of slips and all the various glaze treatments and glaze colors. However, since the principal reason for making porcelain is to achieve a purity, clarity, whiteness, and translucency of body, not many of the decorative treatments suitable for stoneware seem right for porcelain. For example, to cover a white porcelain with a brown slip glaze, or to introduce speckled textures into the slip or glaze, would make the achievement of the porcelanous qualities of whiteness and smoothness of body meaningless. There are ways of finishing porcelain, however, which enhance its very substance.

One of these ways is an intaglio treatment, or the carving into the surface of the clay of designs or patterns. Porcelain surfaces treated in this way have the double advantage of revealing the fineness and smoothness of the paste, and its tendency toward translucence where it is thin, and of allowing the glaze to pool slightly in low places, thus giving a subtle change of color. Thrown porcelain may be given a textural pattern by combing or incising into the soft clay soon after shaping. Such combings may be very free and calligraphic in style, and they need not bite deeply into the clay to show up prominently later when glazed. In fact, the slightest scratch is apt to be quite visible. If a more precise and controlled kind of incised pattern is desired, it may be carried out in the dry ware, or in the soft bisque. The bisqued ware may be carved or incised quite easily with sharp scraping or gouging tools. In this type of surface carving, however, the free sweep of line or form which is characteristic of designs done on the damp clay is impossible.

Another technique which gives marked surface variations is the creation of raised designs on the clay. This may be done by squeezing out lines on the clay with the slip trailer, using the porcelain clay itself as a slip. This gives lines of more or less prominence standing out in low relief from the surface of the piece. In the case of molded or pressed ware, any carving into the mold will, of course, give a corresponding design in relief on the piece.

Even if porcelain is glazed with perfectly clear glaze, carved or incised textures will show up sufficiently to produce a rich and varied surface. If more prominence is to be given to the relief design, a glaze is chosen which is slightly colored and tends to change color somewhat as it pools in slight declivities. The cela-

don type of glaze has always been considered ideal for this kind of decoration, but other types of clear but slightly colored glazes will give similar effects. The effect of clear but colored glazes over relief is one of greatly amplifying the carving; any irregularity of surface is made more prominent in appearance even though the surface is only slightly broken into. And the shadowy flow of glaze lends an enchantment to each line, each nuance of surface.

Porcelain is an ideal vehicle for underglaze painting, although not all the colors which are possible in earthenware firing are effective at the higher temperatures necessary in maturing porcelain. The smooth, white, unbroken surface of porcelain is an excellent, if sometimes frightening, surface for brushwork. In fact, underglaze decoration in cobalt, particularly the blue and white wares of the Ming dynasty and later times in China, became almost synonymous with porcelain. The beautiful dense smoothness of a good porcelain glaze can certainly lend a special quality to various underglaze colors. There are no difficult technical problems involved in doing underglaze decoration on porcelain; the whiteness of the body makes any underlay of engobe unnecessary. One rather interesting technique resembles etching in the appearance of the finished decoration. The tile or piece is given the usual low bisque fire, and the design is then scratched into the surface with a sharp point. A thin wash of underglaze color and water is brushed on the absorbent surface. Some of this color sticks in the scratched lines, the rest is more or less washed off by scrubbing the piece under running water. Different colors may be used for various portions of the design. Some of the color is bound to stick to the surface around the lines even though it is thoroughly scrubbed; this gives the design some color tones as well as lines. The design may be further amplified by areas or brush strokes in underglaze color.

Porcelain has been very frequently used as a vehicle or background for decorations in overglaze enamels. These are fired on at low heat over the already completed piece. While the use of enamels permits the introduction of bright colors, such as red and orange on porcelain, and the development of designs of precise and elaborate detail, the decoration always remains very much on the surface of the glaze and is a part of the glaze only in the sense that it adheres more or less securely to the surface.

Some potters have neither the interest nor the ability to carry out decorative schemes on three-dimensional forms, but prefer to let the form and the color of the pot suffice. The work of Charles Binns is an example. None of his pots was ever decorated, except by the glaze itself and by subtle changes in the color and texture of the glaze. Porcelain is certainly an excellent medium for this kind of expression, since its substance and glaze may have an unusual beauty. As we have seen, porcelain can be decorated in all sorts of ways; in fact, porcelain is usually associated with the overly ornate wares of the later Chinese periods and with the rococo pieces of 18th century Europe. But in modern times, potters have come to appreciate again the possibilities of the simple, naked form, and to be satisfied with the great potential which resides in form and substance alone. Few studio potters today are making porcelain which is decorated in a way that is reminiscent of past styles, but interesting work has been done in adapting various kinds of decoration to porcelain which has not been traditionally associated with this kind of pottery.

Chapter 12

Kilns for High Firing

The design, construction, and operation of pottery kilns is a fascinating subject, and the potter who must depend on others to fire his ware is missing half of the fun of making pottery. He is also missing the chance to complete his work in the process of firing, which is just as creative and requires just as much knowledge, skill, and experience as other phases of the craft.

In acquiring a new kiln for making stoneware or porcelain, a decision must first be made as to the kind of fuel to be used. Natural gas is the ideal fuel, but since it is not available everywhere, and since gas-burning kilns require flues or chimneys which may be impossible to provide, an electric kiln may be the only possibility. Next it must be decided whether to build a kiln permanently in place, or to buy a ready-made portable kiln. Electric kilns are commonly portable, even fairly large ones. Portable kilns for firing with gas or oil are heavy, bulky, and expensive; but if one is working in rented space or does not wish to invest in a permanent kiln, the portable kiln may be the best type to get. Portable kilns made by established manufacturers usually work well. But stationary kilns which are built in place, if properly designed and constructed, are not only cheaper than portable ones but work better and last much longer.

1. Essentials of kiln design

Kilns are actually very simple contrivances—in one form or another they are all insulated refractory boxes which retain the heat put into them either by the combustion of some fuel or by the radiant heat of the electrical heating element. The reason pottery cannot be fired in an open bonfire is not so much the lack of sufficient heat from the fire as the fact that the heat from an open fire is rapidly dissipated by radiation and by convection away from the fire, and while the coals or embers of the fire may be red hot, continuous burning of quantities of fuel is required to keep them that way.

The first pottery was probably fired by simply placing the pots on the ground and building a fire around them. The fire was started slowly at first and then built up into a mass of red-hot embers surrounding the pots. At the height of the fire, wet grass, manure, or a mixture of grass and mud was thrown over the fire; this retained the heat, allowing it to penetrate the pottery and bring it to red heat throughout. Some primitive peoples still fire their ware this way. The trouble with this system is that even the pots which survive the open fire, and perhaps a third of them crack, are only very lightly fired and are therefore sure to be soft and porous. A great improvement over the open fire was the use of a pit for firing. The pots were put in a shallow pit or trench and were protected by layers of broken pots. The fire was then kindled around the pots, and continued until the whole pit was filled with red-hot embers. The earth around the pit served as insulation to retain the heat. When the pots were surrounded by a heavy bed of glowing coals, the pit was covered over with earth or manure, which held in the heat and allowed it to soak thoroughly into the mass of pots. Temperatures of around 800°C can be reached by this method of firing, sufficient to make a soft unglazed earthenware.

Firing carried out in open fires or in pits can never achieve temperatures beyond a dull red heat, because the amount of heat is limited to that produced by the fuel which can be piled around the ware and because so much heat is lost by dissipation into the air. For higher temperatures, some way must be provided for trapping and storing the heat of the fire. It was found that if the hot gases coming from the fire were led *through* a chamber of some sort, a considerable portion of the heat of the fire would be retained by the ware. Kilns were built in very early times (in the Near East and elsewhere) which employed a hollow or cave in the earth or in a hillside in which the pottery was placed for firing. The fire was built at the mouth or opening of the cavity, and a flue or exit for the smoke was made at the top or back. In such an oven the fire could be maintained as long as necessary, and the hot gases of combustion, passing through the chamber containing the pots, transmitted some of its heat to them and to the kiln before passing on out through the flue.

The elements of any kiln are: (1) A firebox, or fire mouth, in which the fuel is burned. This need be only big enough to support a suitably large fire. In kilns which burn solid fuels there must be a grate for holding the burning material and some provision for letting in air for combustion and an opening for the removal of ashes. (2) The chamber in which the pottery is placed. The firebox is directly connected to this, but perhaps with a baffle, or at least a narrowed passage between. Some provision must be made for getting into the firing chamber to place the pottery, either through a door or by crawling through the firebox or through a roof or dome which is replaced with each firing. (3) A flue, or hole, which permits the escape of hot gas and smoke. This may be connected to a chimney of greater or lesser height.

Historically, the development of kilns involved the refinement of the proportions of these elements, and the improvement of construction and materials. The use of prefired bricks rather than mud or clay made the kiln into a permanent, or semipermanent structure, and one which was less likely to crumble or collapse on the ware during firing. Improved design of the fireboxes enabled the burning of more fuel in a given time, and consequently a greater input of heat. Improved devices for setting the ware in the kilns, such as saggers, or shelves, resulted in more even distribution of heat within the kiln and in increased capacity per unit of interior volume. Permanent door openings into the ware chamber made setting the kiln easier and facilitated closing it up for each firing. Dampers were developed to control the size of the flue opening or to shut it off entirely and thus permit the slower cooling of the kiln. Chimneys were extended in height, thus creating enough draft through the kiln to draw sufficient air into the fireboxes for the fierce burning of the fuel and to provide a pull of the hot gases through the kiln, perhaps in downward directions rather than in the more natural upward movement.

It is very hard to generalize on the proper proportions of the various parts of the kiln, because different fuels require differences of design, and because the ratios between the size of the various parts of a kiln do not hold exactly for all sizes of kilns. For instance, smaller kilns will have a larger flue in relation to the size of the firing chamber than will larger kilns. But in a rough way, the following proportions hold true:

1. For burning wood, coal, or other solid fuel, the cubic area of the fireboxes

needs to be about one fifth of the firing chamber. If the fireboxes are too big, valuable space which could be used for ware is being taken up by the fires; if, on the other hand, the fireboxes are too small, a large enough fire cannot be built in them to reach the desired temperature. For burning gas or oil, the fireboxes need not be more than about one tenth of the cubic space of the chamber.

2. The passage between the fireboxes and the setting chamber needs to be about 10 square inches for each cubic foot of setting space in the chamber.

3. The flue should be approximately 5 square inches in area for each cubic foot of setting space.

4. The chimney should be about 1 foot high for each cubic foot of setting space. If wood or coal is used as a fuel, the chimney will have to be somewhat higher.

In designing a kiln, it is wise to leave a certain flexibility in all critical proportions, thus enabling the kiln to be easily changed and adjusted to work well after it is finished. For example, the passage between the fireboxes and the firing chamber may be made considerably bigger than indicated above, and if it is necessary to make it smaller, it is very easy to block off some of the passage with loose bricks. Similarly, the flue can be made somewhat larger than necessary and can later be partially closed off with some loose refractories. If the chimney is not high enough to draw well, it can be extended in height, and it should be so designed that this is possible.

As to the shape and the proportion of the various parts of the kiln, these are mostly governed by common-sense considerations. The fireboxes must be shaped in such a way that the full development of flame can take place. Gas will burn in a very small space, but the combustion of coal, wood, and, to a lesser extent, oil, requires more room. The ware chamber should not be either excessively high or excessively broad. A firing chamber which is roughly as high as it is wide will be easier to heat evenly than one which is, say, twice as high as it is wide. Also, rounded surfaces serve better in conducting the heat than do angles, so that theoretically, a kiln which is igloo-shaped would be more efficient than one which is rectangular. In most cases, however, practical considerations of structure result in rectilinear shapes.

These general rules for the proportioning and the shaping of the kiln are useful only in the broadest sense—the exact design of the kiln must take into consideration the materials used, the type of kiln being built, its intended use, the fuel, and perhaps even the location.

2. Kilns—materials and construction

The chief materials used in constructing kilns are as follows:

1. *Firebricks*. Firebricks are made from fire clay and are sold under one of three classifications—"low-heat duty," "intermediate-heat duty," and "high-heat duty." These classes refer to the degree of heat which the brick will successfully withstand in service. For stoneware kilns, only "high-heat duty" bricks should be used. Firebricks are quite dense and hard and will withstand considerable abrasion and load as well as temperature. They are also manufactured in quite uniform sizes, which permits accurate masonry construction without the use of much mortar. Firebricks are made in a number of standard shapes. The most common shape, or "straight," is 9x4½x2½ inches. This is somewhat larger than a common red brick, such as is used for construction. Other shapes commonly available include:

9x6x2½
9x9x2½
9x2½x2½

Also made are wedge bricks, which taper along the 9″ dimension, and arch bricks which taper along the 4½″ dimension. These are made for forming arches, crowns, and domes.

Firebricks are used for the inner surfaces of fireboxes, firing chambers, flues and chimneys, or for any other place where high heat and the impingement of flame requires a strong, durable, heat-resistant brick. They are moderately efficient as an insulating material.

2. *Insulating Firebricks.* Insulating firebricks are made in such a way that they contain cells, pores, or interstices of air in the structure of the brick. This porosity serves as a dam to heat and gives the bricks a high insulating value. The bricks are made from kaolin or mixtures of kaolin and fire clay. They are graded according to the degree of heat they can withstand in service; for example, "K-20" means that the brick is good for service up to 2000°F. The remarkable insulating properties of light bricks of this type make them ideal for electric kilns and for the insulating of other types of kilns. They do not, however, withstand abrasion nearly as well as regular firebricks, and their use as the inner surface of open-fired kilns burning gas or solid fuels is questionable. Insulating bricks also suffer from "fatigue" more than hard-fire bricks and may begin to crumble after long use. They are easy to use in constructing kilns because they can be sawed or shaped by rubbing. Insulating bricks are much more costly than regular firebricks.

3. *Fire Clay Mortar.* Firebricks are laid in a mortar made from fire clay. Pure plastic fire clay may be used, mixed to the right consistency by the addition of water. For a stronger bond, sodium silicate is added to the mortar. Some ball clay also may be added for better workability. In kiln masonry, only enough mortar is used to level the bricks; after firing, the mortar has no great bonding strength, but is useful more as a leveling bed than as an adhesive to hold the structure together.

4. *Vermiculite.* This is an expanded mica used for insulation. It is in granular form and may be used to fill cavities or to cover the tops of kilns. It is not highly refractory and may not be used on the inside of the kiln.

5. *Diatomaceous Earth.* This is a natural siliceous material composed of the skeletons of a microscopic marine animal, the diatom. It is not highly refractory, but has a high insulating value. It is used loose, as a fill, or sometimes in the form of brick or slabs cut from natural deposits.

6. *Silicon Carbide.* Silicon carbide is made by fusing silica and carbon at high temperatures. It is a hard, refractory substance, used for kiln shelves, muffles, and other kiln furniture. Silicon carbide is an efficient conductor of heat rather than an insulating material.

Kilns are constructed by methods similar to those used for other masonry structures, but there are some important differences. For one thing, since the bricks in the kiln expand considerably when they are heated, expansion joints must be left every so often between bricks. Instead of using heavy beds of mortar between bricks, only a thin layer of fire clay is used, just enough to give a level bed for each brick and to keep it from teetering. The mortar may be spread on with a trowel or dipped onto the brick. Since the bricks do not remain securely stuck to each other with mortar, all kiln structures must be built so they will stand by themselves, or with the help of iron bracing, without any reliance on bond between individual bricks. Arches, crowns, domes, and vaults are built in a manner similar to architectural masonry, except that as little mortar as possible is used.

The following general procedure applies to the building of an open-fired stoneware or porcelain kiln for gas firing: A suitable foundation is required, one which will keep the kiln from settling and cracking. This may be made by pouring a reinforced concrete slab or by building a solid platform of concrete blocks securely laid with cement mortar. The

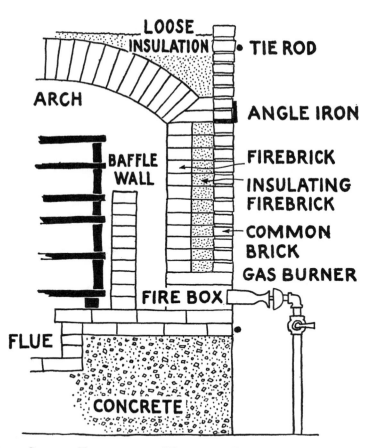

Fig. 2. Cross Section Through the Wall of a Downdraft Kiln, Showing Construction

This cross section shows one half of the kiln, with the shelves and props for ware in place. The flue hole at the bottom leads to the chimney, which is back of the kiln. The foundation may be made of concrete blocks. In this kiln, the wall, which is composed of three layers of brick, is 13½" thick and the arch is made up of 9" wedge brick. The loose fill above the arch may be vermiculite or diatomaceous earth.

floor of the kiln should be made of at least two layers of firebrick, laid so the joints do not coincide, and well grouted with fire clay. On this level platform of firebrick, the walls of the kiln are built. The wall should be made of three layers of brick; the inside wall is of firebrick. Next a course of insulating firebrick is laid, and the outside wall is composed of common red brick laid with cement mortar. These three walls should be lightly tied together by allowing an occasional firebrick to be laid endwise and

extending into the insulating brick layer. The wall is essentially a sandwich composed of firebrick and common brick, with insulating brick in between. All three walls are kept at the same height during construction. Door openings and burner-port openings are lined with firebricks. The outer wall of common red brick can be made to course with the firebrick walls by the use of a thicker bed of mortar. When the structure reaches the height of the top of the door, a wooden form is inserted in the door, and an arch

198

constructed over the opening. Arches are made of fire clay arch brick, and the rise and span of the arch and number and kind of arch brick which will be needed is figured out in advance (from a table furnished by the firebrick manufacturer). The arch rests at either end on a skew block which may be cut especially for the job. Firebricks are cut by scoring and tapping with the brick hammer and brick chisel. Insulating bricks are cut by sawing with a discarded wood saw. When the level of the main arch is reached, the skew blocks for the arch are set, and a wooden form to support the arch during construction is propped up in the kiln. The arch is then laid up, course by course, and the final or keystone brick in each course is tapped into place with the hammer. The arch may be made of arch brick if it is to be 4½″ thick, but in bigger kilns, it should be made of wedge brick 9″ thick. After the arch is completed, the walls of the kiln are finished on the ends. Then the iron supports are put in place. These consist of angle irons at the corners held close to the kiln with iron tie rods. A piece of angle iron may also be inserted just back of the skew of the arch to take the thrust of the arch. When the iron bracing is in place (it is not tightened completely until after the first firing), the wooden arch form may be withdrawn from inside the kiln. If it will not come out, it may be left in place, where it will burn away during the first firing. Proper connection is made to the chimney, and the interior of the kiln is completed by building the floor checkers and the baffle walls. These are laid up dry with no mortar. When the burners are installed, the kiln is dried out over a period of 2 or 3 days with a small flame, after which it is ready for the first firing.

Usually a new kiln will have to be adjusted over a period of several firings before it works well. It may be found that the baffle walls may need to be made higher or lower, that the entrances to the flue need to be made smaller or changed in position, that the flue needs to be smaller, or that the chimney needs to be higher. It may also be found that the burners are inadequate or that they do not supply enough air to burn the fuel. No kiln should be declared a failure until all of these possible sources of trouble have been thoroughly checked and experimented with, and if all the possible adjustments have been made, few kilns indeed will fail to give reasonably good results. Really satisfactory firing usually comes only after considerable experience has been gained in managing the burners, maintaining a satisfactory advance of temperature, maintaining the right atmosphere for the intended effects, and cooling the kiln properly. Each kiln will have its own individual peculiarities.

The first firing of a new kiln should be a very slow one and should be carried only up to red heat rather than to the full heat of stoneware or porcelain temperatures. Because of heat expansion, some cracks are sure to develop in any new kiln when it is first fired. If the kiln is properly constructed with ample expansion joints, these cracks will not get worse and may be disregarded. During the first few firings, crumbs of mortar may fall from the arch into the ware chamber, but after a while this tends to stop. For long life, the kiln should not be either heated or cooled too rapidly; rapid heating is much harder on a kiln than the effects of the actual heat to which it is subjected.

3. Updraft and downdraft kilns

In the updraft kiln, the fire enters the kiln at the bottom, passes upward through the ware chamber, and escapes from a flue at the top into the chimney. This design allows the hot gases to travel in the direction which they naturally take— upward. Figure 4 shows an updraft kiln. The combustion chamber, or firebox, is actually below the firing chamber. The fire passes upward through chinks in the floor, or around the edges of the ware

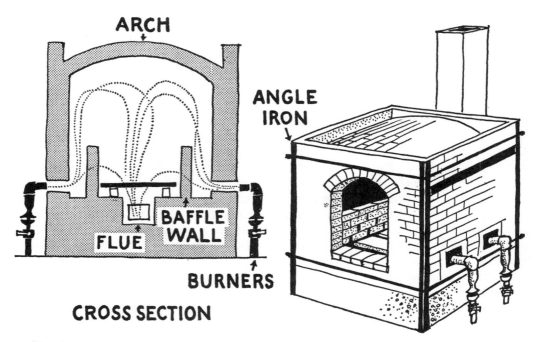

ARCH

ANGLE
IRON

BAFFLE
WALL

FLUE

BURNERS

CROSS SECTION

Fig. 3. A DOWNDRAFT KILN

This type of kiln, which may vary in size from about 10 cubic feet capacity to 30 or more cubic feet, is an ideal kiln for making stoneware and porcelain. Heat from the burners enters the sides of the kiln, is deflected upward by the baffle wall, and is then pulled downward through the ware and out the flue, which is located in the bottom. The downdraft circulation gives perfect control over the heat distribution throughout the firing chamber.

chamber, and is collected at the top of the kiln, where it enters the flue. A damper is provided at this point to control the passage of heat into the chimney. The updraft kiln has the advantage of simplicity of construction—it is essentially a box with openings for the burners at the bottom and a flue hole at the top. But this type of kiln has some serious disadvantages. For one thing, the heat of the fires striking directly on the props and lower shelves of the kiln causes them to deteriorate rapidly. But more serious is the tendency of updraft kilns to be considerably hotter in the bottom than in the top. Slow firing and adjustments of the damper opening may help this somewhat, but in most updraft kilns, the unevenness must be accepted as inevitable, and two different glazes are used, one for ware placed near the bottom and an-

other for the pots which occupy the cooler top. In European porcelain factories large updraft kilns are used which are shaped like a bottle. These sometimes have an upper chamber in which the bisque is fired.

A downdraft kiln is shown in Fig. 3. In this kiln the fire enters at the sides of the kiln and is deflected by a baffle wall which forces the hot gases to travel upward toward the top of the kiln. The flue is in the bottom of the kiln at the rear. The fire is drawn down through the ware into chinks in the floor of the kiln and toward the flue. To force the fire downward in this way requires a lively draft or pull from the chimney. There are several distinct advantages to the downdraft kiln. The flames do not impinge directly on the ware, but strike the baffle wall first. The path of the flame is long, thus permitting a maximum of transfer of heat to the ware. The bottom of the kiln is heated not only by the passage of the fire through it but by radiation through the baffle wall. If the top of the kiln fires hotter than the bottom, a more even heat can be achieved by opening chinks in the baffle wall and allowing more flame to enter the bottom of the kiln directly. Downdraft kilns have a tendency to be hot at the top, but they can be made to fire hot at the bottom by adjustments in the baffle walls. The evenness of heat from back to front can be controlled by opening more or fewer chinks in the floor at the back or toward the front, thus forcing more of the fire to the desired spot.

Both the updraft kiln and the downdraft kiln as described, are open-fired kilns, that is, the pottery is not protected from the flame, which swirls around it as it passes from the burner, through the ware chamber, and toward the flue. This direct exposure to the flame is no disadvantage in the case of wares which are fired in reduction, in fact it may insure the more complete reduction of glazes and bodies. However, if no flashing is desired on the ware, or if the kiln is to be used for lower temperature lead-glazed ware, open firing is not practical, and the ware must be placed in protective saggers or boxes of fire clay.

4. The muffle kiln

Some kilns are built with muffles which protect the ware from the flame. A muffle is, in effect, a protective box inside the kiln in which the ware is placed. The flames are led in passages around the muffle and do not impinge on the ware. Figure 4 shows an updraft muffle kiln. The muffle is constructed of plates of silicon carbide, a good conductor of heat. The space between the interior walls of the kiln and the muffle is fairly narrow, just enough to permit the flame to travel through the kiln to the flue. The muffle has its own arch composed of separate interlocking tiles, and is closed in the front during firing by removable tiles which form the door. The door to the kiln is separate from the door of the muffle, and this enables flames to pass up the front of the kiln as well as the sides and the back. The advantage of a muffle kiln is the complete protection which it affords the ware from the direct contact with the flame. For strictly oxidizing effects, and for firing lead-glazed ware, such a kiln makes the use of saggers unnecessary. Muffle kilns are also constructed by providing fire clay tubes through the ware chamber which carry the flame upward to a collecting chamber which leads to the flue. The ware is heated by radiation from the bottom of the kiln and from the hot muffle tubes.

5. The salt glaze kiln

For salt glazing, an open fired downdraft kiln is required. It need not differ radically from the downdraft kiln already described, except that for salt glazing somewhat more space may be required for the fireboxes to enable adequate volatilization of the salt. The salt is thrown directly into the firebox at the height of the fire, and a sufficient space must be left around the burner to get the salt in. The salt may be thrown in with a small shovel or scoop, or it may be packed in paper cups or cartons and these thrown into the firebox. The life of salt glaze kilns is considerably less than that of other kilns. The salt glazes over the inside of the kiln, but in the fireboxes it tends to corrode the refractories and to eat holes down into the brickwork. The kiln can be given a longer life by frequent washings inside with aluminum oxide and by keeping the fireboxes always in good repair. The effect of the salt on kiln shelves and props is also destructive. Due to the acrid smoke given off by the sale glaze kiln it is absolutely necessary to have a good chimney leading to the open air.

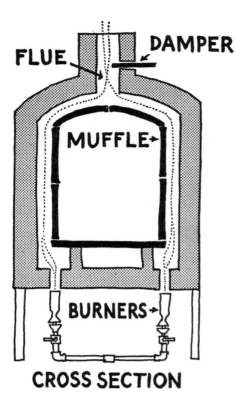

FLUE   DAMPER

MUFFLE→

BURNERS→

CROSS SECTION

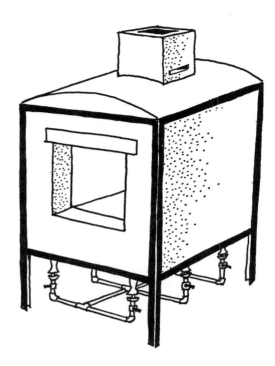

Fig. 4. An Updraft Kiln

Without the muffle, this kiln is a simple box with heat entering from the burners at the bottom and venting through a hole in the top. Six small burners are used. The muffle, which protects the ware from direct contact with the flame, is made of plates of silicon carbide. A small kiln of this type may be held together with an angle iron frame, and little or no mortar is used between the bricks.

6. Fuels and burners

Natural gas is not only the most convenient fuel for kilns, it is apt to be also the cheapest in areas where it is available. For kilns of more than about 10 cubic foot capacity, at least 6 or 8 ounces of gas pressure is required, and for an adequate volume of gas, a 1″ pipe should lead from the gas meter to the kiln. A meter larger than the usual household size may be required to deliver enough gas.

Gas burners may be either the atmospheric type, or the type which uses forced air. In the atmospheric type of burner, the gas emerges from a small orifice or hole into a venturi, or mixing tube. As

the gas enters this tube, it drags some air in along with it. The gas and the air become mixed as they travel through the tube and burn at the mouth of the tube. Atmospheric burners are quiet, dependable, have no moving parts, and do not depend on power for electric motors. The amount of air is regulated by a valve near the orifice.

Forced air burners for gas employ a motor-driven fan to supply the air. The air from the fan is mixed with the gas, either in the blower itself, or in a burner tube, and the mixture emerges ready to burn. With forced air, a more powerful flame can be achieved, since the air supply is not limited to the amount which

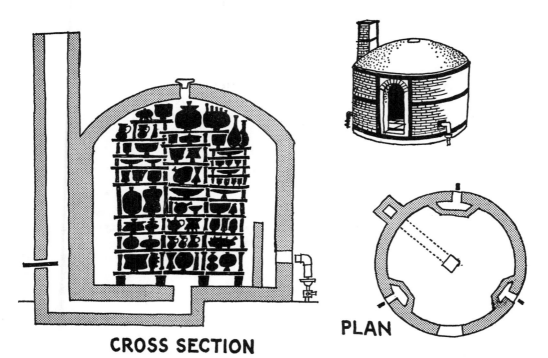

CROSS SECTION **PLAN**

Fig. 5. A Walk-in Downdraft Kiln

> *This kiln might be 6' or more high inside. It is an excellent type of kiln where larger production requires a large firing capacity. The shelves and their supports can be arranged to give an even distribution of temperature. Gas or oil is used for fuel.*

can be entrained by the gas. Exact mixtures of various proportions of gas and air can be had by regulating valves controlling the flow of both. In situations where the chimney is of limited height, forced air burners may be necessary to secure a positive draft through the kiln.

Bottled gas (liquefied petroleum gas) gives results in firing which are in every way comparable to natural gas. It is considerably more expensive, however. To fire with bottled gas, ample storage must be provided for the gas. A tank of several hundred gallons capacity is desirable, even for a modest-sized kiln. Burners for bottled gas are very similar to those used for natural gas, but will require larger orifices.

If natural gas is not available, oil should be considered as a fuel. It costs somewhat more to fire with oil than it does with

gas, but the results are equally good. Firing with oil is relatively inconvenient compared to firing with gas. Storage must be provided for the oil, and to insure against running out of oil during a firing, and to prevent the necessity of too frequent deliveries, the tank should be quite large, at least 200 gallons, even for a small kiln. For safety reasons it is preferable to have the tank buried in the ground, but this necessitates a pump for delivering the oil to the burners. If the tank is placed above the level of the burners, the oil can be made to flow to the burners by gravity. The piping from tank to burners should be carefully constructed, not only to minimize the danger of fire but to prevent unsightly and odorous leaks. Oil burners depend on forced air to atomize the oil and to supply the air for combustion. A rather powerful blower is re-

203

quired for even a small kiln, and the blower is apt to be very noisy. Sometimes the blower is covered with an insulated box to muffle the noise. The air is led from the blower to the burners in a 2″ pipe. The burners may be adjusted for different intensities of flame and for more or less air. One difficulty with oil burners is that they usually do not work well when adjusted to give a very small flame, especially at first when the kiln is being warmed up and the fireboxes are still cold. Great care must be taken at this stage of firing so as not to crack the pots by a too rapid advance of heat. Once the fireboxes are red hot, a good oil burner will give a flame which is similar to that of gas and just as easily controlled. The flame from oil burners is longer than gas and tends to lick through the ware to a greater extent. For this reason, more flashing will be noticed in oil firing, and reduction is accomplished by simply diminishing the air supply until the kiln is filled with yellow flame. If oil burners are not working properly, or if the fireboxes are too small, deposits of carbon may build up in the fireboxes during firing. These must be removed between firings, and sometimes they are very hard and have to be chiseled away.

The number of burners needed on a gas-fired kiln will vary with the size of the kiln. Kilns up to about 10 cubic foot capacity may be fired with two burners. A kiln with a capacity of 15 cubic feet will require four burners, and one of 20 cubic feet may require six. Fewer oil burners than gas burners are required for kilns of similar capacity; thus, a 20 cubic foot kiln can be fired with two oil burners, provided that the burners have sufficient capacity and provided the fireboxes are sufficiently large.

Firing with wood, formerly the usual, everyday fuel of the potter, has now become so rare in this country as to be almost a curiosity. Actually firing with wood is not so expensive, tedious, uncertain, or limited in temperature as one

might think. The wood-burning kiln should be of the downdraft type and should have ample firebox space to support the fire. An iron grate, and an ashpit, is required for each burner, as well as an opening through which the wood can be stoked. The stokeholes need not be large; just enough to admit the pieces of wood one by one. Since the amount of wood which can be burned in a given time depends on the amount of air being sucked into the kiln by the draft, relatively high chimneys are needed for wood firing, especially if stoneware temperatures are desired. Even a fairly small kiln may need a chimney about 20 feet high to give enough pull. Well-seasoned, soft wood makes the best fuel. The wood should be split into pieces about the length of the firebox, and not more than two inches across. As the firing proceeds and the heat advances in the kiln, the fires are plied with more and more wood. Toward the end of the firing, when top temperature is being reached, the size of the pieces of wood should be smaller to enable a rapid release of heat. There is certainly an excitement about wood firing which is entirely lacking in working with other kinds of kilns. The smell of the wood smoke, the subdued, throaty roar of combustion in the firebox, and the look of the long yellow flames sweeping down through the ware all contribute to the feeling that one is really *firing*, not just watching over some mechanical contrivance. However, the constant attention required during firing and the work of splitting the wood may add up to an amount of effort which in most cases is hardly justified.

In wood firing, considerable amounts of ash are carried through the kiln with the flame, and this ash, when it settles on the ware, tends to form a semiglazed surface. The ash alighting on the shoulders and tops of glazed pots changes the color and melting characteristic of the glazes. If it is desired to protect the ware from the effects of ashes, saggers may be used. The ashes also affect the cones, causing them to subside much before their normal deformation temperature. Cones should be protected by putting them in a little open box of brick or tile where they will be protected from the ash, but will still be plainly visible from the spy-hole.

7. Electric kilns

The electric kiln is certainly the most convenient type of kiln to operate, although it may be somewhat more expensive to fire than fuel-burning kilns. The electric kiln is compact, requires no chimney or fuel storage, fires the same each time, and requires only the turning of knobs or switches to operate. Furthermore, most electric kilns are equipped with swinging doors rather than with doors which have to be bricked in for each firing, and access is as convenient as to a refrigerator.

The electric kiln is heated by the radiant heat given off by electrical elements which offer resistance to the flow of electricity. For low temperature work, up to about 1100°C, ni-chrome elements are usually used. Care must be taken not to exceed the maximum temperatures recommended by the manufacturer of the kiln, or the elements will be damaged. For middle and high temperature work, canthol wire or ribbon elements are used, or globar elements, which are rods of silicon carbide. The walls of electric kilns are constructed of insulating firebricks, usually laid without mortar, and backed up by additional insulation. The structure is held together by a case made of metal or asbestos cement board. The rate of heating is controlled by the number of elements which are turned on, and by the amount of current. Since the firing does not involve the flow of gases through the kiln, the atmosphere in the kiln during firing is quiet, inert, and on the whole, oxidizing. From the point of view of one interested in high temperature work, this is the chief disadvantage of the electric

kiln; it will not reduce. Reduction which is accomplished by adding carbonaceous matter into the chamber of the kiln during firing is rarely satisfactory, and is hard on the kiln besides. In many situations, however, the electric kiln is the only practical type, and if this is the case, the potter must be content with the range of possible colors and textures which electric firing can provide. This range is, of course, considerable.

8. Temperature indication and control

In former times, the draw-trial was the only means of determining when a firing was completed, and if all of our pyrometric cones and pyrometers were taken away, we could still successfully gauge kiln temperatures in this way. But the pyrometric cone is certainly a convenient device. The cone, being made of ceramic materials of the same sort which are used for glazes, measures not only the temperature but the degree to which the materials of the pottery have been affected by the combined factors of both time and temperature. In ceramics, a lower temperature held over a longer period of time may have the same effect as a higher temperature held for a shorter length of time. In other words, it is not merely the degree of heat which is important but also the time during which the ware is subjected to the heat. Cones should be set in their plaques at a slight angle, about 8 degrees, and should be placed in the kiln so they are plainly visible. It is important to put the cones well inside the kiln, not just on the other side of the spy-hole, so they will be actually in among the pots. When temperatures in excess of cone 9 are reached, the cones become very difficult to see in the yellow glare of the kiln. Observing them through a smoked or colored glass may help. Cones are particularly hard to see during periods of reduction, and sometimes the atmosphere has to be cleared up before a good look can be had of the cone plaque. Some potters consider a cone down when its tip bends over level with its base, while others do not consider the cone down until it is completely melted and is entirely flat. The inexperienced fireman is apt to get panicky and to shut off the kiln before the cone desired is actually all the way down. An excellent booklet on pyrometric cones and their use is published by the Edward Orton Ceramic Foundation, Columbus, Ohio.

Cones are so reliable an indication of the end point of firing that pyrometers, or devices for measuring the exact temperature, are really not needed to determine when to shut off the kiln. However, the pyrometer is very useful in indicating the advance of temperature during firing and its subsidence during cooling. This enables the exact following of a firing schedule which allows for the slow ap-proaching of critical temperatures, and the more rapid and hence more economical firing at periods in the schedule where this is safe.

The pyrometer consists of two parts: a thermocouple and a device for measuring the electric current coming from the thermocouple. The thermocouple is inserted into the firing chamber during firing. It consists of two wires of dissimilar metal joined together. When the joint is heated, a small current of electricity is set up in the wire. This current is proportionate to the degree of heat. The current is measured and recorded by an ammeter outside the kiln, which may be calibrated to read in degrees of temperature. The thermocouples used in high temperature work must be made of platinum or platinum alloy and are relatively expensive.

Chapter 13

The Shop and Rhythms of Work

The pottery shop need not be an elaborate or expensive affair. Space is not always easy to find or to create, and the first essential to pleasant working conditions, in pottery as in other kinds of work, is enough space so that one does not feel crowded. The amount of one's production is important as far as space requirements go. If one is making pottery on a fairly small scale, or as a part-time occupation, a space about the size of a single garage may be adequate, but if the shop is intended for full-time work or for occasional periods of full production, a space twice that size will hardly be enough. In a small shop, it is wise to keep all the work areas quite flexible, so that if throwing is being done, the whole shop can be devoted to this process, and to drying, trimming, slipping, and all the other related work which goes on when a group of pots are being made. Then, when glazing is being done, the same areas can be used for vats of glaze and for pots in various stages of completion. The most useful work surface is a large central table. This can be about 3 feet wide, as long as possible, and about 33 inches high—high enough to work at comfortably while standing or seated on a high stool. Wedging and kneading is done on a lower surface, preferably one which is the exact height of one's hand from the floor when standing. Worktables and wedge tables should be sturdily built and surfaced with smooth planks. Unfinished wood is the ideal work surface for pottery making. It is slightly absorb-

ent, which keeps the plastic clay from sticking to it excessively, and its relatively soft, resilient surface seems just right for all pottery processes. Wood surfaces which have been used for some time get a worn and scrubbed look that is very pleasant.

The most direct way to mix clay is to weigh out the dry ingredients into a pile on a clean cement floor. The dry ingredients are mixed together with a hoe, then water is gradually added until all the clay has become damp and soft. The mass of wet clay is then shoveled into the clay bin, where it is left to temper for a week or so. It may then be taken out, wedged, and stored for aging. Clay in small quantities may be stored in concrete laundry tubs or galvanized iron cans with lids. Larger quantities of clay can be kept in pits made of concrete or brick, or in large boxes lined with zinc. After a satisfactory body has been developed, it is best to mix clay in fairly large quantities. This avoids constant interruptions while more clay is being prepared and allows the clay to age before it is used. If there is enough clay storage capacity, a new batch of clay can be made up long before the old is used up, thus assuring constant supplies of well-aged clay. Clay in storage should be slightly softer than desired for use, which makes it possible to wedge the clay thoroughly without having it get too stiff. Clay scraps are thrown into a container and wet down from time to time. If just the right amount of water is added to the scrap, it will slake and soften, and after it has been allowed to temper for a week or so it may be taken out and reused. The clay scrap bin should be easily accessible to the working areas so that if one takes a sudden dislike to a pot it may be tossed without further ado into the discard. Potters who pay for and who labor to make up their own clay are apt to be saving of it, and every scrap is swept into the soaking pit rather than onto the floor.

An ample ware rack is needed to store pots in progress. This should be made up of crosspieces of wood or pipe which hold removable ware planks. The ware boards should be made of 8″ lumber, preferably redwood, about 3′ long. The ware boards can be used to receive freshly thrown pots, for carrying glazed ware to the kiln, and for storing pots in any stage of completion. The potter will feel happy when the ware boards are crowded with pots of promise.

Glazes can be mixed simply by combining the ingredients together with the right amount of water and passing the resultant slip through a screen two or three times. If glazes are stored in tightly closed containers, the work of rewetting and rescreening dried-out glaze will be avoided, and the glazes will always be ready for use after thorough stirring. Too many glazes are the curse of the pottery shop. The hundred or more jars of glazes commonly seen in shops are usually not being actively used, and if they all are, it is to the detriment of the pottery. A dozen good glazes are enough. They can be stored under a bench, or on the shelves and always kept in stock.

The kiln, especially if it is a gas- or oil-burning kiln, is best put in a space other than the workshop proper. The heat, noise, and smell of the kiln, if it is right in the workshop, is likely to bring all work to a halt during firing. The kiln room should contain storage space for kiln furniture, cones, clay for wadding in the door, and other appurtenances pertaining to firing, and perhaps storage space also for bisqued pots.

Somewhere in the shop a place should be provided where a few good pots can be shown more or less by themselves and in surroundings which enable them to be seen distinctly as objects for their own sake. It is easy to become discouraged with pots, not so much because they are not all they should be as because they are too often seen in dust-covered confusion and profusion. The conditions of the average workshop are perhaps the worst possible environment for the viewing of pottery.

The pottery shop does not have to be a place of dirt, dust, confusion, congestion, and disorder. If the equipment is simple and well designed, and the arrangement of things is spacious within whatever limitations exist, the shop can be pleasant and orderly while still having the feeling of a place where work is going forward.

Pots should originate not as isolated orphans but as families and clans of pots which are related and come into being as the result of consecutive work resulting from convictions and ideas that require more than one example for adequate expression. This does not mean that pottery must consist of a boring repetition of shapes; on the contrary, each pot, although it is a member of a series, may be a fresh and new statement of an idea. But by the very nature of the processes of pottery, pots can and should be created spontaneously, rhythmically, and in some quantity. The material is abundant and dirt cheap, the clay is plastic, mobile, easily shaped, easily changed. And the process of throwing, and even of modeling and coiling pots is, or should be, fast. A pot can be thrown in two minutes or less—why take longer? It springs into existence at the touch of the fingers. A skillful potter does not even have to look at a small pot while he is making it, any more than a pianist must look at his hands, and the process of throwing can be almost effortless. Larger forms take a lot of work and more time, but even big pots are quickly made compared to the pace of work common to other more intractable materials. Since pots are quickly and easily made, and since the materials and the process is essentially inexpensive, pots have been cheap. They have served in a thousand ways in everyday life and have always been considered more or less expendable. If the pot breaks, another one is readily available.

It is in this matter of pace and rhythm that the potter finds his strength. Throwing should take the form of an overflow of pots—forms should spring from the wheel in happy profusion. Enough clay should be wedged up to last for half a day and shaped into balls which are piled like cannon balls at the wheel. Groups of pots of similar size are made as a series, so the hands become comfortable with a given sized wad of clay. The preliminary part of the throwing—centering and pulling up—proceeds with accuracy and directness. But it is at the very end of the process of throwing that the potter's judgment, his feeling, his hunches about the rightness or wrongness of the form, must be especially alert. The nuances of shape, and the final accents which may make a pot a coherent design are accomplished by exceptionally delicate pressures on the slowly revolving, soft clay. The final shaping of each pot should occur during a moment of contemplative decision. The damp pots should line up in ranks for drying, and all of those which do not measure up to the quality of the group as a whole should be ruthlessly thrown back in the soaking pit. This is the answer to the problem of the "bad pot"—it is aborted in an embryonic stage. Since the clay can be reclaimed and the work at this stage represents only a small investment of time, no regrets should be experienced at the loss. It is true that to destroy pots at any stage takes courage and self-discipline. But it is never wise to fire pots which are inferior to one's normal best, nor is it really possible to rescue a weak form with a successful glaze.

The work of trimming, adding feet, handles, lids, knobs, or spouts should likewise be done on groups of pots. In these operations, the timing and the organization of the work require experience. Trimming needs to be done at just the right stage of dryness, and handles must be pulled ahead of time so they will reach just the right degree of stiffness when they are attached. The processes of texturing, applying slips, and of performing other plastic operations on the pots must be carefully staged. Here again the work is tremendously facilitated if a group of pots is being made, all of which are being treated in somewhat the same manner. Thus one or two slips can be made up and with them a whole table full of pots can be dipped or trailed. The advantage of working on the surfaces of pots in this way is that one soon loses the fear of ruining any one piece, and approaches each in a spirit of relaxation and hopefulness, rather than with timidity and apprehension. The hand, instead of being tight and trembly, is relaxed and at the service of one's best intentions.

In glazing as well as making, the production of groups of pots rather than of isolated ones greatly facilitates the work. A quantity of glaze can be made and when the glaze is at the right consistency and a number of pots are ready to be dipped, the work can go along easily, surely, and with a good chance that the glazes will be applied properly for the intended results. Firing also is a much more easily organized and controlled job if groups of related pieces are being fired rather than isolated individual pots having all sorts of different forms and glazes.

The most efficient, and certainly the most enjoyable way to make pottery, is to create pieces in fairly large groups and to divide the work into the natural divisions of forming, decorating, bisquing, glazing, and firing. Each operation is carried out on numerous pieces, and the work, instead of being fragmented into innumerable unrelated small actions, becomes rhythmical, rapid, expressive. The object of organizing the work in this fashion is not so much to make more pieces of pottery with a given amount of effort (although it certainly has this effect) as it is to *free the creative intelligence and its expression through the physical skills of craftsmanship.* Fully matured ability in pottery making is not unlike a mastery of the dance; it is based on a control over the various movements which enable one to think and feel, not about the movement itself but about the thing which is being created.

What makes one pot have a measure of life while another seems dull and dead is as difficult to account for as any other evidence of the workings of human personality and expression. Most potters have had the experience of making a number of pieces, all perhaps more or less similar, and of having one or two stand out as if they belonged in another class of objects altogether. This distinction of liveliness or vitality may defy analysis. But it has something to do with the flow of intention from the potter into the pot, with nothing intervening between. Although concentrated effort is required to establish and to sustain such a flow, a quality of relaxation, even of thoughtlessness, must also enter in, rather than a feeling of struggle, doubt, or uncertainty. Good work is probably always the indirect result of a long effort to learn the craft, to get the operations of potting under control and to know where the real values reside. But, as in the case of a good shot with the bow, the actual accomplishment of something meaningful, the hitting of the target, seems to have an ease almost as if done by someone else.

Like other activities which are done for their own sake, potting seems to derive its central value from the degree to which the potter is able to put himself into the work. But if the potter is to extend himself through his work, to pour a little of himself into the pots, he must have a firm grip on the methods of pottery making. In many ways pottery is an exacting craft. The ease with which a lump of clay can be made to assume different shapes by the untutored hand is deceptive. Until one gains control of the manual processes involved, and learns to understand the temperament of clay as it dries and changes, and until one is able to foresee and to use the changes and transformations of the fire, one is really at the mercy of the medium rather than in control of it, and the results, although they may be expressive of process to a degree, will not be something capable of being ripened and developed. All the processes of pottery, when carried out with skill and understanding, have an expressive potential; this potential is fulfilled only when the process becomes second nature, when the work can proceed with *élan.*

The events of the pottery process must always be examined and re-examined for new riches. What is a flaw to one potter may prove to be the basis for a career to another. Today we should not be restrained by prejudice or precedent from taking what we find is good in pottery and using it to the fullest extent. If we are honest with ourselves, it does not matter whether what we find has the sanction of either the past or the present. The growth of forms, their turning and roundness, or their angularity and restraint, the springing upward of forms and their terminations, the scale of parts, the cupping and the closing in as of a gourd or the palms of the hands—these qualities in pots are the real raw materials of the art. The tooth of fired clay, its earthiness or its quartzlike quality, its burnt and rocky colors, the unctuous or icy flow of glaze—these are the colors and textures not only of pots but of the earth itself. Every good pot is a new landscape.

The dilemma of pottery is that it may

express both sculptural and painterly values. Its forms are limitless, bounded only by the imagination of the potter; its surfaces, too, may run the gamut of values, hues, configurations, shapes, textures, reliefs, gravings, projections, transparencies and opacities, reflectance or mattness. The resolution of these two visions or ways of expression—form on the one hand and the two-dimensional qualities of surface color and complexity on the other— is a difficult thing. In most pots there is an uneasy balance between the two, a feeling of uncertainty as to which emphasis, form, or surface is the significant one. Many of the great pots of the past have resolved the dilemma in favor of one or the other; either they are primarily expressions of form, with surface qualities which are truly outgrowths of the form and which are intended to enhance, and to suitably *clothe* the form, without in any way dominating it or smothering it; or, on the other hand, they have been concerned primarily with the surface variations of color, decoration, glaze quality, or even illustrative drawing, with the form serving primarily as a support for surface. Chinese pottery, at least the early wares, seems usually to be concerned primarily with form, while Persian pottery, with its strong orientation toward color and figurative styles of decoration, seems to have been more intensely preoccupied with surface.

The tension and the uncertain relationship between form and surface can, of course, be resolved by the dominance of one or the other. A sculptural expression in ceramics can be fully carried out with forms which are unbroken by color change, brushwork, changes of texture, or by glazes which in themselves tend to dominate the expression. On the other hand, a painterly genius can find expression in plates, tiles, or other relatively two-dimensional forms which give free and undisputed play to the surface.

The resolution of this problem is one of the most important and intriguing problems of pottery. Perhaps the answer can be found in nature, where the bark of the tree in no way conflicts with or contradicts the shape or the essence of the tree, or the surface of a shell which, far from having the look of having been pasted on as an afterthought, is *actually expressive, in a structural way, of the manner of growth and actual substance of the shell.* Pottery techniques and pottery qualities are full of hints as to how surface can relate to form in ways which are fundamental rather than superficial. The striations of tools and fingers on the turning forms, the stamp and scratch of tools, the rhythm of throwing marks, the textures of trimming, the surface evidences of joinings, additions, and deformations, the pour of slip and glaze over rounded surfaces, the high water marks of dipping, even the flashings of the fire— all of these are full of possibilities for an expression in which surface is an *outgrowth* of form, neither subordinate nor dominate, but of the form itself. In the delicate balance of surface and form, perhaps in tensions between them, or in surprising or even seemingly contradictory elements in them, the potter finds his chance. No other art quite attempts this synthesis.

Many, if not most, pots are overworked and have the look of having served merely as the vehicle for experiment in the decorative processes. It is too often a case of malaprop lines, brushwork, patches of color, bands and stripes, or the accidental droolings of slip and glaze, applied to forms which were not meant to take such a profusion of décor. In pottery it is easy to be carried away with enthusiasm for the processes themselves and to lose all sense of restraint or fitness in the application of them. "Decoration" can be almost a disease, and it seems to afflict those who are least able to cope with the problem of fitness of surface for form and function. Part of the reason for this difficulty is that surface features are applied to pots as an *afterthought*. The pot is first made on the wheel, with no thought as to what color, texture, or treatment it is to receive later. Then, when the ware is bisqued, the potter, perhaps weeks or months after he made the pot, decides on color, brushings, lines, markings, and glaze involvements, and each pot becomes the hapless victim of an experiment in process, in no sense related to the original idea for the pot, if indeed such an idea ever existed. It is essential that the way always be left open for the intuitive creation of form and surface, but this creation, if it is to be truly successful, must take place within some frame or boundary which precludes mere waywardness. When a group of pots are made, a certain predication should be made as to the eventual character of them all. Thus one could say that all the pots of the group would receive slip treatments limited to certain colors, and that all would then be glazed with certain limited glazes. The stage is then set, and the potter proceeds with half a picture in his mind's eye of the finished pots; he knows, within certain limits, what their colors and surfaces are to be, but each pot, each *specific* embodiment of the idea is as yet unborn. Then, if the potter feels like hurling a jar of slip at the piece, he may do so with a true sense of the meaning of his act in terms of the finished pot. There is a meaningful and vital relationship between his actions as a potter and the final result.

No potter would wish to preclude all accidents, happy or otherwise, from his work, but there are ways of setting the stage for the happy accident. It is frequently observed that the happiest accidents always occur in the work of the potter who is perfectly capable of allowing *no* accidents to happen if he so desires. This does not mean that he is not allowing the materials and processes to speak freely, but it does indicate that he knows how to establish the conditions of the accident, and how to limit them and

give them meaning. The happiest accidents seem to grow out of intimacy with the materials. A sense of thickness and thinness, a sense of the probable results when one layer falls over another, a sense of the colors and textures which will probably result from certain combinations of glazes, slips, and clays, all of these acquired judgments are really the potter's intelligence, an intelligence developed out of experience.

Pottery making is a kind of adventure in which, if one is successful, one finds, in the end, oneself. It involves the risk of self-revelation. It offers the chance of making a synthesis of one's physical self, the co-ordination of hand and eye, the "handwriting" of one's skills, with a philosophy, a point of view, a statement of values. It requires patience and skill, but these will be valueless without feeling and insight. It calls upon deep strata of our intuition. When the craft of pottery becomes an art, it can never be codified, hedged with rules or principles, or fully explained, any more than can any other art.

And unlike some forms of art, which may aim for the heroic, epic, or monumental expression, pottery is basically humble. It is made out of earth—materials of no particular value in themselves. Its creation is firmly bound to manual processes, to digging, to kneading, to shaping with the hands and simple tools. Its substance retains the mark of earthy origins and can never be mistaken for any precious material. Pots have been created always to fulfill basic everyday needs. They have been made always by men who received little or no financial reward from pottery making. The greatest pots were never intended for museums, were never shown in exhibits. Most of the greatest pots were not signed by their makers, but were completely anonymous contributions. The pot can be nothing—a piece of fired clay to be used, broken, and discarded. Or it can be much.

Index